T0207394

Lecture Notes in Computer Science   12812

More information about this subseries at http://www.springer.com/series/7410

Thomas Groß · Luca Viganò (Eds.)

Socio-Technical Aspects in Security and Trust

10th International Workshop, STAST 2020
Virtual Event, September 14, 2020
Revised Selected Papers

 Springer

Editors
Thomas Groß (ID)
Newcastle University
Newcastle upon Tyne, UK

Luca Viganò (ID)
King's College London
London, UK

ISSN 0302-9743   ISSN 1611-3349   (electronic)
Lecture Notes in Computer Science
ISBN 978-3-030-79317-3   ISBN 978-3-030-79318-0   (eBook)
https://doi.org/10.1007/978-3-030-79318-0

LNCS Sublibrary: SL4 – Security and Cryptology

This Springer imprint is published by the registered company Springer Nature Switzerland AG
The registered company address is: Gewerbestrasse 11, 6330 Cham, Switzerland

Preface

The 10th International Workshop on Socio-Technical Aspects in Security (STAST 2020) aimed at creating an exchange of ideas and experiences on how to design systems that are secure in the real world where they interact with non-expert users. The term "socio-technical," in this context, means a reciprocal relationship between technology and people. The 2020 workshop focused especially on the interplay of technical, organizational, and human factors in achieving or breaking computer security, privacy, and trust.

As typical for STAST, the workshop received a wide range of inter-disciplinary submissions with a number of distinct methodologies - 11 submissions used quantitative methods, such as statistical inference, to make their argument, whereas 21 submissions employed qualitative methods, such as semi-structured interviews. We received five submissions in protocol design (with underpinning in cryptography or formal methods) and five submissions in security analysis (on vulnerabilities or attacks). Two submissions were review papers. Seven submissions focused on research methodology, that is, instrument evaluation, meta-research, or research synthesis.

The peer-review was organized as a double-blind process. Each submission received a minimum of three reviews. Submissions with appreciable variance in review scores were assigned a fourth review as a tiebreaker. On average, we had 3.2 reviews per submission. The peer-review process included an active discussion phase, facilitated by a designated discussion lead for each submission, who subsequently summarized the discussion outcome and agreed conclusions in a meta-review.

STAST benefited from a strong conflict-of-interest management system, allowing the chairs to submit papers themselves while ensuring that an other chair could govern the submission, maintaining a strict separation-of-duty policy.

Of the 42 papers initially submitted to the workshop, 35 papers were retained by the chairs for peer-review after an initial check against the stipulations of the call for papers. Eventually, we accepted 11 submissions for publication in this volume, yielding an acceptance rate of 31%, not counting the chairs' desk rejections.

We prepared this volume with the following sections. First, *Personality and Behavior* includes investigations on the impact of personality and traits on behavior. Second, *Behavior in Face of Adversaries* considers human behavior when confronted with a range of real-world attacks. Third, *Smart Environments* focuses on emergent smart systems, such as smart buildings and smart homes. Fourth, *Decentralized Systems and Digital Ledgers* includes analyses of decentralized systems, especially ledgers. Finally, *Reflections on Socio-Technical Aspects of Security* includes analyses of, and positions on, the past and future of the field itself.

Simon Parkin and Yi Ting Chua were recognized with the STAST 2020 Best Paper Award for their paper *Refining the Blunt Instruments of Cybersecurity: A Framework to Coordinate Prevention and Preservation of Behaviours.*

Overall, we are very pleased with the quality of STAST's 10th anniversary volume. We are grateful for the high-quality work of the authors involved and for the invaluable contributions of the 33 Program Committee members and 4 external reviewers, whose dedication and attention to details enabled this volume.

December 2020   Thomas Groß
                                                          Luca Viganò

Message from the Workshop Organizers

It has been ten years since we had the idea of founding a workshop dedicated to socio-technical aspects of cyber-security. At that time, something was missing in the landscape of events in security research: a venue in which to discuss security in a broader manner, a manner that combined technical discussion with other topics traditionally linked to usability and human computer interaction research, yet much broader than just these. There was a need to discuss attacks that exploit technical hacking in combination with social engineering and, equally, there was a need to discuss user practices, organizational processes, and social culture as instruments to establish security or, by contrast, as possible vectors to break it.

Discussing such matters was, and still is, relevant since evidence shows that designing systems that are secure when analyzed from a merely technical perspective, regardless of the values and merits of the approach, does not guarantee that security works as expected once deployed. The common and arguable explanation is that the human, the "weakest link," did not comply. However, blaming users neither helps nor gives us instruments to design stronger systems. We have learned by experience that a better strategy is to holistically conceive systems whose security emerges by harmonizing the technical features with the modalities in which humans, organizations, and societies operate. The manifesto of addressing security problems socio-technically means exactly that all the components are addressed as a whole. We have also learned that such a manifesto has a very wide impact, encompassing virtually all application areas where human beings may play a role in the effectiveness of security measures; hence, it concerns virtually every ICT application that must be protected from criminals.

Looking at the proceedings of this year's edition of the workshop, the published contents clearly attest that the idea outlined above has rooted well. As a result, the International Workshop on Socio-Technical Aspects in Security (STAST) is now fully mature. Its aims have come to a clear focus, and the affiliation with the European Symposium on Research in Computer Security (ESORICS) is naturally well principled and practically fruitful.

We would like to thank all the Program Chairs and Program Committee members who over the last decade have helped STAST become a successful event. And we are particularly grateful to this year's Program Chairs, Thomas Groß and Luca Viganò: they have done an impeccable job and brought, with a top-level Program Committee, this year's edition to an unmatched success with a great scientific program.

December 2020

Giampaolo Bella
Gabriele Lenzini

Organization

General Chairs

Giampolo Bella   University of Catania, Italy
Gabriele Lenzini   University of Luxembourg, Luxembourg

Program Committee Chairs

Thomas Groß   Newcastle University, UK
Luca Viganò   King's College London, UK

Programme Committee

Luca Allodi   Eindhoven University of Technology, Netherlands
Kalliopi Anastasopoulou   University of Bristol, UK
Panagiotis Andriotis   University of the West of England, UK
Ingolf Becker   University College London, UK
Giampaolo Bella   University of Catania, Italy
Zinaida Benenson   University of Erlangen-Nuremberg, Germany
Tobias Blanke   University of Amsterdam, Netherlands
Michael Carter   Queen's University Belfast, UK
Lynne Coventry   Northumbria University, UK
Sarah Diesburg   University of Northern Iowa, USA
Verena Distler   University of Luxembourg, Luxembourg
Lothar Fritsch   Karlstad University, Sweden
Rosario Giustolisi   IT University of Copenhagen, Netherlands
Thomas Groß   Newcastle University, UK
Pieter Hartel   University of Twente, Netherlands
Ulrike Hugl   Innsbruck University, Austria
Markus Jakobsson   ZapFraud, USA
Kat Krol   Google, UK
Shujun Li   University of Kent, UK
Jean Martina   Universidade Federal de Santa Catarina, Brazil
Maryam Mehrnezhad   Newcastle University, UK
Masakatsu Nishigaki   Shizuoka University, Japan
Jason Nurse   University of Kent, UK
Simon Parkin   University College London, UK
Saša Radomirovic   University of Dundee, UK
Karen Renaud   Abertay University, UK
Peter Y. A. Ryan   University of Luxembourg, Luxembourg
Diego Sempreboni   King's College London, UK

Kerry-Lynn Thomson   Nelson Mandela Metropolitan University, South Africa
Theo Tryfonas   University of Bristol, UK
Luca Viganò   King's College London, UK
Konrad Wrona   NCI Agency/Military University of Technology in Warsaw,
      Poland

Additional Reviewers

Susanne Barth
Lucas Palma
Borce Stojkovski
Samuel Wairimu

Publicity and Web Site Chairs

Borce Stojkovski   University of Luxembourg, Luxembourg
Itzel Vazquez Sandoval   University of Luxembourg, Luxembourg

Sponsors

Fonds National de la
Recherche Luxembourg

securityandtrust.lu

UNIVERSITÀ
degli STUDI
di CATANIA

UNIVERSITÉ DU
LUXEMBOURG

Contents

Personality and Behavior

How Can Personality Influence Perception on Security of Context-Aware
Applications? 3
  *Nelly Condori-Fernandez, Franci Suni-Lopez, Denisse Muñante,
and Maya Daneva*

Refining the Blunt Instruments of Cybersecurity: A Framework
to Coordinate Prevention and Preservation of Behaviours 23
  Simon Parkin and Yi Ting Chua

Behavior in Face of Adversaries

Natural Strategic Abilities in Voting Protocols 45
  Wojciech Jamroga, Damian Kurpiewski, and Vadim Malvone

A Study of Targeted Telephone Scams Involving Live Attackers 63
  Ian G. Harris, Ali Derakhshan, and Marcel Carlsson

Smart Environments

User Privacy Concerns and Preferences in Smart Buildings 85
  Scott Harper, Maryam Mehrnezhad, and John C. Mace

Work in Progress: Towards Usable Updates for Smart Home Devices 107
  Julie M. Haney and Susanne M. Furman

Decentralized Systems and Digital Ledgers

WARChain: Blockchain-Based Validation of Web Archives 121
  Imre Lendák, Balázs Indig, and Gábor Palkó

Cyber 9/11 Will Not Take Place: A User Perspective of Bitcoin
and Cryptocurrencies from Underground and Dark Net Forums 135
  Simon Butler

Self-Governing Public Decentralised Systems: Work in Progress 154
  Moritz Platt and Peter McBurney

Reflections on Socio-Technical Aspects of Security

Statistical Reliability of 10 Years of Cyber Security User Studies 171
    Thomas Groß

Privacy, Security and Trust in the Internet of Neurons 191
    Diego Sempreboni and Luca Viganò

Author Index 207

Personality and Behavior

How Can Personality Influence Perception on Security of Context-Aware Applications?

Nelly Condori-Fernandez[1,2(✉)], Franci Suni-Lopez[3], Denisse Muñante[4], and Maya Daneva[5]

[1] Universidade da Coruña, A Coruña, Spain
n.condori-fernandez@vu.nl, n.condori.fernandez@udc.es
[2] Vrije Universiteit Amsterdam, Amsterdam, The Netherlands
[3] Universidad Nacional de San Agustín, Arequipa, Peru
fsunilo@unsa.edu.pe
[4] SAMOVAR, Télécom SudParis, Institut Polytechnique de Paris, Paris, France
munante@telecom-sudparis.eu
[5] University of Twente, Enschede, The Netherlands
m.daneva@utwente.nl

Abstract. [**Context and Motivation**] Our lives are being transformed by context-aware software applications with important social, environmental, and economic implications. [**Question/Problem**] Experts recognized that quality attributes, e.g. security, are the cornerstone to get healthy social implications of these applications. However, do end-users (service consumers) perceive these attributes as so important? [**Methodology**] To answer this question, we designed a survey, to understand how end-users perceive security of context-aware software applications and how the users' personality traits might influence their perceptions. To this end, we did a web-based survey that embeds two animated-demonstration videos in order to present i) the functionality of a context-aware mobile app, and ii) some vulnerabilities of the mobile app. It involved 48 subjects divided in two groups: subjects with software engineering (SE) background (Group A) and subjects without any SE background (Group B). [**Results**] Our study found that the importance of *confidentiality* and *integrity* is more clearly perceived by subjects with SE backgrounds (Group A). *Accountability* is more difficult to be perceived by subjects. And this difficulty can be even more pronounced for subjects without any SE background (Group B). Our findings suggest that importance preferences on security are influenced by personality types. For instance, open-minded people have a higher propensity to perceive the importance of *confidentiality* and *integrity*. Whilst, people with a high level of agreeableness hold quite different perceptions regarding the importance of *authenticity* and *accountability*. Analyzing the level of association between personality and the perceived importance on security, we found that the importance perceptions on *confidentiality* are influenced by the personality of subjects from Group B. And, the changes (positive an negative) in the importance perception on confidentiality are very strongly influenced by personality, even more so by the personality of subjects from Group B.

© Springer Nature Switzerland AG 2021
T. Groß and L. Viganò (Eds.): STAST 2020, LNCS 12812, pp. 3–22, 2021.
https://doi.org/10.1007/978-3-030-79318-0_1

Keywords: Security · Users perception · Personality test · Survey · Context aware applications

1   Introduction

Context-aware software applications are transforming our daily lives with important social, environmental, and economic implications, for example, in domains such as transportation, health-care, telecommunication and banking. It is expected that in the near future software-intensive systems will behave autonomously thanks to the continuous sensing and monitoring.

Given the complexity of this kind of systems, and the social implications behind emerging wearable sensing technologies, Condori-Fernandez and Lago [10] investigated how quality attributes can contribute to the social, technical, economic and environmental sustainability dimensions from a developer perspective. These authors found that experts recognized that security quality attributes are the cornerstone to get healthy social implications of software-intensive systems. Even though the efforts made in conceiving secured software millions of dollars in losses are still the result of attacks on systems harming directly service consumers. Many security breaches occur in software due to errors in analysis, design and implementation [3,4]. Hence, security in software engineering (SE) is a critical issue that is clearly gaining more emphasis in the recent years [17,20]. However, to incorporate security in the software development is especially challenging because software designers/architects must consider not only security software mechanisms but also interactions among people, organizations, hardware, and other software systems, as it is described by Dalpiaz *et al.* in [13]. Despite the efforts made by the security engineers to consider both social and technical aspects, there is still a gap to be filled: we still understand relatively little about the end-user's behavior in adopting security, even more when software applications are used massively. Specifically, there is no published research on the possible relationships between personal attributes traceable to personality traits, and the ways in which end-users act and react when facing security issues in context-aware applications.

To address this gap of knowledge, it is necessary to investigate security from an end-user perspective, *i.e.,* how end-users perceive the importance on security of context-aware software applications. So, the present research makes a step in this direction. We start from the hypothesis that end-users perceive the importance of software functionalities in different ways due to their different profiles (e.g. educational backgrounds, ages, genders, personality traits) [9,21]. Furthermore, although there is a substantial evidence in the literature about factors such as personality traits that influence end-users perceptions on technology acceptance (e.g. [24,27]), there is not yet enough empirical research on how personality and certain contextual factors (e.g. educational background) of end-users can influence the perceived importance of security implementation (*i.e.,* security policies and security software technology) for context-aware software applications. Moreover, regarding to security, it becomes more challenging to be studied because, as West indicated [29], security is hard to be appreciated by end-users due to: *end-users do not think they are at risk, safety is an abstract concept, security is considered as a secondary task* and *losses perceived disproportionately to gains.*

In this paper, we aim to investigate this phenomenon trough a survey questionnaire, by focusing on four specific quality attributes related to security such as confidentiality, authenticity, accountability and integrity. To this end, we did a web-based survey that embeds two animated-demonstration videos. Two experiments were conducted with SE experts who were attendees of REFSQ [11] and students from the Education department of the Universidad Nacional de San Agustin (Peru). In total, our study involved 48 subjects. Our study found that the importance of some security attributes (i.e. accountability) was more difficult to be perceived by end-users than others. And this difficulty was even more pronounced for end-users without any SE background, which is reflected in the variability of their answers (perceptions). Also our findings suggest that importance preferences on security are influenced by personality types and educational background. However our empirical results cannot be conclusive, therefore we call for more studies on this topic.

From a methodological perspective, our study highlights the importance of i) taking into account of personality tests for complementing the characterization of end-users and, in turn, get a better understanding on user perceptions about security, and ii) employing animated-demonstration videos as a medium to help in the importance recognition of security. Although the idea of using positive and negative scenarios in the user reactions assessment of interactive products was already considered in previous studies (i.e., [6,23]), as far we know, the use of these artifacts in the context of security is novel.

The remainder of this paper is organized as follows. Section 2 introduces our study design. Sections 3 and 4 present our results and threats to validity, respectively. Section 5 discusses some related empirical research publications. Finally, Sect. 6 describes our next steps and conclusion.

2 Study Design

This section first presents a realistic scenario which serves as a motivating example for our work. We then present our research questions and research goal. Next, we describe the participant selection, we then present the formulated hypothesis, variables and metrics. Finally we introduce the survey implementation and the survey validation and conduction[1].

2.1 Motivating Scenario Example

Frank lives in a city where the amount of parking spaces per motor vehicle is becoming scarce. Given the difficulty of finding a parking space, Frank uses a mobile application called happyParking. The application uses multiple input

---

[1] The artifacts used in this study were published in the following link: https://osf.io/wupd6/?view_only=30d712fee72243098fabd6bfee357567.

sources of i) external contextual information to provide a certain degree of probability of finding a parking spot in different locations; and ii) internal contextual information (i.e. emotional states) for assessing quality of User Experience (UX). happyParking is built based on a context-aware quality assurance framework.

For example, by knowing the current situation of other circulating cars, happyParking can recommend the fastest route by avoiding congested hot spots. However, despite the reduced time for finding a public parking space, sometimes Frank was not fully satisfied with happyParking because i) the navigation information was overloaded and difficult to interpret, or ii) space of the available parking spot was not large enough for Frank's car, or iii) the closest space recommended by happyParking was meanwhile taken.

In this situation, interacting with happyParking was annoying and stressful for Frank. This emotional information is derived from physiological data collected through wearable sensors of the E4-Wristband[2] device at runtime. Exploiting this emotional information, happyParking is able to measure the actual quality of UX, and consequently increase awareness of potential issues with the software services (e.g. finding a closest space), what could eventually lead to actions addressing the issue.

2.2 Goal and Research Questions

The goal of the study presented in this paper is to *understand* perceived importance with respect to security attributes *from the viewpoint of* service consumer[3], *in the context of* the smart parking happyParking. From this goal, the following research questions are derived:

RQ₁: *How do service consumers perceive the importance of security of a context-aware software intensive system?*
RQ₂: *Does the personality influence on the importance perceived of security of context-aware software applications?*

To answer these RQs we planned and executed a survey with volunteer participants as potential service consumers of happyParking. Our survey design draws on the methodological guidelines of Kitchenham and Pfleeger [16], and Molleri et al. [19].

2.3 Participant Selection

Considering the importance of modeling the diversity in users for identifying right subjects [26], we considered the educational background. This results in two groups: *Group A* consists of subjects at University education level, with background in SE. *Group B* includes subjects at University level with background in Education without an SE background.

---

[2] https://www.empatica.com/en-eu/research/e4/.
[3] We refer to end-users as to service consumers, as the applications usually provide services to their users.

2.4 Hypothesis, Variables and Metrics

We identify as a *hypothesis* that the personality influences the perceived importance of security attributes of software applications. From this hypothesis, we identified the following variables:

Response variables: the perceived importance of security, which is defined in terms of authenticity, confidentiality, accountability, and integrity attributes, is measured by means of i) four items formulated in 5-points ordinal scale (from "not at all important" to "extremely important"); ii) ranking ten domain-specific items, where at least five of them should be rated.

Factors: as the main functionality and some vulnerabilities of the happyParking app are illustrated through animated-demonstration videos. In this study, we identified the videos as a factor that could affect the response variables.
Personality is another important factor identified in our study. To measure it, we use the Big Five Inventory questionnaire (BFI) [14], which is a self-report inventory designed to measure the so-called Big Five dimensions: Extraversion, Agreeableness, Conscientiousness, Neuroticism, and Openness to experience.

2.5 Web-Based Survey Implementation

We implemented a web-based survey using the Qualtrics tool. Figure 1 presents the process of survey execution. The survey takes 35 min and it is composed of two parts:

A pre-questionnaire: aiming to collect demographic and personality information. The *demographic part* consists of nine questions (*e.g.,* sex, age, educational degree, domain expertise).

The *Personality test* based on "The BFI questionnaire" that consists of 44 items for measuring five dimensions: Extraversion, Agreeableness, Neuroticism,

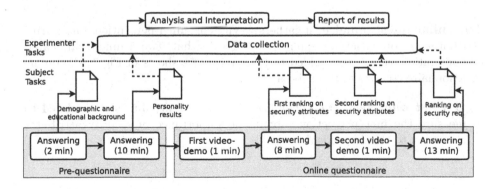

Fig. 1. An overview of the survey conduction

Openness, and Conscientiousness. However, for the purpose of reducing the average duration of the survey, we considered only those items related to the following dimensions:

i) Agreeableness: it refers to a person's tendency to be compassionate and cooperative toward others. Low Agreeableness is related to being suspicious, challenging, and antagonistic towards other people. Agreeableness is composed of the nine following items: *A1-Tends to find fault with others, A2-Is helpful and unselfish with others, A3-Starts quarrels with others, A4-Has a forgiving nature, A5-Is generally trusting, A6-Can be cold and aloof, A7-Is considerate and kind to almost everyone, A8-Is sometimes rude to others, A9-Likes to cooperate with others.*

ii) Neuroticism: it refers to the extent to which a person's emotions are sensitive to the environment, thus identifying individuals prone to psychological distress, anxiety or excessive urges. Those who have a low score in Neuroticism are calmer and more stable. Neuroticism is composed of the eight following items: *N1-Is depressed, blue, N2-Is relaxed, handles stress well, N3-Can be tense, N4-Worries a lot, N5-Is emotionally stable, not easily upset, N6-Can be moody, N7-Remains calm in tense situations, N8-Gets nervous easily.*

iii) Openness: it refers to the extent to which a person is open to experiencing a variety of activities. People low in Openness tend to be more conservative and close-minded. Openness is composed of the ten following items: *O1-Is original, comes up with new ideas, O2-Is curious about many different things, O3-Is ingenious, a deep thinker, O4-Has an active imagination, O5-Is inventive, O6-Values artistic, aesthetic experiences, O7-Prefers work that is routine, O8-Likes to reflect, play with ideas, O9-Has few artistic interests, O10-Is sophisticated in art, music, or literature.*

According to [22], these constructs (dimensions) were found as the most relevant for understanding the personality characteristics in the context of software technology. All of the scale items were in the Five-point Likert Response Format (where the lowest point of 1 means "strongly disagree" and the highest point of 5 means "strongly agree").

The online questionnaire: it gathers service consumer perceptions on security attributes of context-aware applications. To do that, two 1-minute animated demonstration videos were added to the survey. As shows in Fig. 1, the online questionnaire consists of two sub-parts:

i) First one: items (*i.e.,* definitions of security attributes) formulated to measure the first perceptions about the importance of security attributes according to the first video[4].

---

[4] happyparking.mp4 file in the OSF repository link (see Sect. 2).

ii) Second one: questions for re-evaluating the importance of security attributes (after watching the second video[5]) are formulated. Finally, a set of security requirements to keep quality of the case study high should be prioritized by subjects[6]. It helps us to confirm the importance provided in the second round, however the analysis of these requirements is not part of this paper.

2.6 Survey Validation and Conduction

Survey validation: a pilot study that used our survey design was performed in October 9, 2018 in the MEGSUS workshop at ESEM 2018 [18]. Therein, we collected feedback from seven subjects working on topics of software sustainability. Their feedback was used to improve the questionnaire design regarding: i) the clarity and relevance of the questions, and ii) the duration of the survey. The completing process of the survey took about 40–60 min. In this version, all items of the BFI dimensions were considered, which demanded more than 20 min. In order to reduce this time, we shortened the BFI questionnaire by considering items from three dimensions only (instead the total of five dimensions) as explained.

Survey Conduction

A. Data collection: considering the characteristics of our target audience, we planned our data collection in three stages. The first two collection stages were already conducted whilst the third one is planned for future work. They are described as follows:

First stage: the survey was conducted as part of the Live Study track of the International Working conference on Requirements Engineering: Foundations for Software Quality (REFSQ). Voluntary researchers and practitioners with background in Requirements Engineering completed this survey, which was opened from 18 March until 3th April 2019. General instructions were given during one of the plenary sessions of REFSQ [11].

Second stage: the survey was conducted with Students from the Education department of the Universidad Nacional de San Agustin (Peru) in June 18, 2019. With the purpose of avoiding some internet connection issues, the collection was carried out using the paper and electronic forms for the data collection. All subjects gave an informed consent before performing the study. The averaged actual time of executing the survey took about 35 min.

Regarding the *third collection stage*, we plan to conduct the survey with teenagers and elderly people with basic educational background.

This new data will be independently analyzed and compared to our results obtained from the first two stages.

---

[5] happyparking-vulnerabilities.mp4 file in the OSF repository.
[6] SecurityRequirements.pdf file in the OSF repository link.

B. Data validation: it ensures that the survey questionnaire is completed and contains consistent data. In this paper, we focus on the analysis of the data collected from the two first stages of data collection described above. Overall, 20 subjects accepted to participate in Stage 1, whereas 33 Subjects participated in Stage 2. However, incomplete questionnaires were discarded (four were from the first stage, and only one from the second stage). Moreover, verifying the target group of all subjects involved in both stages, by means of some demographics (i.e., educational background), we identified four subjects involved in Stage 2 were categorized as Group A because of their mixed background in Education and SE. Therefore, we found that 20 subjects were categorized as Group A and 28 as Group B.

3   Results

As mentioned, data collected from a total of 48 subjects was used in our analysis. The demographics are presented in Table 1. We note that the subjects from Group B (with background in Education) are younger than the subjects in Group A (with Software Engineering background). We can also see that Group A tends to use the mobile phone with less frequency than Group B. The mobile feature most used were camera, and text messaging for Group A, whereas internet browsing/apps was for Group B. Moreover, Group A included men and women subjects, whereas over 90% of subjects from Group B were female.

Table 1. Demographics of subjects from Group A and B

Characteristics	Group A	Group B
Age	20–70 years old	20–28 years old
Sex	35% female, 65% male	93% female, 7% male
Background	Software engineering	Education
Frequency of mobile usage (per day)	15% <30 min	11% ≥ 30 min and <1 h
	20% ≥ 30 min and <1 h	18% ≥ 1 h and <2 h
	55% ≥ 1 h and <2 h	21% ≥ 2 h and ≤ 3 h
	10% ≥ 2 h and ≤ 3 h	50% >3 h
Mobile feature most used	Camera, text messaging (each <30 min)	Internet browsing/apps (>2 h)

In the following, we proceed to analyze the gathered data through the survey in order to answer our research questions.

3.1   RQ$_1$: How Do Service Consumers Perceive the Importance of Security of a Context-Aware Software Intensive System?

To answer RQ1, we analysed the frequency distribution per security attribute regarding the perceived importance, which is measured in a 5-points ordinal

Table 2. Comparison between answers on perceived importance of security attributes: 20 Subjects of Group A and 28 Subjects of Group B. Where: *1st Vid = first video, 2nd Vid = second video, NI = not at all important, SI = slightly important, MI = moderate important, VI = very important and EI = extremely important.*

		Confidentiality		Authenticity		Accountability		Integrity	
		1st Vid	2nd Vid	1st Vid	2nd Vid	1st Vid	2nd Vid	1st Vid	2nd Vid
Group A	NI	0	1	3	1	3	2	1	0
	SI	2	0	2	1	6	2	0	0
	MI	2	1	2	3	5	4	2	3
	VI	5	6	8	6	4	6	8	4
	EI	11	12	5	9	2	6	9	13
	% VI+EI	80%	90%	65%	75%	30%	60%	80%	85%
Group B	NI	0	5	0	4	0	6	0	4
	SI	3	3	4	6	2	2	3	4
	MI	10	5	7	5	12	6	11	6
	VI	9	10	12	9	11	8	10	9
	EI	6	5	5	4	3	6	4	5
	% VI+EI	54%	54%	61%	46%	50%	50%	50%	50%

scale. Table 2 presents the importance of security attributes perceived by subjects from Group A and B. As this measure was taken in two different moments, we added two columns to each security attribute: "1st Video" columns represent number of subject's answers about how a security attribute is perceived after watching the first video (main functionalities of happyParking), whereas "2nd Video" columns represent the number of answers to the same question but after watching the second video (happyParking with security breaches).

From this data, we can see that most of the security attributes were more clearly perceived as important by subjects from Group A than by subjects from Group B. Particularly, *Integrity* and *Confidentiality* were deemed extremely important security attributes by subjects from Group A. Interestingly, we noticed that the importance of both attributes could be perceived from the beginning (first video), whereas the importance for other security attributes, like *authenticity* or *accountability*, was most hardly perceived. For instance, most of the subjects from Group A realized the importance of accountability only after watching the second video. We can also observe that after watching the second video more subjects from Group A rate all security attributes as very and extremely important. It may also be the fact that the second video, which exhibits a scenario in which security breaches can damage service consumers, helps subjects to understand the value of keeping security attributes high.

The variation in the perceptions of the importance of security attributes seems to be even broader in case of subjects with non-technical background, i.e. different from SE, such as subjects from Group B. Another interesting observation was that subjects from Group B tend to perceive the importance of security attributes from the beginning but with not so much intensity such as it was with the subjects of Group A. For example, as shown in Table 2 for Group B, about 35% of subjects perceived confidentiality, accountability, and integrity as security attributes with a moderate importance level. And, only around 50% of subjects from Group B perceived confidentiality and integrity as very or extremely important in contrast to the 80% of subjects from Group A.

Moreover, more or less 14% of subjects from Group B changed their perceptions after watching the second video, by considering the security attributes as not all important. This unexpected result may be due to the lack of adequate understanding on the security attributes definitions by subjects with a non-technical background. Another possible explanation for this may be related to the socio-cultural issues, e.g. vulnerabilities illustrated in the video could not have been considered as so critical in comparison with actual vulnerabilities experienced in real-life. Overall, we consider that this combination of results provides some support for the conceptual premise stated by West [29]: *"security is hard to be appreciated because end-users do not think they are at risk"* or *"losses perceived disproportionately to gains"*.

> **In response to RQ1:** Confidentiality and integrity are more clearly perceived as important by service consumers with technical (SE) background. Whilst accountability is more difficult to be perceived as important by service consumers, even more pronounced for those without any SE background. Moreover, after watching a dangerous scenario in which security vulnerabilities were exploited, service consumers with SE background reassert their perception on the importance of security attributes (confidentiality, authenticity, accountability, integrity). Contrary to service consumers without SE background, where some of them (around 18%) perceived security attributes as not at all important.

In order to understand better these results, in the next sub-section, we will investigate how personality traits influence subjects' answers in this study.

3.2   RQ2: Do the Personality Influence on the Importance Perceived of Security of Context-Aware Software Applications?

To answer RQ2, our analysis consists of three steps: 1) characterizing each subject by means of three personality dimensions; 2) analyzing the influence of personality on the perceived importance of security attributes; 3) analyzing the personality's influence on change in security perceptions.

Step 1: characterizing each subject by means of three personality dimensions. To characterize each subject through the three personality dimensions (i.e. agreeableness, neuroticism, openness), we have first calculated the scores self-reported by means of the personality test. To do this, for each dimension (construct), the scores of the corresponding items were added. Then, in order to make comparable our dimensions, each result was normalized to a common ratio scale with values between 0 and 1. Next, for each subject, we chose

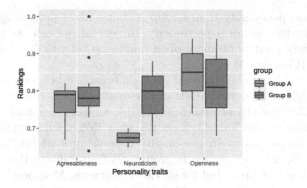

Fig. 2. Personality distributions of subjects from Group A and B

the maximum value of these normalized values. If this value was greater than 0.75 we labeled it as high level of the personality. Otherwise, if this value was greater than 0.5 we labeled it as a moderate level, else the subject will not be characterized by any personality trait studied in this paper. Analysing our data set we found that all subjects were characterized by high or moderate levels of personalities. Notice that two subjects from Group B presented the same maximum value for two different dimensions. To analyse both personality dimensions, we have duplicated the entries related to these subjects. This is the reason why we have 50 Subjects in total (instead of 48) for the analysis of RQ_2.

Figure 2 depicts the personality distributions of the subjects from Group A and B. We observe that Group A tends to have a greater level of *openness* and a lower level of *neuroticism* than Group B. Both groups seem to have a similar level of *agreeableness*, however Group B contains three subjects who are outside of the range. On the other hand, Table 3 introduces the percentages of subjects from Group A and B who are characterized by a personality in two levels: high and moderate values. From this table we notice that both groups have equivalent percentages of subjects characterized by the *Neuroticism* personality. Moreover, Group B has a slightly greater percentage of subjects who were characterized by

Table 3. Percentages of subjects characterized by a personality trait

Groups	Values	Personality traits		
		Agreeableness	Neuroticism	Openness
A	High	20	0	45
	Moderate	10	10	15
	% Total	30	10	60
B	High	30	6.67	40
	Moderate	6.67	3.33	13.33
	% Total	36.67	10	53.33

the *agreeableness* personality than Group A, but a lower percentage of subjects characterized by the *openness* personality. In general, we can say that the subjects of our study tend to be more open-minded (Columns 5) and cooperative toward others (Columns 3).

For the rest of our analysis, we do not differentiate between subjects characterized by high or moderate levels of personality types. However, we should keep in mind that the characterization of subjects using personality test is not trivial. For instance, from Table 3, we notice that 35% of subjects from Group A were characterized as a certain personality type using moderate values. In the case of Group B, this percentage is around 23%. It reflects the variability of personality tendencies presented by service consumers. Moreover, the fact that people could present different combinations of personality types increases the difficulty of characterization. As mentioned, we considered only the type of personality with highest value. However for future work, a deep analysis of users characterization will be needed.

Step2: analyzing the influence of personality on the perceived importance of security attributes. To investigate whether personality types influence on the perceived importance of security attributes, we firstly analyzed the distribution of our data set[7] (see Table 4). From this table, we can see that subjects with a high level of *openness* have a higher propensity to perceive the importance of certain security attributes like *confidentiality* and *integrity*. However, subjects hold quite different perceptions regarding the importance of *authenticity* and *accountability*.

This variability is even greater for those subjects with a high level of *agreeableness* (who are assumed to be kind, considerate, likable, helpful, and cooperative). It is interesting to note that most of these kind of respondents from Group B considered security attributes like *confidentiality, accountability* and *integrity* as not at all important (see Table 4, Column 9, on the right). It is somewhat surprising since this perception was after watching the second video (scenarios with vulnerabilities of the mobile app). A possible explanation for this might be that the mobile app such as happyParking could have been perceived as so useful that security was not considered as important. The first part of this observation seems to be consistent with other research which found that *"individuals with a high level of agreeableness have a higher propensity to perceive smart phone technology as more useful"* [22]. However, further research needs to be carried out in order to get a better understanding whether the importance of security can be more difficult perceived by people with a high level in agreeableness.

The relationships between our categorical variables (personality type in a nominal scale and perceived importance in a ordinal scale) were analyzed by means of cross-tabulation. Then, in order to determine the strength of association between both variables, we used the Cramer's V measure[8], whose value

---

[7] You can find the data set (SecurityPerception.csv file) in the OSF repository.

[8] According to [1], the strength of association is interpreted as follows: >0.25 very strong; >0.15 strong; >0.10 moderate; >0.05 weak; >0 to 0.05 no relationship.

Table 4. Frequency distribution about the perceived importance of security attributes. Where: *NI = not at all important, SI = slightly important, MI = moderate important, VI = very important and EI = extremely important.*

Personality dimension		Group	First video					Second video				
			NI	SI	MI	VI	EI	NI	SI	MI	VI	EI
Confident.	Agreeableness	A	0	0	1	1	4	0	0	0	2	4
		B	0	1	5	4	1	4	0	3	1	3
	Neuroticism	A	0	0	0	1	1	0	0	0	1	1
		B	0	2	0	1	0	1	1	0	1	0
	Openness	A	0	2	1	3	6	1	0	1	3	7
		B	0	1	6	4	5	1	3	2	8	2
Authent.	Agrecableness	A	0	0	1	3	2	0	0	0	2	4
		B	0	2	4	4	1	2	4	2	2	1
	Neuroticism	A	0	0	1	1	0	0	0	1	0	1
		B	0	1	0	2	0	1	1	1	0	0
	Openness	A	3	2	0	4	3	1	1	2	4	4
		B	0	3	3	6	4	2	2	2	7	3
Account.	Agreeableness	A	0	0	3	2	1	0	0	0	3	3
		B	0	1	5	5	0	4	1	2	2	2
	Neuroticism	A	0	2	0	0	0	0	1	1	4	5
		B	0	1	1	1	0	1	1	0	0	1
	Openness	A	3	4	2	2	1	2	1	3	3	3
		B	0	1	7	5	3	2	1	4	6	3
Integrity	Agreeableness	A	0	0	0	4	2	0	0	1	1	4
		B	0	2	6	3	0	3	2	2	3	1
	Neuroticism	A	0	0	1	1	0	0	0	0	1	1
		B	0	0	1	1	1	1	1	0	1	0
	Openness	A	1	0	1	3	7	0	0	2	2	8
		B	0	2	4	6	4	1	2	4	5	4

varies between 0 and 1. The Cramer's V values calculated from our data set are presented in Table 5. As we can notice from this table, the *p-values* suggest non-significant results to reject the null hypothesis (*i.e.*, that variables are independent). According to our first descriptive data analysis (Fig. 2), three data points were located outside the whiskers of the box plot. Considering these data points as outliers, we recalculated the Cramer's V values. For this, we obtained one significant result, which is related to personality types of Group B and the *confidentiality* attribute (first video). We obtained 0.04 as *p-value* and 0.5 as Cramers'V value, so it suggests a very strong association between service consumers' personality types and the importance perception on confidentiality. The complete results are not shown for space limitation reasons.

Table 5. Cramer's V measure to evaluate the association between personality traits and security attributes

		First video				Second video			
		Conf.	Authent.	Account.	Integr.	Conf.	Authent.	Account.	Integr.
Total	p-value	0.35	0.56	0.15	0.60	0.43	0.63	0.40	0.66
	Chi-square	6.69	6.76	12.10	6.42	8.01	6.19	8.36	5.87
	Cramer's V	0.26	0.26	0.35	0.25	0.28	0.25	0.29	0.24
GrpA	p-value	0.84	0.34	0.20	0.25	0.94	0.70	0.24	0.84
	Chi-square	2.71	9.00	10.94	7.85	1.81	5.56	10.42	1.41
	Cramer's V	0.26	0.47	0.52	0.44	0.21	0.37	0.51	0.19
GrpB	p-value	0.09	0.67	0.55	0.50	0.15	0.60	0.59	0.72
	Chi-square	11.05	4.08	4.94	5.37	12.06	6.42	6.52	5.38
	Cramer's V	0.43	0.26	0.29	0.30	0.45	0.33	0.33	0.30

Step3: analyzing the personality's influence on change in security perceptions. To investigate whether personality type influence on changes in the importance perceived by service consumers, we firstly calculated the delta values (*i.e.*, $perception\_value_{second\_video} - perception\_value_{first\_video}$). Then, the Cramer's V values were calculated to analyze the level of association between the different (positive and negative) delta values and personality types (see Table 6). From this table, we notice that the positive and negative delta values of the importance on *confidentiality* are very strongly influenced by the subjects' personality traits (the *p-values* are 0.02 and 0.05, and the *Cramer's values* are 0.84 and 0.54, see Column 3 and 7). It does not depend on the subjects' education background. This result is even more clear for the positive delta values whose *p-values* is 0.02 and the *Cramer's V value* is = 0.84 (see Column 3).

Table 6. Cramer's V measure to evaluate the association between personality traits and changes in security perceptions (delta)

		Positive delta				Negative delta			
		Conf.	Authent.	Account.	Integr.	Conf.	Authent.	Account.	Integr.
Total	p-value	0.02	0.74	0.87	0.51	0.05	0.25	0.29	0.33
	Chi-square	7.76	0.61	1.23	1.33	9.48	5.40	4.99	4.62
	Cramer's V	0.84	0.21	0.19	0.33	0.54	0.42	0.46	0.42
GrpA	p-value	0.32	0.55	0.69	0.30				
	Chi-square	1.00	1.20	2.25	2.40				
	Cramer's V	0.50	0.39	0.34	0.63				
GrpB	p-value	0.03	1.00	0.46	1.00	0.07	0.32	0.29	0.36
	Chi-square	7.00	0.00	1.56	0.00	8.61	4.67	4.99	4.37
	Cramer's V	1.00	0.00	0.47	0.00	0.54	0.41	0.46	0.43

Analysing each group, we notice that Group A does not have enough negative variations to calculate the chi-square and Cramer's V values. It could be explained by the fact of the subjects from Group A, having a SE background, understand better the importance of security attributes. So, their perceptions could not be changed in a negative way. Regarding Group B, we note that the positive variations of perceptions on confidentiality are perfectly associated to the subjects personality types (the *p-value* is 0.03 and the *Cramer's V value* is 1.0). And, the negative variations of perceptions on confidentiality could be very strongly associated to the subjects personality types if we accept the *p-value* = 0.07 (the *Cramer's V value* is = 0.54). For the rest of the calculated Cramer's V values, we obtained non-significant results to reject the null hypothesis.

In response to RQ2: Open-minded service consumers have a higher propensity to perceive the importance of confidentiality and integrity. Whilst, service consumers with levels of openness or agreeableness hold quite different importance perceptions on authenticity and accountability. Moreover, according to Cramers'V values, the importance perceptions on confidentiality are influenced by the personality of service consumers without SE background. And, the (positive or negative) changes in the importance perception on confidentiality are also very strongly influenced by the personality of service consumers without SE background.

---

4   Threats to Validity

Internal validity: As the survey was conducted with two different target audiences, we translated the original instruments (questionnaires, personality test and videos) from English to Spanish. To mitigate any error in the translation, Spanish native speakers reviewed the instruments used in our study. Another potential threat is regarding the unequally sized gender groups, which can impact on our results.

Construct validity: We mitigated the threat related to the following two social factors by implementing specific actions: (i) regarding *Hypothesis guessing*, we did not reveal the research goal before conducting the survey, and (ii) regarding *Evaluation apprehension*, we made the completion of both personality test and online questionnaire anonymous as some people are afraid of being evaluated. Regarding the threats related to the design of the study: the most important is *mono-operation bias*; as we included only one treatment (happyParking app), the study could be under-representing the identified constructs (perceived importance on security). To mitigate this threat, we carefully selected the software domain (IoT systems for the smart parking sector in which security and privacy are crucial [2]), which we think it is representative enough for measuring our response variables. Also we considered other relevant factors as personality, which was measured by means of the BFI questionnaire, defined and validated in the psychology field [14]. Moreover, the BFI model has been widely used in the SE field (*e.g.,* the analysis of developers' personalities in the Apache ecosystem pre-sented by Calefato *et al.* [8]). For our analysis, we focused especially on a sub set of constructs that have an effect on the Technology acceptance [22] (i.e. agreeableness, neuroticism, openness). However, our current analysis is limited in considering only one personality type by subject (the maximum value of the three personality dimensions). Further work is needed to characterize individuals by considering other levels of personality dimensions. For example, a subject can be high in openness, but moderate in agreeableness, and low in neuroticism.

Regarding the questions in ordinal scale (importance level) we added the option: "No opinion" to avoid forcing respondents in choosing one of the other levels of importance.

External validity: concerns the *generalization* of the findings beyond the validation settings. As our sample corresponds to a selective proportion of end-users (48 subjects) of a context-aware software application (*i.e.,* happyParking mobile app), our results can not be generalized. This threat is partly reduced by the fact that the survey was first conducted with volunteer attendees from REFSQ 2019, then replicated in Peru with volunteer education students.

5   Related Work

The 2015 mapping study of Cruz *et al.* [12] on empirical research on personality types in SE, indicated a broad array of contexts in which SE researchers analyzed the role and the effect of personality, e.g. pair programming, individual performance team process, team effectiveness, leadership performance, software process allocation, and SE education. Although this mapping study covers a 40 years long period of research publication activity, very few papers were found on the topic of linkages between personality types and security engineering.

For instance, Shropshire *et al.* [25] propose a method for identifying those individuals in an organization that are most likely to commit IT security infractions, based on some dimensions of their personality. However, the authors just motivate and propose an empirical research design, without reporting how it is executed in a study with real-world subjects. Furthermore, Uffen *et al.* [28] empirically investigated the relationship between personality traits and attitudes towards security risks of security executives. These authors hypothesized relationships between the construct of the five-factor model (FFM) and technical and non-technical dimensions (e.g. culture, compliance, organization, strategic management) of information security management. Next, Bansal empirically examined the relation of the FFM constructs and concerns of security and privacy on websites [5]. This study found that neuroticism, conscientiousness and extraversion are positively related with concerns for security. Personality traits of agreeableness and openness are significantly associated with concern for privacy. Moreover, Junglas et al. [15] used protection motivation theory to look into any possible relationship between privacy concerns and agreeableness, conscientiousness, and openness. These authors found that personality traits affect the concern for privacy in location-based services. Finally, Bulgurcu *et al.* [7] investigated how personality influences employees' intention to comply with the requirements of an organization's security policies. The authors's empirical design is grounded on the theory of planned behavior and the rational choice theory and investigates the possible relationships between the constructs of these theories and individual intention to comply with the requirements of the information security policies. Using data of 110 practitioners in a company, this study shows that the individual intention to comply is significantly influenced by attitude, normative beliefs, and self-efficacy to comply.

To the best of our knowledge, our approach is the first designed to analyse empirically end-users (*i.e.,* service consumers who are outside of a company) perception on security attributes of context-aware software applications. Moreover, our approach differs from previous works on the methodology employed to collect end-users perceptions on the importance of security attributes. In particular, none of these approaches used contra-version scenarios to analyse users profile (user's personality types and educational background) in perceiving security.

6 Conclusions and Further Work

In this paper we studied how end-users perceive security attributes of context-aware software applications. To do that, we performed a survey in two stages: firstly, it was with voluntary participants of the REFSQ conference. Secondly, it as with volunteers of education students of the Universidad Nacional San Agustin (Peru). The survey allowed us to understand how a selective proportion of end-users (48 subjects) perceives security in two different scenarios of a mobile app (with and without security vulnerabilities), and how the users personality types affect these perceptions and changes in them.

From this sample of potential service consumers, the results showed that subjects' educational background influenced their perception on security. After watching the second video, Group A (subjects with SE background) considered security attributes more important, whilst Group B (subjects with education background) deemed them less important. This phenomenon could be traceable to the use of technical terms in security, which were probably better understood by software engineers than educators.

The research has also shown that subjects with a higher level of openness would have a much better perception on the importance of confidentiality and integrity. However, the importance of security attributes like accountability and authenticity was not appreciated by subjects from Group B with a highest level of agreeableness. Considering the Cramer's V values, we found a significant very strong association between personality traits of subjects from Group B and the importance perception on confidentiality. We also obtained that users personality types is very strongly associated to the changes in the importance perception on confidentiality. This conclusion is even more clear for subjects from Group B.

For the next step of our study we plan to replicate the survey with a broader group of participants, and consider other variables such as gender and the frequency of mobile apps usage.

Acknowledgment. We thank the participants of the study. N. Condori-Fernandez and F. Suni-Lopez acknowledge the financial support of the KUSISQA Project - World Bank, through Fondo Nacional de Desarrollo Cientfico, Tecnolgico y de Innovacin Tecnolgica (FONDECYT). Also, this work has been partially supported by Datos 4.0 (TIN2016-78011-C4-1-R) funded by MINECO-AEI/FEDER-UE.

References

1. Akoglu, H.: User's guide to correlation coefficients. Turk. J. Emerg. Med. **18**(3), 91–93 (2018)
2. Al-Turjman, F., Malekloo, A.: Smart parking in IoT-enabled cities: a survey. Sustain. Cities Soc. **49**, 101608 (2019)
3. Anderson, R.J.: Security Engineering: A Guide to Building Dependable Distributed Systems, 2nd edn. Wiley, Hoboken (2008)
4. Anderson, R., et al.: Measuring the cost of cybercrime. In: Böhme, R. (ed.) The Economics of Information Security and Privacy, pp. 265–300. Springer, Heidelberg (2013). https://doi.org/10.1007/978-3-642-39498-0_12
5. Bansal, G.: Security concerns in the nomological network of trust and big 5: first order vs. second order. In: Galletta, D.F., Liang, T. (eds.) Proceedings of the International Conference on Information Systems, ICIS 2011, Shanghai, China, 4–7 December 2011. Association for Information Systems (2011). http://aisel.aisnet.org/icis2011/proceedings/ISsecurity/9
6. Bødker, S.: Scenarios in user-centred design setting the stage for reflection and action. Interact. Comput. **13**(1), 61–75 (2000). https://doi.org/10.1016/S0953-5438(00)00024-2
7. Bulgurcu, B., Cavusoglu, H., Benbasat, I.: Information security policy compliance: an empirical study of rationality-based beliefs and information security awareness. MIS Q. **34**(3), 523–548 (2010)
8. Calefato, F., Lanubile, F., Vasilescu, B.: A large-scale, in-depth analysis of developers' personalities in the apache ecosystem. Inf. Softw. Technol. **114**, 1–20 (2019). https://doi.org/10.1016/j.infsof.2019.05.012
9. Condori-Fernández, N.: HAPPYNESS: an emotion-aware QoS assurance framework for enhancing user experience. In: Uchitel, S., Orso, A., Robillard, M.P. (eds.) Proceedings of the 39th International Conference on Software Engineering, ICSE 2017, Buenos Aires, Argentina, 20–28 May 2017 - Companion Volume, pp. 235–237. IEEE Computer Society (2017). https://doi.org/10.1109/ICSE-C.2017.137
10. Condori-Fernández, N., Lago, P.: Characterizing the contribution of quality requirements to software sustainability. J. Syst. Softw. **137**, 289–305 (2018). https://doi.org/10.1016/j.jss.2017.12.005
11. Condori-Fernández, N., Muñante, D., Lopez, F.S.: Exploring users perception on security and satisfaction requirements of context-aware applications: an online survey. In: Spoletini, P., et al. (eds.) Joint Proceedings of REFSQ-2019 Workshops, Doctoral Symposium, Live Studies Track, and Poster Track Co-Located with the 25th International Conference on Requirements Engineering: Foundation for Software Quality (REFSQ 2019). CEUR Workshop Proceedings, Essen, Germany, 18 March 2019, vol. 2376. CEUR-WS.org (2019). http://ceur-ws.org/Vol-2376/LS_paper1.pdf
12. Cruz, S.S.J.O., da Silva, F.Q.B., Capretz, L.F.: Forty years of research on personality in software engineering: a mapping study. Comput. Hum. Behav. **46**, 94–113 (2015). https://doi.org/10.1016/j.chb.2014.12.008

13. Dalpiaz, F., Paja, E., Giorgini, P.: Security Requirements Engineering: Designing Secure Socio-Technical Systems. MIT Press, Cambridge (2016)
14. John, O.P., Srivastava, S.: The big five trait taxonomy: history, measurement, and theoretical perspectives. In: Pervin, L.A., John, O.P. (eds.) Handbook of Personality: Theory and Research, 2nd edn, pp. 102–138. Guilford Press, New York (1999)
15. Junglas, I.A., Johnson, N.A., Spitzmüller, C.: Personality traits and concern for privacy: an empirical study in the context of location-based services. Eur. J. Inf. Syst. **17**(4), 387–402 (2008). https://doi.org/10.1057/ejis.2008.29
16. Kitchenham, B.A., Pfleeger, S.L.: Principles of survey research part 2: designing a survey. ACM SIGSOFT Softw. Eng. Notes **27**(1), 18–20 (2002). https://doi.org/10.1145/566493.566495
17. Laverdière, M., Mourad, A., Hanna, A., Debbabi, M.: Security design patterns: survey and evaluation. In: Proceedings of the Canadian Conference on Electrical and Computer Engineering, CCECE 2006, Ottawa Congress Centre, Ottawa, Canada, 7–10 May 2006, pp. 1605–1608. IEEE (2006). https://doi.org/10.1109/CCECE.2006.277727
18. Lopez, F.S., Condori-Fernández, N., Muñante, D.: End-user perceptions on social sustainability in context-aware applications: validation of an experiment design. In: Condori-Fernández, N., Bagnato, A., Kern, E. (eds.) Proceedings of the 4th International Workshop on Measurement and Metrics for Green and Sustainable Software Systems Co-Located with Empirical Software Engineering International Week (ESEIW 2018). CEUR Workshop Proceedings, Oulu, Finland, 9 October 2018, vol. 2286, p. 31. CEUR-WS.org (2018). http://ceur-ws.org/Vol-2286/paper_4.pdf
19. Molléri, J.S., Petersen, K., Mendes, E.: Survey guidelines in software engineering: an annotated review. In: Proceedings of the 10th ACM/IEEE International Symposium on Empirical Software Engineering and Measurement, ESEM 2016, Ciudad Real, Spain, 8–9 September 2016, pp. 58:1–58:6. ACM (2016). https://doi.org/10.1145/2961111.2962619
20. Muñante, D., Chiprianov, V., Gallon, L., Aniorté, P.: A review of security requirements engineering methods with respect to risk analysis and model-driven engineering. In: Teufel, S., Min, T.A., You, I., Weippl, E. (eds.) CD-ARES 2014. LNCS, vol. 8708, pp. 79–93. Springer, Cham (2014). https://doi.org/10.1007/978-3-319-10975-6_6
21. Muñante, D., Siena, A., Kifetew, F.M., Susi, A., Stade, M.J.C., Seyff, N.: Gathering requirements for software configuration from the crowd. In: IEEE 25th International Requirements Engineering Conference Workshops, RE 2017 Workshops, Lisbon, Portugal, 4–8 September 2017, pp. 176–181. IEEE Computer Society (2017). https://doi.org/10.1109/REW.2017.74
22. Özbek, V., Alnıaçık, Ü., Koc, F., Akkılıç, M.E., Kaş, E.: The impact of personality on technology acceptance: a study on smart phone users. Procedia. Soc. Behav. Sci. **150**, 541–551 (2014)
23. Price, B.A., et al.: Contravision: presenting contrasting visions of future technology. In: Mynatt, E.D., Schoner, D., Fitzpatrick, G., Hudson, S.E., Edwards, W.K., Rodden, T. (eds.) Proceedings of the 28th International Conference on Human Factors in Computing Systems, CHI 2010, Extended Abstracts Volume, Atlanta, Georgia, USA, 10–15 April 2010, pp. 4759–4764. ACM (2010). https://doi.org/10.1145/1753846.1754227
24. Rad, M.S., Nilashi, M., Dahlan, H.M.: Information technology adoption: a review of the literature and classification. Univ. Access Inf. Soc. **17**(2), 361–390 (2018). https://doi.org/10.1007/s10209-017-0534-z

25. Shropshire, J., Warkentin, M., Johnston, A.C., Schmidt, M.B.: Personality and IT security: an application of the five-factor model. In: Rodríguez-Abitia, G., B., I.A. (eds.) Connecting the Americas. 12th Americas Conference on Information Systems, AMCIS 2006, Acapulco, Mexico, 4–6 August 2006, p. 415. Association for Information Systems (2006). http://aisel.aisnet.org/amcis2006/415
26. Soikkeli, T., Karikoski, J., Hämmäinen, H.: Diversity and end user context in smartphone usage sessions. In: Al-Begain, K., Belimpasakis, P., Balakrishna, C. (eds.) 5th International Conference on Next Generation Mobile Applications, Services and Technologies, NGMAST 2011, Cardiff, United Kingdom, 14–16 September 2011, pp. 7–12. IEEE (2011). https://doi.org/10.1109/NGMAST.2011.12
27. Svendsen, G.B., Johnsen, J.K., Almås-Sørensen, L., Vittersø, J.: Personality and technology acceptance: the influence of personality factors on the core constructs of the technology acceptance model. Behav. Inf. Technol. **32**(4), 323–334 (2013). https://doi.org/10.1080/0144929X.2011.553740
28. Uffen, J., Kaemmerer, N., Breitner, M.H.: Personality traits and cognitive determinants—an empirical investigation of the use of smartphone security measures. J. Inf. Secur. **04**(04), 203–212 (2013)
29. West, R.: The psychology of security. Commun. ACM **51**(4), 34–40 (2008). https://doi.org/10.1145/1330311.1330320

Refining the Blunt Instruments of Cybersecurity: A Framework to Coordinate Prevention and Preservation of Behaviours

Simon Parkin[1(✉)] and Yi Ting Chua[2]

[1] University College London, London, UK
s.parkin@ucl.ac.uk
[2] University of Cambridge, Cambridge, UK
yiting.chua@cl.cam.ac.uk

Abstract. Background. Cybersecurity controls are deployed to manage risks posed by malicious behaviours or systems. What is not often considered or articulated is how cybersecurity controls may impact legitimate users (often those whose use of a managed system needs to be protected, and preserved). This oversight characterises the 'blunt' nature of many cybersecurity controls.

Aim. Here we present a framework produced from a synthesis of methods from cybercrime opportunity reduction and behaviour change, and a consideration of existing risk management guidelines.

Method. We illustrate the framework and its principles with a range of examples and a potential application focusing on online abuse and social media controls, relating in turn to issues inherent in cyberbullying and tech-abuse.

Results. The framework describes a capacity to improve the precision of cybersecurity controls by examining shared determinants of negative and positive behaviours in a system. This identifies opportunities for risk owners to better protect legitimate users while simultaneously acting to prevent malicious activity in a managed system.

Conclusions. We describe capabilities for a novel approach to managing sociotechnical cyber-risk which can be integrated into typical risk management processes. This includes consideration of user activities as a system asset to protect, and a consideration of how to engage with other stakeholders to identify behaviours to preserve in a system.

Keywords: Risk management · Cyber risk · Sociotechnical security

1 Introduction

Cyber-risk controls are deployed within a managed IT system, such as in a business or an online service platform, to manage cyber risks and address unknown or anticipated malicious behaviour. Implicit in common security and privacy risk

© Springer Nature Switzerland AG 2021
T. Groß and L. Viganò (Eds.): STAST 2020, LNCS 12812, pp. 23–42, 2021.
https://doi.org/10.1007/978-3-030-79318-0_2

management practices is that if a control is well-intentioned, it will not do any harm to those it is meant to protect. Cyber threats can impose a range of different harms upon legitimate users [3], however so can cybersecurity risk controls if not carefully considered [17]. This can result in e.g., legitimate users being removed from a system, or their activity being misclassified. Such *unintended harms* may be more severe for specific user groups who lack targeted support (such as the technical skills assumed to follow basic advice), or are inadvertently treated as malicious entities (e.g., by rules for identifying suspicious activity on a social media platform).

The potential for risk controls to harm legitimate users is pronounced in modern IT systems. The *hyperconnectivity* they embody [50] means that malicious and legitimate human activity in the same IT environment can have some of the same observable behaviours and use of the same infrastructure (e.g., accessing an online account through the same interface). We must ensure in advance that a candidate risk control does not impact the existing activities of legitimate users.

Many methods exist for analysing a whole system to discourage a malicious behaviour [19,22], or to promote positive behaviours [58], i.e., behaviours to encourage in an IT environment (Sect. 2). We consider the latter schools of science together, as a means to avoid 'blunt' controls which reduce malicious behaviours at a cost to legitimate behaviours. An example would be changing system features to stop an attack, but making other benign activities difficult or impossible. To our knowledge, the interplay between these two groups of approaches has not been considered within cyber-risk management, though formative and disparate activities can be found (Sect. 2.3). This leads to approaches to address the sociotechnical *precision* of cyber-risk controls, to target only malicious or unwanted behaviours (Sect. 3).

We describe extensions to address gaps in existing risk management approaches, to explicitly consider user behaviour as an asset to protect; identifying shared determinant factors between negative and positive behaviours in a *sphere of interference*, and; the need to engage with stakeholders in the sociotechnical system in key risk management decisions. This acts as a foundation for a holistic cyber-risk management which is "user-friendly while abuser-unfriendly" [29]. We apply the novel approach to a case study on abusive behaviours on Social Media Platforms (SMPs), where there are many cross-cutting concerns (Sect. 4). We close with discussion (Sect. 5) and directions for future work (Sect. 6).

2   Managing Security for an Ecosystem of Behaviours

With IT systems underpinning so much of what people do in their normal lives, legitimate users and malicious actors are using the same infrastructure and technologies, making it more difficult to distinguish between them. To address this, we explore the synthesis of crime science and crime prevention (Sect. 2.1), with behaviour change science (Sect. 2.2), alongside information security management standards (Sect. 2.3). This identifies gaps in existing cyber-risk approaches, and opportunities to refine the precision of sociotechnical security controls (Sect. 2.6), couched within existing cyber-risk management approaches.

2.1 Discouraging Malicious Security-Related Behaviours

Scholars have explored the applicability of existing crime prevention theoretical frameworks and approaches to the domain of cybercrime. Both social learning theory and general theory of crime have been applied to examine cybercrime, such as hacking behaviours [12,56,57], where both theories focus at the level of the individual. Other crime prevention approaches focus on the opportunity structures and immediate environment as causes of criminal acts. *Situational crime prevention (SCP)* has shown success in addressing numerous offline crimes such as burglary and car theft [19], and online crimes such as data breaches [23].

SCP is a framework of strategies aiming to reduce criminal opportunities arising from the immediate environment [18,19]. Rather than viewing crime as a result of criminal predispositions, it views crime as the result of one's deliberate choices and decisions [18], affected by a person's immediate situation and circumstances. This shapes the three inter-related features of *SCP*, being specificity of the crime, the immediate environment, and the individual's perception and decision to commit a malicious act [18,19]. Associated techniques fall under five categories, each containing five techniques: increasing efforts, increasing risks, reducing reward, reducing provocations, and removing excuses [19,24,73]. These *opportunity reduction techniques* target the potential components of criminal opportunities [19,20,24,73], affording precision in targeting malicious behaviour.

Routine Activity Theory (RAT) emphasises the circumstances around when crimes occur [22,37]. Its main proposition is that crime occurs as the convergence in space and time of a suitable target, a motivated offender, and the absence of a capable guardian [22,37]. This last element refers to any person or object with the potential capabilities to prevent the occurrence of a crime [22]. Although generally associated with formal guardians such as police officers, capable guardians can have informal roles, such as pedestrians on the street or security cameras in stores. *RAT* has been adapted to explain victimisation as a result of online lifestyle and routine behaviours, while conceptualising computer and cybersecurity features as effective guardians [15]. Here we focus on risk owners within a managed IT infrastructure as 'guardians' of legitimate users in a system, acting to reduce the opportunities and capacity to conduct malicious activity.

2.2 Encouraging Positive Security-Related Behaviours

A range of factors are critical to encouraging an individual to adopt a positive behaviour. The COM-B model [58] distills critical factors for promoting behaviour change, namely capability, opportunity, and motivation. The authors position these factors alongside complementary layers of intervention and policy activities (such as environment design). These then complement the broader range of levers found in situational crime prevention (Sect. 2.1); it also indicates that there is a shared environment where interventions to prevent and to promote behaviours may all be happening in the same place. Similarly, the 'B = MAP' behaviour change framework [38] encompasses the need for a combination of Motivation, Ability, and Prompt for new behaviours to form. Prompts have been explored for security elsewhere (in security advice for consumers [61]).

Clear [21] outlines principles necessary to position and sustain a good behaviour, and de-emphasise unwanted behaviours. The latter can include making a behaviour more difficult to accomplish, less visible, or less desirable. If risk controls are not targeted sufficiently, they may induce effects upon otherwise positive behaviours which mirror the same techniques used to break bad habits. Similarly, the Theory of Planned Behaviour (TPB) [4] highlights the importance of self-efficacy (a person's belief that they can enact a behaviour toward an intended outcome), which is critical for security-related behaviours [34]. Regarding controls themselves, if a behaviour is seen as undermined and unlikely to succeed, this reduces (positive) control beliefs.

Intervention Mapping [7], within the health domain, identifies relationships between critical factors for an intervention aimed at an 'at risk' group. The approach acknowledges that development and deployment of an intervention is a collaborative activity involving a variety of stakeholders. The approach identifies behavioural and environmental causes of problems, producing *determinants* of problem behaviours. The approach also advocates *"reframing problem behaviors and environmental causes of health problems as desirable behaviors and environmental outcomes"*. Subgroups are further differentiated through targeted performance objectives and determinants. Being precise is then framed as key to encouraging and sustaining good behaviours. These principles have been applied in targeting cybersecurity awareness initiatives [63].

Again looking to the health domain, the PRECEDE-PROCEED intervention framework [40] includes a PRECEDE phase, which diagnoses factors critical to an intervention, including behavioural and environmental factors. This phase includes identifying the activities of actors which can affect the environment. Here we develop an approach for cybersecurity for actors, such as cyber-risk owners, to engage in this kind of diagnosis. PRECEDE-PROCEED emphasises the development of more specific interventions to target a particular group and behaviour, including factors which promote or prevent a behaviour. Here we argue that the need for such precision should be emphasised similarly in the design of cybersecurity interventions, rather than *after* an intervention has been enacted as may be seen if they contribute to harms.

2.3   Risk Management for Systems of Behaviours

We refer to *risk owners* as the stakeholders in an IT environment who have the authority and decision-making responsibility to enact changes to the cybersecurity apparatus within that environment (including technical and sociotechnical controls). This is aside from a risk owner potentially being the person assigned responsibility in an organisation. We refer to risk management literature aimed primarily at organisations, as it is indicative of how security-related behaviours may be managed and allows us to build on practices familiar to risk managers.

Various risk management approaches have hinted at issues tangential to our aims, albeit without directly addressing the linked impacts between efforts to *prevent* and *preserve* different IT-facilitated behaviours concurrently. ISO/IEC 27005:2011 ('Information security risk management') [51] explicitly includes

'Identification of consequences', though focusing on the consequences of a threat upon an asset, with no explicit examination of the impacts a control may have upon that asset. The broader ISO/IEC 31000:2018 'risk management' guidelines [13] acknowledge that risk management efforts may produce unintended consequences, noting that implementation of risk treatment plans ought to ensure that controls are effective when they are deployed, or otherwise that any risks they introduce are managed.

Related 'Risk management techniques' in ISO/IEC 31010:2009 [47] outline *consequence analysis*, to capture impacts including those affecting different objectives and different stakeholders. It is also advised to capture how consequences relate to the original objectives, and secondary consequences, with further consideration of *hazards*, including physical harm. The potential for knock-on impacts from managing one risk upon another risk are highlighted, but not further developed. The need to ensure a 'freedom from risk' is acknowledged in the digital domain within standards for software development (as in ISO 25010 [48]). Techniques exist in cyber-risk management standards which can minimise unintended harms to legitimate users, but are not being coordinated to do so.

The NIST 'Risk Management Framework for Information Systems and Organizations' standard [52] brings attention to "potential adverse effects on individuals", and that some capabilities must be upheld to meet stakeholder needs. Our framework addresses a need for *existing* security and non-security capabilities to escape impact from subsequent countermeasures. The OCTAVE risk management process [5] considers how a risk management strategy itself can impact 'exposed assets'. We argue that users and behaviours linked to known, permitted capabilities within a system should be explicitly regarded as assets to protect, echoing directions outlined by a successor to OCTAVE, OCTAVE Allegro [14].

2.4   Existing Examples

The following are examples of where consideration of the interplay between malicious behaviours and legitimate user activities has resulted in precise targeting of negative outcomes while preserving positive behaviours.

- **Phishing reduction through token authentication.** Google employees were provided with two-factor authentication (2FA) tokens [55]. Rather than relying solely on training to avoid phishing attacks, this recognises that email links and service access can be typical in work, and that malicious/fake links etc. may be difficult to spot all of the time, making them difficult to separate. By using physical tokens to enable system access, a 'successful' phishing attack does not gain enough credentials to compromise a system (nullifying the value of knowledge-based credentials). This also means that employees are not under pressure to identify malicious links themselves to avoid compromise at all cost, and as a result warp their treatment of legitimate emails.
- **'Loan-phones' during digital forensics activities.** When a personal phone is being analysed for evidence of domestic abuse, some police forces in

the UK provide a temporary phone, while some may not (which can factor in grave consequences [10]). A temporary phone preserves a person's capacity to reach their social support network or seek help. Here, a control to collect data of malicious activity (from smartphones) inadvertently removes the smartphone from its user; provision of loan phones reduces the impact to positive behaviours.

– **Socio-technical password controls.** There have been approaches in UK policy[1] to shift effort in managing passwords from end-users to background technical controls, so that legitimate users do not face the same difficulties that are created to dissuade malicious behaviour. For instance, system monitoring may be able to detect suspicious system activity and block access to legitimate login sites. 2FA tokens, as above, is a similar measure, reducing the heavy reliance on legitimate users to protect their passwords.

2.5 Related Work

The SCENE framework [25] suggests to develop cybersecurity behaviour change options so that the most secure options are most accessible, ideally as 'defaults' (as applied for Wi-Fi selection [71]). Similar to behaviour change and crime reduction approaches, SCENE advocates co-creation of solutions with target audience and stakeholders. We posit that the available options for using IT securely may be reduced by efforts to reduce malicious activity.

Agrafiotis et al. describe a taxonomy of *cyber harms* [3] which may be observed in organizations. The taxonomy comprises five broad themes, including digital harm, and social and societal harm. The authors posit that analytical tools are necessary to reduce these harms, and as part of risk assessment. Similarly, Chua et al. [17] encourage risk managers to explore the potential for *unintended harms* to emerge as a result of their own risk controls. The authors' framework emphasises the need to support vulnerable populations who may experience harms if risk controls work against them rather than for them. We identify factors which contribute to unintended harms, rather than consequences.

The Security Function Framework (SFF) [28] surfaces design considerations for sustainable crime reduction solutions, and creation of new products. Ekblom notes that malicious actors and their (potential) victims may have *script clashes* [31], with a need to design solutions to "favour the good guys". Where a crime reduction solution has a *niche* [30] in how it relates to "other products, people and places in the human, informational and material ecosystem", we pursue a similar notion of *precision*. As we consider user communities in IT ecosystems, this involves users, user behaviours, and infrastructure.

2.6 Synthesis of Sociotechnical Risk-Related Research

We have shown in the above analysis that activities to reduce behaviours are linked to activities to promote or sustain behaviours, arguably more so in

---

[1] "Password policy: updating your approach": https://www.ncsc.gov.uk/collection/passwords/updating-your-approach.

hyperconnected IT systems. Risk management standards hint at the need to balance these efforts, but do not sufficiently articulate and address the needs to protect users and existing user behaviours. Both negative behaviour and positive behaviour change approaches iterate over an intervention to reach a *more precise solution*. Behaviours are regarded as the result of a combination of individual factors (motivations, personal beliefs, self-control), capabilities of the individual, behavioural factors, and environmental factors (opportunity, rewards and punishments). *Linkages* between definitions of positive and negative behaviours can then be identified, as a measure that acting on one can impact the other, creating what we refer to here as *interference*.

Techniques in both crime reduction and behaviour change both act to move from an undesirable behaviour to a new target behaviour. Risk management and crime reduction approaches focus on undoing negative behaviours, but given the interconnected nature of cyber-risks, what is missing is a consideration to protect existing positive behaviours while doing so.

When identifying determinants from the perspective of crime prevention, the first step is having a specific definition of a malicious behaviour, regardless of the level of determinants [19]. Small variations in malicious behaviour are the results of a combination of factors [19, 22, 24, 37]. Specifying a malicious behaviour allows for more precise identification of determinants. Behaviour change approaches, such as Intervention Mapping, are similarly *specific in defining behaviours*.

We make a simplifying assumption that a risk owner is afforded more sight than any other stakeholder of candidate risk controls and their features. This means they can better develop an awareness of causal factors for user behaviours as defined in a control [67]. *Engagement with stakeholders* (including guardians managing offenders, targets, and places) is encouraged to reach effective solutions, in both crime reduction and positive behaviour change. We see in our Case Study (Sect. 4) examples of action taken by parents to protect their children online. Those managing or encouraging positive behaviours are best-placed to identify potential consequences. We then focus on those mechanisms under the view of a risk owner which can result in changes to other parts of the system (Sect. 3.1).

The identification and involvement of stakeholders in shaping controls appears somewhat open-ended in current risk management approaches. Risk management standards are generally quite detailed in determining how the actors and constituent elements in a system may be adversely affected by an incident or malicious activity, but this same rigour is not applied to the controls themselves. Where ISO 27005:2011 [51], for instance, refers to the 'scope and boundaries' for a risk control, the notion of 'boundaries' in cyber-risk management requires development in terms of how user needs are identified with stakeholders. Techniques may be adapted relating to guardianship in *RAT*, or crime preventers and promoters in the work of Ekblom [30]. There needs to be greater *proactive effort to identify stakeholders* to avoid harms from deploying a risk control.

We argue that positive behaviours exhibited by legitimate users need to be an explicit part of cyber-risk assessment, but that there is a pronounced gap in existing cyber-risk management approaches, where *sociotechnical assets* are not directly considered despite being represented in systems as user profiles, behaviour data, and system management decisions/rules which act upon them. Risk management is at present centred around data and artefacts of value, but the behaviour of legitimate users is not directly considered. However, changes in how aspects of existing risk management approaches are emphasised can realise more holistic, user-centred outcomes. We address this in the next section, toward *sociotechnical risk management*. We also consider the shared language of mediations between preventative behaviour management and positive behaviour change in secured systems, as a means of moving beyond blunt instruments in cybersecurity.

3   Framework for Precision in Sociotechnical Controls

3.1   Prevention and Preservation of Behaviours

Risk controls in an IT environment potentially restrict behaviour, users, and infrastructure [17], in turn affecting actual user behaviour, through their representations in IT systems. A risk owner making decisions about IT-security and related technical systems is unlikely to have a direct view of what users are doing. Instead they have access to systems which record or prohibit particular activities on systems, as data. There is then a lack of explicit acknowledgement of the connections between what would normally be considered assets to protect, such as data and systems, and the legitimate user activities that use those assets.

For our purposes, this is directly addressed by adopting the mechanistic approach to cybersecurity described by Hatleback and Spring [43]. With this, a behaviour can be an *indexed entity*, as a file or data, but also exist as an activity in a system, producing a visible phenomenon. An example would be a 'delete' function which exists as rules, but can also be enacted as an activity which is run within the system.

A foundation for precision in sociotechnical security controls extends the definition of an asset to include indexed entities (Fig. 1). This relates (positive and negative) real-world behaviours to identifiable data and systems which a cyber-risk owner imposes decisions upon. Critically, there is a feedback loop between System Assets and People—if there are rules about how data can be created in a system, these rules may restrict the activities of People. Examples include restrictions on credentials necessary to make a new account on a system, or checks for particular kinds of behaviour which are permitted.

If we are able to represent behaviour as an indexed entity in a managed system, this leads to the challenge of coordinating two up-to-now distinct efforts. The first is removal of negative/malicious behaviours from the system, e.g., inflammatory posts on social media. The second is maintaining positive behaviours already in the system, e.g., allowing users to share posts on social media. Where risk management often involves maintaining a *risk register* of top risks, a specific risk management activity is generally missing to address the

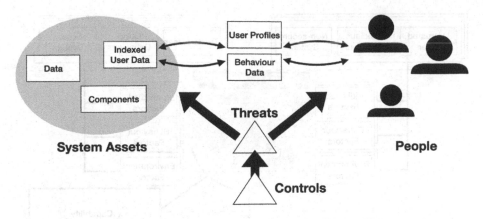

Fig. 1. Extending risk management artefacts to accommodate sociotechnical risk management. Individual People may interact with a system in such a way that User Profiles and Behaviour Data are generated and maintained. These are then Indexed User Data, generated as system activities alongside the behaviours of People using a system.

second of these efforts, and record user behaviours which are active in the system and must be preserved. An example would be that a legitimate user from a particular geographic location should be able to make regular posts to a social media platform and share links if they would want to, but that malicious activity seeming to emerge from the same area, posting fake messages and sharing malicious links, ought to be stopped, as may happen in online romance scams [17]. The capacity to populate a (positive) *behaviour register* is needed, where this is a natural extension to existing risk management techniques, aligning with behaviour intervention approaches (Sect. 2.3).

3.2   Intersection of Behaviours to Prevent or Preserve

As in Fig. 2, we describe a method of sociotechnical cyber-risk management to coordinate refinement of precision in security controls. Existing (cyber)crime reduction techniques and behaviour change approaches amply describe how to manage individual behaviours. As a first step, we propose to consider the Capability, Opportunity, and Motivation of a behaviour [58], as common terminology from both domains, to allow for comparison between two sets of specific behaviours and allow for refinement of controls. For simplicity, a 'positive' behaviour can include continuing not to do a behaviour which is detrimental [39]. If separating legitimate and malicious behaviours is difficult, this indicates where *linkages* between them are strongest, and the need to unpick them more critical so as to avoid unintended harms to positive behaviours.

A further step is to identify sufficiently detailed definitions of User, User Behaviour, and Infrastructure, as these are elements familiar to a cyber risk owner, but which also influence the COM factors in behaviours (as evidenced by risk controls preventing malicious behaviours). The extended asset definition

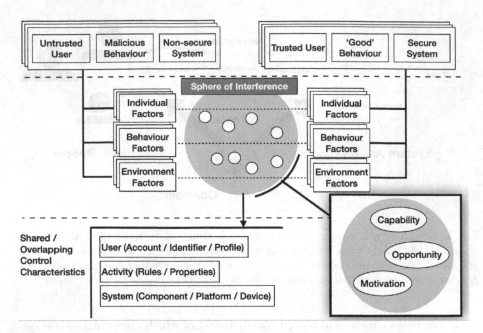

Fig. 2. Overview of proposed unison of negative and positive behaviours in a managed (cyber) system, and related controls.

in Fig. 1 supports this. An extended behaviour definition that relates to user behaviours also serves as a *trading zone* [67] between cyber-risk management, reduction of negative behaviours, and retention of positive user behaviours.

Crime reduction techniques (Sect. 2.1) are advocated here to identify negative behaviours, and in turn interact with risk management approaches (Sect. 2.3) to identify candidate controls. The behaviour change approaches in Sect. 2.2 are leveraged to identify positive behaviours to preserve. The latter requires a retrospective view of which behaviours are to be retained in the system, which is not exactly what behaviour change approaches do, but indicates a need to catalogue behaviours much like there can be a record of the technologies deployed in an IT environment.

3.3   Identifying Lack of Precision in Risk Controls

From prior analysis in Sect. 2, our method includes the following steps:

Step 1. Record behaviours in the system.

1A. **Identify active behaviour reduction activities.** This requires a catalogue of (malicious) behaviours being actively targeted, $R_1 - R_N$. See both cybercrime reduction approaches in Sect. 2.1, and risk management approaches, Sect. 2.1.

1B. **Identify active behaviours to be preserved**. This set, $P_1 - P_N$, includes behaviours being promoted as part of active intervention programmes. This requires communication with other stakeholders in the system, as in common behaviour change approaches, Sect. 2.2. In organisations, the extraction of permitted behaviours can begin with access control policies, computer fair use policies, and include discussions with team managers to understand regular work activities [53]. In IT environments more broadly, this requires discussions with user representatives and local community experts (as with responding to tech-abuse [60]).

1C. **Identify candidate controls.** This identifies controls $C_1 - C_N$, and applies to managing both negative behaviours and protecting positive behaviours. Involving stakeholders will make this more tractable. Once conducted, assessments may be reusable, making it less demanding over time and akin to maintaining an ongoing *risk register*. Such a register would describe concerns to manage (left-side of Fig. 2), and a *behaviour register* of existing behaviours to preserve (right-side of Fig. 2). It may not be possible to confirm that all behaviours and associated controls in the system have been identified, but efforts to do so should be documented.

Step 2. Map connections between behaviours and system assets.

2A. **Identify sociotechnical representations of behaviours.** For each Control C in $C_1 - C_N$ identify the Environment, or *cyberplace* [49], the Behavioural determinants, Individual factors, and related data representations as recorded in IT systems (the *indexed assets*) that it acts upon. User activities must translate to user or behaviour representations (data or rules, Fig. 1), or system elements, for a cyber-risk manager to be able to work directly with the information. Behaviour change approaches emphasise that it is critical to involve stakeholders in identifying target behaviours.

2B. **Map behaviour determinants to technical features.** This will relate the impacts of controls on Environment and Behaviour to the Individual. For specific behaviours and their candidate controls, map data and systems to COM-B properties [58]. This can, for instance, map Capabilities to rules for permitted activity, or account properties; map Opportunity to restrictions on account access (such as registration requirements, or rules for signalling malicious behaviour); map Motivation to assumptions about workload/effort around what users will need to do to have access to a service (including technical knowledge). Having an Opportunity facilitated in technology does not necessarily mean that it is easily accessible. For instance, target-hardening efforts may make a system less accessible to legitimate users. For this reason, a user having access to—and being present in—an IT environment should be managed as a conscious Control decision.

Step 3. Address linkages between negative and positive behaviours and/or controls. Controls are engineered mechanisms [43]—it may be assumed but is not always assured that a control precisely addresses only the entity or activity it is intended to act upon. This means there is scope to address linkages. Controls and Behaviours must both be assessed together in an iterative manner. If it is found that any mapping of COM-B features to user, activity, or system entities overlaps between the *negative* and *positive* sets, it should be assumed that there is a legitimate group of users which will be affected by a cyber-risk management control if it is deployed. For instance, specific access restrictions may be activated by particular device or account details, but these rules might affect legitimate users sharing the same traits. A stark example is when one US police force was prevented from rapidly registering temporary email addresses after a ransomware attack, as systems treated this as activity associated with a spam campaign [9]. Linkages would require *remediation* (see Sect. 3.4) to break, or record and compensate for, the shared dependency between positive and negative behaviours. The number of linkages is a basic indicator of potential harms and a lack of precision in the candidate control.

3.4   Managing for the Precision of Risk Controls

If a control affects both positive and negative behaviours, there may be a need to *reconsider* it. This would involve searching for a candidate Control which does not act on shared determinants, but only on negative behaviour determinants. With adaptation, current risk management processes would accommodate this, including searching for existing solutions already available to the risk owner. This highlights the need to take a mechanistic approach to understanding the role of security-related technologies in real-world systems [67]. Precise approaches for achieving this must be developed, where existing risk management guidelines can be adapted to identify controls which appropriately address a risk, relative to other activities already active in the system.

If a Control is adaptable, it can be *refined*—this applies more so to Controls which can be configured in how they interact with People, such as detection rules for system/online behaviour. We make an assumption that cybersecurity controls are generally deployed without an initial check of whether they carry the kind of *residual risk* which can result in *unintended harms*. There must be agreement with stakeholders that a control adequately minimises or avoids harms. If there is an expectation of potential harms to legitimate users—where negative and positive behaviour determinants interact—there may be a choice to *compensate* for the harm, and accept a candidate control but with additional compensatory measures. This may happen if a control is deemed necessary but expected to be short-lived (such as to address an emergent security threat). Refinements may be realised through, e.g., configuration of data processing rules, policies for user identification and verification, user behaviour detection rules, and device detection and management rules.

Any lack of knowledge or expectations around the knock-on effects of a cyber-security control should be logged as a residual risk ('unidentified risk' as in 27005:2011 [51]). This may be the case if a control is relatively novel. This relates to *ongoing attentiveness* to making systems work together (Sect. 5), realised most readily by measuring the performance of the system. The process should include input from non-security stakeholders, where their perception of consequences of cyber-risks must be considered [3]. Existing risk management approaches already advocate this, but not necessarily the residual risk of controls for legitimate users, or how to identify this particular kind of risk.

4   Use Case—Online Abuse Controls for Social Media

Here we consider a potential application of the framework to a real-world environment, specifically use of online social media platforms and prevention of online abuse. This is a domain in which platform operators have needed to iterate controls for security and privacy, to ensure that a range of different legitimate users can use social media with confidence. At the same time, there is a need to identify and prevent malicious activity. Online abuse continues to be an issue as technology and the Internet are interleaved with our everyday lives. Some common behaviours considered as online abuse include trolling, online harassment, stalking, bullying, and online threats [42,45,69]. The increased use of social media platforms (*SMPs*) like Facebook and Twitter allow for continuous contact between offenders and targets without regard for physical and temporal distance [45]. This constitutes negative behaviour to be prevented on SMPs.

To address the negative behavior, SMPs introduce controls to minimise its occurrence and impacts on users (e.g., [35,66,70]). The necessity of such controls is increasing as the use of SMPs continues to grow among teenagers and adults [62] and is encouraged for their beneficial effects [33]. In this instance, there are two positive outcomes to be preserved: encouraging continued use of SMPs, while also lowering users' risks of becoming targets as they converge with offenders in the same online social space. Personal privacy controls are realised in part through security controls which maintain a safe environment which users can trust. A user may exercise a privacy decision through a service—security controls can serve to create the environment which enforces those decisions. An example would be ensuring that a user on an SMP cannot be reached by another user who they have blocked or not explicitly provided visibility to.

4.1   Factors in Positive and Negative Behaviours

One factor affecting the utilisation of controls is the 'privacy paradox', where there is a disparity between expressed privacy concerns and privacy-related behaviours [6]. For instance, users have reported utilizing features such as friends-only content accessibility, but at the same time accepting large numbers of friend requests from individuals who may not be seen as friends beyond the context of the SMP [27]. Another factor is the possible overlap between offenders and targets in cyberbullying and cyber-interpersonal violence [16,72]. This overlap is exacerbated by a reliance on users to be proactive.

Current literature establishes a range of factors contributing to the rise of online abusive behaviors. Factors to consider at the individual level include pro-victim attitudes [32], perceptions of norms and injustice [11], and the contexts of exchanges [11,72]. Other relevant factors of cyberbullying relate to features of cyberspace, such as the anonymity and distance between users which can result in a sense of impunity and deindividuation. This can lead to adoption of online aggressive behaviours [42,44,64]. The nature of online media also means that users are removed from direct confrontation or consequence for their own behaviours [44,64]. Another feature is the scalability of the Internet, which allows multiple individuals to participate simultaneously in bullying behaviours [44].

There is some evidence supporting the effectiveness of SMP controls. Younger users of SMPs tend to be more proactive in adopting existing accessibility controls and settings [2,6,26,27,54]. A comprehensive review on cyberbullying also found that blocking cyberbullies is among the most common strategies used and recommended among children and adolescents [2,41]. Some factors affecting the effectiveness of existing controls, especially privacy controls, are users' engagement, proactivity toward privacy, and technical skills [6,8]. These must be balanced with users' aims to communicate with others, potentially opportunistically or openly. This points to a combination of COM-B elements [58]. This can require approachable means for finding other users on the same SMP, reaching others with messages they potentially were not expecting, and being able to tune interests to define the messages which are received from other accounts. In terms of security and privacy, this would require a blend of controls to prevent negative behaviours and realise user intentions.

4.2   Risk Controls

Here we are examining features and controls which have been deployed, rather than the design process behind them. Nonetheless, to combat the above issues, various SMPs have introduced controls to counter online abuse. There is the use of privacy settings and controls that allow account holders to manage accessibility to content via blocking or filtering [35,66,70]. Facebook later introduced the "friend list" feature to dictate the types of content each list has access to [36]. Snapchat provides finer granularity in controls, such as "Who can view my Story" and "Who can contact me" [66].

Another type of control is the introduction of clear community rules. The Snapchat community guidelines explicitly prohibit harassment, bullying, impersonation or violence, and encourage account holders to report these behaviours [65]. SMPs listed punishments of different severity in guidelines, from the removal of content, to termination of an account, to the possibility of activity being reported to law enforcement agencies [65]. In some cases, the platforms attempt to include other stakeholders in their controls. Snapchat encourages parents to help adolescents in managing their accounts [66]. Parents have also advised their children to manage privacy by providing false information [26].

4.3   Refining Risk Controls

In general, SMP controls address different COM-B characteristics that affect both behaviours that we wish to preserve (use of trustworthy SMPs) and prevent (online abuse). First, there is an inherent source of interference in the nature of the environment and users' motivations. The primary purposes for using SMPs include expressing one's identity digitally, maintaining and enhancing existing offline and online relationships, and creating new social relationships [74]. To reach their goals, both legitimate and malicious users share some degree of information such as names and email addresses [68,74]. These requirements, along with the small to moderate effects between privacy concerns and users' utilization of privacy controls [6,8,27,54], suggest increased opportunity for malicious behaviours as existing controls do not fully align with legitimate behaviours.

This raises the need for security controls to be in place to contribute to an environment which allows legitimate users to interact with other users, while also not preventing them from accessing the platform. The accessibility of personal controls for both privacy and security is also part of this need. Complications arise in the tension that stems from differences in the dynamics of online and offline social relationships. Online SMPs tend to oversimplify social ties into friends and not-friends [74]. Such dichotomous definitions do not always reflect the fluidity of social relationships in the offline world, adding to the effort required to maintain online privacy. In addition, users of online SMPs assign different values to different types of personal and sensitive information in cyberspace [1,2,54,68]. Variations in value assignment can interfere with perceptions of risks and opportunities, in turn affecting users' utilization of existing controls.

These studies highlight possible sources of interference between users' needs of SMPs and controls introduced on SMPs to protect user groups from unintended harms. What is also highlighted are the potentially subtle ways in which well-intentioned controls may impact legitimate users. Both sources of interference suggest a need for proactive consideration of legitimate behaviours in the design of the controls, to limit misuse or ignorance of these controls. Risk managers would benefit from an understanding of these issues, so as to also avoid the displacement of users to other platforms that provide a stronger sense of agency via easy-to-use privacy controls [2], or the reliance on alternative options [46].

5 Discussion

Our framework combines existing capabilities across disciplines, highlighting where adjustments can better manage sociotechnical risks. An existing risk register can be extended to log existing positive behaviours, but this may require concerted effort and knowledge of activities in the system which have positive effects. Communication is required with specific stakeholders such as Human Resources departments, user advocacy groups, etc. This is more tractable than determining where users have been 'forgotten' or removed by harmful risk controls [17].

A risk owner may not be willing—or able—to *reconsider* or *refine* a control (Sect. 3.4). At an extreme, they may act to remain ignorant of potential harms created by a cybersecurity control, as 'organised irresponsibility' [3]. This introduces its own risk, of assuming that a control will not have impacts for legitimate users or that impacts transferred to users are trivial, which undermines security assurances. This would be a form of *risk acceptance*, which in light of unintended harms would be *imposed acceptance* on users (as risk dumping [17]).

We propose an approach to risk management which combines prevention and preservation of behaviours to avoid linkages between them. This would bolster what Molotch [59] advocates in safety management, to *"add to rather than subtract from our well-being"*, by providing secure IT environments which are accessible to intended users. Molotch also advocates *ongoing attentiveness* to the management of risks, which in this context would be regular oversight and dialogue with stakeholders. At present, security guidelines signpost seemingly few points at which to engage parties with localised knowledge of user needs.

We make a number of initial recommendations for moving practice toward more precise sociotechnical cyber-risk management, including to **extend the definition of digital assets to include user** *activities*. In cyber-risk management processes, we must go beyond only considering data and components involved in activities within risk registers, to include representations of active user behaviour. OCTAVE Allegro [14] advocates similar initiatives. There is also scope to **develop control portfolios to accommodate precision**. There must be capacity to tailor controls to match specific negative behaviour controls, and leave positive behaviours alone. The work of Hatleback and Spring [43], and Chua et al. [17], provide a basis for terminology to navigate between prevention and preservation of behaviours. Risk management also requires **measurement of control precision**, and with this an understanding of how unintended impacts upon legitimate users manifest in a system. We present a simple measure, of the number of overlapping factors between negative and positive behaviours (e.g., legitimate activities and phishing attacks both use hyperlinks).

6 Conclusion

We describe a framework for management of the concurrent prevention and promotion of different security and privacy behaviours in a managed IT environment. This framework leverages risk management approaches familiar to practitioners, and a synergy of approaches from (cyber)crime reduction and behaviour change science. The definition of digital assets for risk management must explicitly include representations of user behaviour in managed systems; the role of stakeholders and how to engage with them is underspecified in cyber-risk management standards, and; more must be done to measure unintended harms upon legitimate users, and develop candidate cyber-risk controls with a precision that avoids impacts on determinants of protected user behaviours.

As future work, we will explore the notion of sociotechnical precision in cyber-security and cyber-risk management, with a real-world environment, related stakeholders, and discernible vulnerable populations. Future work will also explore how existing cyber-risk management standards can be adapted and extended to promote precision in sociotechnical risk management.

References

1. Acquisti, A., Gross, R.: Imagined communities: awareness, information sharing, and privacy on the Facebook. In: Danezis, G., Golle, P. (eds.) PET 2006. LNCS, vol. 4258, pp. 36–58. Springer, Heidelberg (2006). https://doi.org/10.1007/11957454_3
2. Adorjan, M., Ricciardelli, R.: A new privacy paradox? Youth agentic practices of privacy management despite "nothing to hide" online. Can. Rev. Sociol. **56**(1), 8–29 (2019)
3. Agrafiotis, I., et al.: Cyber harm: concepts, taxonomy and measurement. Saïd Business School WP 2016-23 (2016)
4. Ajzen, I., et al.: The theory of planned behavior. Organ. Behav. Hum. Decis. Processes **50**(2), 179–211 (1991)
5. Alberts, C., Behrens, S., Pethia, R., Wilson, W.: Operationally critical threat, asset, and vulnerability evaluation (OCTAVE) framework, version 1.0. Technical report CMU/SEI-99-TR-017, Software Engineering Institute, Carnegie Mellon University (1999)
6. Barnes, S.B.: A privacy paradox: social networking in the United States. First Monday **11**(9) (2006). https://doi.org/10.5210/fm.v11i9.1394
7. Bartholomew, L.K., Parcel, G.S., Kok, G.: Intervention mapping: a process for developing theory and evidence-based health education programs. Health Educ. Behav. **25**(5), 545–563 (1998)
8. Baruh, L., Secinti, E., Cemalcilar, Z.: Online privacy concerns and privacy management: a meta-analytical review. J. Commun. **67**(1), 26–53 (2017)
9. BBC News: Google thwarts Baltimore ransomware fightback (2019). https://www.bbc.co.uk/news/technology-48380662. Accessed 15 Sept 2020
10. BBC News: Katrina O'Hara murder: coroner recommends phone access changes (2020). https://www.bbc.co.uk/news/uk-england-dorset-51557476. Accessed 13 July 2020
11. Blackwell, L., Chen, T., Schoenebeck, S., Lampe, C.: When online harassment is perceived as justified. In: Twelfth International AAAI Conference on Web and Social Media (2018)
12. Bossler, A.M., Burruss, G.W.: The general theory of crime and computer hacking: low self-control hackers? In: Cyber Crime: Concepts, Methodologies, Tools and Applications, pp. 1499–1527. IGI Global (2012)
13. BS, ISO: BS ISO 31000:2018 – Risk management – Guidelines. BS ISO (2018)
14. Caralli, R., Stevens, J., Young, L., Wilson, W.: Introducing octave allegro: improving the information security risk assessment process. Technical report CMU/SEI-2007-TR-012, Software Engineering Institute, Carnegie Mellon University (2007)
15. Choi, K.S.: Computer crime victimization and integrated theory: an empirical assessment. Int. J. Cyber Criminol. **2**(1), 308–333 (2008)
16. Choi, K.S., Lee, J.R.: Theoretical analysis of cyber-interpersonal violence victimization and offending using cyber-routine activities theory. Comput. Hum. Behav. **73**, 394–402 (2017)
17. Chua, Y.T., et al.: Identifying unintended harms of cybersecurity countermeasures. In: 2019 APWG Symposium on Electronic Crime Research (eCrime), pp. 1–15. IEEE (2019)
18. Clarke, R.V.: Situational crime prevention: its theoretical basis and practical scope. Crime Justice **4**, 225–256 (1983)
19. Clarke, R.V.: Situational Crime Prevention: Successful Case Studies. Harrow and Heston Publishers, Albany (1997)

20. Clarke, R.V., Homel, R.: A revised classification of situational crime prevention techniques. In: Lab, S.P. (ed.) Crime Prevention at a Crossroads, pp. 17–27. Anderson Publishing Co. (1997)
21. Clear, J.: Atomic habits: an easy & proven way to build good habits & break bad ones. Penguin (2018)
22. Cohen, L.E., Felson, M.: Social change and crime rate trends: a routine activity approach. Am. Sociol. Rev. **44**(4), 588–608 (1979)
23. Collins, J.D., Sainato, V.A., Khey, D.N.: Organizational data breaches 2005–2010: applying SCP to the healthcare and education sectors. Int. J. Cyber Criminol. **5**(1), 794–810 (2011)
24. Cornish, D.B., Clarke, R.V.: Opportunities, precipitators and criminal decisions: a reply to Wortley's critique of situational crime prevention. Crime Prev. Stud. **16**, 41–96 (2003)
25. Coventry, L., Briggs, P., Jeske, D., van Moorsel, A.: SCENE: a structured means for creating and evaluating behavioral nudges in a cyber security environment. In: Marcus, A. (ed.) DUXU 2014. LNCS, vol. 8517, pp. 229–239. Springer, Cham (2014). https://doi.org/10.1007/978-3-319-07668-3_23
26. Davis, K., James, C.: Tweens' conceptions of privacy online: implications for educators. Learn. Media Technol. **38**(1), 4–25 (2013)
27. Debatin, B., Lovejoy, J.P., Horn, A.K., Hughes, B.N.: Facebook and online privacy: attitudes, behaviors, and unintended consequences. J. Comput.-Mediat. Commun. **15**(1), 83–108 (2009)
28. Ekblom, P.: The security function framework. In: Ekblom, P. (ed.) Design Against Crime: Crime Proofing Everyday Products, Chap. 2, pp. 9–36. Lynne Rienner Publishers (2012)
29. Ekblom, P.: Crime prevention through product design. In: Handbook of Crime Prevention and Community Safety, pp. 207–233. Taylor & Francis, Abingdon (2017)
30. Ekblom, P.: Technology, opportunity, crime and crime prevention: current and evolutionary perspectives. In: Leclerc, B., Savona, E.U. (eds.) Crime Prevention in the 21st Century, pp. 319–343. Springer, Cham (2017). https://doi.org/10.1007/978-3-319-27793-6_19
31. Ekblom, P., Gill, M.: Rewriting the script: cross-disciplinary exploration and conceptual consolidation of the procedural analysis of crime. Eur. J. Crim. Policy Res. **22**(2), 319–339 (2016). https://doi.org/10.1007/s10610-015-9291-9
32. Elledge, L.C., Williford, A., Boulton, A.J., DePaolis, K.J., Little, T.D., Salmivalli, C.: Individual and contextual predictors of cyberbullying: the influence of children's provictim attitudes and teachers' ability to intervene. J. Youth Adolesc. **42**(5), 698–710 (2013). https://doi.org/10.1007/s10964-013-9920-x
33. Ellison, N.B., Steinfield, C., Lampe, C.: The benefits of Facebook "friends:" social capital and college students' use of online social network sites. J. Comput. Mediat. Commun. **12**(4), 1143–1168 (2007)
34. European Union Agency for Cybersecurity (ENISA): Cybersecurity culture guidelines: behavioural aspects of cybersecurity (2018). https://www.enisa.europa.eu/publications/cybersecurity-culture-guidelines-behavioural-aspects-of-cybersecurity
35. Facebook: Abuse resources (2020). https://www.facebook.com/help/726709730764837/?helpref=hc_fnav. Accessed 10 Sept 2020
36. Facebook: Friend lists: Facebook Help Centre (2020). https://www.facebook.com/help/204604196335128. Accessed 08 Dec 2019
37. Felson, M., Cohen, L.E.: Human ecology and crime: a routine activity approach. Hum. Ecol. **8**(4), 389–406 (1980)

38. Fogg, B.J.: Tiny Habits: The Small Changes that Change Everything. Houghton Mifflin Harcourt, Boston (2019)
39. Fogg, B.J., Hreha, J.: Behavior wizard: a method for matching target behaviors with solutions. In: Ploug, T., Hasle, P., Oinas-Kukkonen, H. (eds.) PERSUASIVE 2010. LNCS, vol. 6137, pp. 117–131. Springer, Heidelberg (2010). https://doi.org/ 10.1007/978-3-642-13226-1_13
40. Green, L.W.: Toward cost-benefit evaluations of health education: some concepts, methods, and examples. Health Educ. Monogr. 2(1_suppl), 34–64 (1974)
41. Hamm, M.P., et al.: Prevalence and effect of cyberbullying on children and young people: a scoping review of social media studies. JAMA Pediatr. 169(8), 770–777 (2015)
42. Hardaker, C.: Trolling in asynchronous computer-mediated communication: from user discussions to academic definitions. J. Politeness Res. 6(2), 215–242 (2010)
43. Hatleback, E.N., Spring, J.M.: A refinement to the general mechanistic account. Eur. J. Philos. Sci. 9(2) (2019). Article number: 19. https://doi.org/10.1007/ s13194-018-0237-1
44. Hinduja, S., Patchin, J.: Cyberbullying: identification, prevention, & response. Cyberbullying Research Center (2018)
45. Holt, T.J., Bossler, A.M.: An assessment of the current state of cybercrime scholarship. Deviant Behav. 35(1), 20–40 (2014)
46. Househ, M., Borycki, E., Kushniruk, A.: Empowering patients through social media: the benefits and challenges. Health Inform. J. 20(1), 50–58 (2014)
47. IEC, ISO: 31010: 2009 risk management – risk assessment techniques (2009). https://doi.org/10.3403/30183975
48. IEC, ISO: BS ISO/IEC 25010:2011 - Systems and software engineering. Systems and software quality requirements and evaluation (SQuaRE). System and software quality models. IEC, ISO (2011)
49. Ife, C.C., Davies, T., Murdoch, S.J., Stringhini, G.: Bridging information security and environmental criminology research to better mitigate cybercrime. arXiv preprint arXiv:1910.06380 (2019)
50. Islam, T., et al.: A socio-technical and co-evolutionary framework for reducing human-related risks in cyber security and cybercrime ecosystems. In: Wang, G., Bhuiyan, M.Z.A., De Capitani di Vimercati, S., Ren, Y. (eds.) DependSys 2019. CCIS, vol. 1123, pp. 277–293. Springer, Singapore (2019). https://doi.org/10.1007/ 978-981-15-1304-6_22
51. ISO, IEC: IEC 27005: 2011 (EN) information technology-security techniques-information security risk management. ISO/IEC (2011)
52. Joint Task Force: Risk management framework for information systems and organizations: a system life cycle approach for security and privacy (final public draft) (SP 800-37 Rev. 2). Technical report, National Institute of Standards and Technology (2018)
53. Kirlappos, I., Parkin, S., Sasse, M.: Learning from "shadow security": why understanding non-compliant behaviors provides the basis for effective security. In: Workshop on Usable Security and Privacy (USEC 2014), pp. 1–10 (2014)
54. Kokolakis, S.: Privacy attitudes and privacy behaviour: a review of current research on the privacy paradox phenomenon. Comput. Secur. 64, 122–134 (2017)
55. Krebs, B.: Google: security keys neutralized employee phishing (2018). https://krebsonsecurity.com/2018/07/google-security-keys-neutralized-employee-phishing/. Accessed 13 July 2020
56. Lee, J.R., Holt, T.J.: Assessing the factors associated with the detection of juvenile hacking behaviors. Front. Psychol. 11, 840 (2020)

57. Marcum, C.D., Higgins, G.E., Ricketts, M.L., Wolfe, S.E.: Hacking in high school: cybercrime perpetration by juveniles. Deviant Behav. **35**(7), 581–591 (2014)
58. Michie, S., Atkins, L., West, R.: The Behaviour Change Wheel. A Guide to Designing Interventions, 1st edn., pp. 1003–1010. Silverback Publishing, Great Britain (2014)
59. Molotch, H.L.: Against Security: How We Go Wrong at Airports, Subways, and Other Sites of Ambiguous Danger. Princeton University Press, Princeton (2014)
60. Parkin, S., Patel, T., Lopez-Neira, I., Tanczer, L.: Usability analysis of shared device ecosystem security: informing support for survivors of IoT-facilitated tech-abuse. In: New Security Paradigms Workshop (NSPW 2019). ACM (2019)
61. Parkin, S., Redmiles, E.M., Coventry, L., Sasse, M.A.: Security when it is welcome: exploring device purchase as an opportune moment for security behavior change. In: Workshop on Usable Security and Privacy (USEC 2019). Internet Society (2019)
62. Pew Research Center: Demographics of social media users and adopters in the United States (2019). https://www.pewresearch.org/internet/fact-sheet/social-media/
63. Renaud, K., Warkentin, M.: Using intervention mapping to breach the cyber-defense deficit. In: 12th Annual Symposium on Information Assurance (ASIA 2017), June 2017, pp. 7–8 (2017)
64. Sambaraju, R., McVittie, C.: Examining abuse in online media. Soc. Pers. Psychol. Compass **14**(3), e12521 (2020)
65. Snapchat: community guidelines (2020). https://www.snap.com/en-US/community-guidelines
66. Snapchat: privacy settings (2020). https://support.snapchat.com/en-GB/article/privacy-settings2. Accessed 07 Mar 2020
67. Spring, J.M., Moore, T., Pym, D.: Practicing a science of security: a philosophy of science perspective. In: 2017 New Security Paradigms Workshop (NSPW 2017). ACM (2017)
68. Taddicken, M.: The 'privacy paradox' in the social web: the impact of privacy concerns, individual characteristics, and the perceived social relevance on different forms of self-disclosure. J. Comput.-Mediat. Commun. **19**(2), 248–273 (2014)
69. The Crown Prosecution Service: Cyber/Online Crime (2020). https://www.cps.gov.uk/cyber-online-crime. Accessed 07 Mar 2020
70. TikTok: Safety center (2020). https://www.tiktok.com/safety/resources/anti-bully?lang=en. Accessed 07 Mar 2020
71. Turland, J., Coventry, L., Jeske, D., Briggs, P., van Moorsel, A.: Nudging towards security: developing an application for wireless network selection for android phones. In: 2015 British HCI Conference, pp. 193–201 (2015)
72. Whittaker, E., Kowalski, R.M.: Cyberbullying via social media. J. Sch. Violence **14**(1), 11–29 (2015)
73. Wortley, R.: A classification of techniques for controlling situational precipitators of crime. Secur. J. **14**(4), 63–82 (2001). https://doi.org/10.1057/palgrave.sj.8340098
74. Zhang, C., Sun, J., Zhu, X., Fang, Y.: Privacy and security for online social networks: challenges and opportunities. IEEE Netw. **24**(4), 13–18 (2010)

Behavior in Face of Adversaries

Natural Strategic Abilities in Voting Protocols

Wojciech Jamroga[1,2], Damian Kurpiewski[2(✉)], and Vadim Malvone[3]

[1] Interdisciplinary Centre on Security, Reliability and Trust, SnT,
University of Luxembourg, Luxembourg City, Luxembourg
[2] Institute of Computer Science, Polish Academy of Sciences, Warsaw, Poland
d.kurpiewski@ipipan.waw.pl
[3] Télécom Paris, Paris, France

Abstract. Security properties are often focused on the technological side of the system. One implicitly assumes that the users will behave in the right way to preserve the property at hand. In real life, this cannot be taken for granted. In particular, security mechanisms that are difficult and costly to use are often ignored by the users, and do not really defend the system against possible attacks.

Here, we propose a graded notion of security based on the complexity of the user's strategic behavior. More precisely, we suggest that the level to which a security property φ is satisfied can be defined in terms of (a) the complexity of the strategy that the voter needs to execute to make φ true, and (b) the resources that the user must employ on the way. The simpler and cheaper to obtain φ, the higher the degree of security.

We demonstrate how the idea works in a case study based on an electronic voting scenario. To this end, we model the vVote implementation of the Prêt à Voter voting protocol for coercion-resistant and voter-verifiable elections. Then, we identify "natural" strategies for the voter to obtain receipt-freeness, and measure the voter's effort that they require.

Keywords: Electronic voting · Coercion resistance · Natural strategies · Multi-agent models · Graded security

1 Introduction

Security analysis often focuses on the technological side of the system. It implicitly assumes that the users will duly follow the sequence of steps that the designer of the protocol prescribed for them. However, such behavior of human participants seldom happens in real life. In particular, mechanisms that are difficult and costly to use are often ignored by the users, even if they are there to defend those very users from possible attacks.

For example, protocols for electronic voting are usually expected to satisfy *receipt-freeness* (the voter should be given no certificate that can be used to break the anonymity of her vote) and the related property of *coercion-resistance* (the voter should be able to deceive the potential coercer and cast her vote in

© Springer Nature Switzerland AG 2021
T. Groß and L. Viganò (Eds.): STAST 2020, LNCS 12812, pp. 45–62, 2021.
https://doi.org/10.1007/978-3-030-79318-0_3

accordance with her preferences) [8,18,19,30,31,35]. More recently, significant progress has been made in the development of voting systems that would be coercion-resistant and at the same time *voter-verifiable*, i.e., would allow the voter to verify her part of the election outcome [13,37]. The idea is to partly "crowdsource" an audit of the election to the voters, and see if they detect any irregularities. Examples include the Prêt à Voter protocol [36] and its implementation vVote [14] that was used in the 2014 election in the Australian state of Victoria.

However, the fact that a voting system includes a mechanism for voter-verifiability does not immediately imply that it is more secure and trustworthy. This crucially depends on how many voters will actually verify their ballots [42], which in turn depends on how understandable and easy to use the mechanism is. The same applies to mechanisms for coercion-resistance and receipt-freeness, and in fact to any optional security mechanism. If the users find the mechanism complicated and tiresome, and they can avoid it, they will avoid it.

Thus, the right question is often not *if* but *how much* security is obtained by the given mechanism. In this paper, we propose a graded notion of *practical security* based on the complexity of the strategic behavior, expected from the user if a given security property is to be achieved. More precisely, we suggest that the level to which property φ is "practically" satisfied can be defined in terms of (a) the complexity of the strategy that the user needs to execute to make φ true, and (b) the resources that the user must employ on the way. The simpler and cheaper to obtain φ, the higher the degree of security.

Obviously, the devil is in the detail. It often works best when a general idea is developed with concrete examples in mind. Here, we do the first step, and look how the voter-verifiability can be assessed in vVote and Prêt à Voter. To this end, we come up with a multi-agent model of vVote, inspired by interpreted systems [20]. We consider three main types of agents participating in the voting process: the election system, a voter, and a potential coercer. Then, we identify strategies for the voter to use the voter-verifiability mechanism, and estimate the voter's effort that they require. We also look at how difficult it is for the coercer to compromise the election through a randomization attack [30]. The strategic reasoning and its complexity is formalized by means of so called *natural strategies*, proposed in [26,27] and consistent with psychological evidence on how humans use symbolic concepts [9,21].

To create the models, we use the UPPAAL model checker for distributed and multi-agent systems [5], with its flexible modeling language and intuitive GUI. This additionally allows to use the UPPAAL verification functionality and check that our natural strategies indeed obtain the goals for which they are proposed.

Related Work. Formal analysis of security that takes a more human-centered approach has been done in a number of papers, for example with respect to insider threats [23]. A more systematic approach, based on the idea of *security ceremonies*, was proposed and used in [6,7,11,33], and applied to formal analysis of voting protocols [32]. Here, we build on a different modeling tradition, namely on the framework of *multi-agent systems*. This modeling approach was only used in [24] where a preliminary verification of the SELENE voting protocol

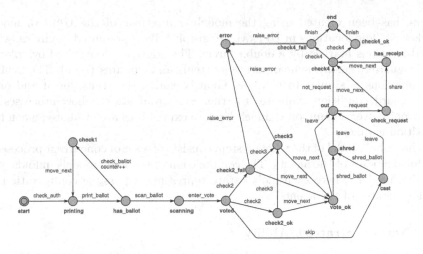

Fig. 1. Voter model

was conducted. Moreover, to our best knowledge, the idea of measuring the security level by the complexity of strategies needed to preserve a given security requirement is entirely new.

Other (somewhat) related works include social-technical modeling of attacks with timed automata [16] and especially game-theoretic analysis of voting procedures [3,10,15,28]. Also, strategies for human users to obtain simple security requirements were investigated in [4]. Finally, specification of coercion-resistance and receipt-freeness in logics of strategic ability was attempted in [41].

2   Methodology

The main goal of this paper is to propose a framework for analyzing security and usability of voting protocols, based on how easy it is for the participants to use the functionality of the protocol and avoid a breach of security. Dually, we can also look at how difficult it is for the attacker to compromise the system. In this section we explain the methodology.

2.1   Modeling the Voting Process

The first step is to divide the description of the protocol into loosely coupled components, called agents. The partition is often straightforward: in our case, it will include the voter, the election infrastructure, the teller etc.

For each agent we define its local model, which consists of locations (i.e., the local states of the agent) and labeled edges between locations (i.e., local transitions). A transition corresponds to an action performed by the agent. An example model of the voter can be seen in Fig. 1. For instance, when the voter has scanned her ballot and is in the state *scanning* she can perform action *enter_vote*, thus moving to the state *voted*. This local model, as well as the

others, has been created using the modeling interface of the UPPAAL model
checker [5]. The locations in UPPAAL are graphically represented as circles, with
initial locations marked by a double circle. The edges are annotated by colored
labels: guards (green), synchronizations (teal) and updates (blue). The syntax
of expressions is similar to C/C++. Guards enable the transition if and only
if the guard condition evaluates to true. Synchronizations allow processes to
synchronize over a common channel. Update expressions are evaluated when the
transition is taken.

The global model of the whole system consists of a set of concurrent processes,
i.e., local models of the agents. The combination of the local models unfolds into
a global model, where each global state represents a possible configuration of
the local states of the agents.

2.2 Natural Strategic Ability

Many relevant properties of multi-agent systems refer to *strategic abilities* of
agents and their groups. For example, voter-verifiability can be understood as
the ability of the voter to check if her vote was registered and tallied correctly.
Similarly, receipt-freeness can be understood as the inability of the coercer, typically with help from the voter, to obtain evidence of how the voter has voted [41].

Logics of strategic reasoning, such as ATL and Strategy Logic, provide neat
languages to express properties of agents' behavior and its dynamics, driven by
individual and collective goals of the agents [2,12,34]. For example, the ATL for-
mula $\langle\langle cust\rangle\rangle$F ticket may be used to express that the customer *cust* can ensure
that he will eventually obtain a ticket, regardless of the actions of the other
agents. The specification holds if *cust* has a strategy whose every execution path
satisfies ticket at some point in the future. Strategies in a multi-agent system are
understood as conditional plans, and play central role in reasoning about pur-
poseful agents [2,40]. Formally, strategies are defined as functions from sequences
of system states (i.e., possible histories of the game) to actions. A simpler notion
of positional strategies, that we will use here, is defined by functions from states
to actions. However, real-life processes often have millions or even billions of
possible states, which allows for terribly complicated strategies – and humans
are notoriously bad at handling combinatorially complex objects.

To better model the way human agents strategize, we proposed in [26,27]
to use a more human-friendly representation of strategies, based on lists of
condition-action rules. The conditions are given by Boolean formulas for positional strategies and regular expressions over Boolean formulas in the general
case. Moreover, it was postulated that only those strategies should be considered whose complexity does not exceed a given bound. This is consistent with
classical approaches to commonsense reasoning [17] and planning [22], as well as
the empirical results on how humans learn and use concepts [9,21].

2.3 Natural Strategies and Their Complexity

Natural Strategies. Let $\mathcal{B}(Prop_a)$ be the set of Boolean formulas over atomic
propositions $Prop_a$ observable by agent a. In our case, $Prop_a$ consists of all

the references to the local variables of agent a, as well as the global variables in the model. We represent natural positional strategies of agent a by *ordered lists of guarded actions*, i.e., sequences of pairs $\phi_i \rightsquigarrow \alpha_i$ such that: (1) $\phi_i \in \mathcal{B}(Prop_a)$, and (2) α_i is an action available to agent a in every state where ϕ_i holds. Moreover, we assume that the last pair on the list is $\top \rightsquigarrow \alpha$ for some action α, i.e., the last rule is guarded by a condition that will always be satisfied. A *collective natural strategy* for a group of agents $A = \{a_1, \ldots, a_{|A|}\}$ is a tuple of individual natural strategies $s_A = (s_{a_1}, \ldots, s_{a_{|A|}})$. The set of such strategies is denoted by Σ_A.

The "outcome" function $out(q, s_A)$ returns the set of all paths (i.e., all maximal traces) that occur when coalition A executes strategy s_A from state q onward, and the agents outside A are free to act in an arbitrary way.

Complexity of Strategies. We will use the following complexity metric for strategies: $compl(s_A) = \sum_{(\phi, \alpha) \in s_A} |\phi|$, with $|\phi|$ being the number of symbols in ϕ, without parentheses. That is, $compl(s_A)$ simply counts the total length of guards in s_A. Intuitively, the complexity of a strategy is understood as its level of sophistication. It corresponds to the mental effort needed to come up with the strategy, memorize it, and execute it.

3 Specification and Verification of Voting Properties Based on Natural Strategies

To reason about natural strategic ability, the logic NatATL was introduced in [25, 26] with the following syntax:

$$\varphi ::= \mathsf{p} \mid \neg\varphi \mid \varphi \wedge \varphi \mid \langle\!\langle A \rangle\!\rangle^{\leq k} \mathsf{X}\, \varphi \mid \langle\!\langle A \rangle\!\rangle^{\leq k} \mathsf{F}\, \varphi \mid \langle\!\langle A \rangle\!\rangle^{\leq k} \mathsf{G}\, \varphi \mid \langle\!\langle A \rangle\!\rangle^{\leq k} \varphi\, \mathsf{U}\, \varphi.$$

where A is a group of agents and $k \in \mathbb{N}$ is a complexity bound. Intuitively, $\langle\!\langle A \rangle\!\rangle^{\leq k} \gamma$ reads as "coalition A has a collective strategy of size less or equal than k to enforce the property γ." The formulas of NatATL make use of classical temporal operators: "X" ("in the next state"), "G" ("always from now on"), "F" ("now or sometime in the future"), and U (strong "until"). For example, the formula $\langle\!\langle cust \rangle\!\rangle^{\leq 10} \mathsf{F}$ ticket expresses that the customer can obtain a ticket by a strategy of complexity at most 10. This seems more appropriate as a functionality requirement than to require the existence of *any* function from states to actions. We note in passing that the path quantifier "for all paths" from temporal logic can be defined as $\mathsf{A}\gamma \equiv \langle\!\langle \emptyset \rangle\!\rangle^{\leq 0} \gamma$.

3.1 How to Specify Voter-Verifiability

NatATL can be used to specify interesting properties of the voting system. For example, *voter-verifiability* captures the ability of the voter to verify what happened to her vote. In our case, this is represented by the *check4* phase, hence we can specify voter-verifiability with formula $\langle\!\langle voter \rangle\!\rangle^{\leq k} \mathsf{F}$ (check4_ok $\vee$ error). The intuition is simple: the voter has a strategy of size at most k to successfully perform *check4* or else signal an error.

A careful reader can spot one problem with the formalization: it holds if the voter signals an error regardless of the outcome of the check (and it shouldn't!). A better specification is given by $\langle\!\langle voter \rangle\!\rangle^{\leq k} F$ (check4_ok $\vee$ check4_fail), saying that the voter has a strategy of size at most k so that, at some point, she obtains either the positive or the negative outcome of $check4$.

3.2 Towards Dispute Resolution

Moreover, we can use formula AG (check4_fail $\rightarrow$ $\langle\!\langle voter \rangle\!\rangle^{\leq k} F$ error) to connect the negative outcome of the check with the voter's ability to report the problem. This property, which can be called "error signalling," captures one aspect of *dispute resolution*. To characterize dispute resolution in full, we would need to significantly extend our model of the election. For instance, it would have to include a process that handles submitting the relevant evidence to the right authority (electoral commission, the judge, etc.), the deliberation and decision-making steps to be taken by that authority, and finally the way the final decision is to be executed (e.g., the election being declared void and repeated). We conjecture that dispute resolution would require not only more complex models than voter verifiability, but also higher mental complexity of the voter's behaviour, i.e., more complex natural strategies to achieve it.

3.3 Strategic-Epistemic Specifications

The above specification of voter-verifiability is rather technical and relies on appropriate labeling of model states (in particular, with propositions check4_ok and check4_fail). On a more abstract level, one would like to say that the voter has a strategy to eventually know how her vote has been treated. Crucially, this refers to the *knowledge* of the voter. To capture the requirement, we would need to extend NatATL with knowledge operators K_a, where $K_a \varphi$ expresses that agent a knows that φ holds. For instance, K_{voter}voted$_i$ says that the voter knows that her vote has been registered for the candidate i. Then, voter-verifiability could be re-formalized as:

$$\langle\!\langle voter \rangle\!\rangle^{\leq k} F \bigwedge_{i \in Cand} (K_{voter}\text{voted}_i \vee K_{voter}\neg\text{voted}_i).$$

3.4 Receipt-Freeness

The conceptual structure of receipt-freeness is similar. In that case, we want to say that the voter has no way of proving how she has voted, and that the coercer (or a potential vote-buyer) does not have a strategy that allows him to learn the value of the vote, even if the voter cooperates [30]:

$$\bigwedge_{i \in Cand} \neg\langle\!\langle coerc, voter \rangle\!\rangle^{\leq k} G (\text{end} \rightarrow (K_{coerc}\text{vote}_i \vee K_{coerc}\neg\text{vote}_i)).$$

That means that the coercer and the voter have no strategy with complexity at most k to learn, after the election is finished, whether the voter has voted for i or not. Note that this is only one possible formalization of the requirement. For example, one may argue that, to violate receipt-freeness, it suffices that the coercer can detect *whenever the voter has not obeyed*; he does not have to learn the exact value of her vote. This can be captured by the following formula: $\bigwedge_{i \in Cand} \neg \langle\!\langle coerc, voter \rangle\!\rangle^{\leq k} G\, ((\text{end} \wedge \neg \text{vote}_i) \to K_{coerc} \neg \text{vote}_i)$. We note in passing that the related notion of *vote anonymity* can be specified as $\bigwedge_{a \in Agents \setminus \{voter\}} \bigwedge_{i \in Cand} AG\, (\neg K_a \text{vote}_i \wedge \neg K_a \neg \text{vote}_i)$.

Combining strategic and epistemic aspects poses a number of semantic problems [1,29]. To avoid those, we will concentrate on properties that use only strategic operators, such as the "technical" specification of voter-verifiability.

3.5 Using Verification Tools to Facilitate Analysis

The focus of this work is on modeling and specification; the formal analysis is done mainly by hand. However, having the models specified in UPPAAL suggests that we can also benefit from its model checking functionality. Unfortunately, the requirement specification language of UPPAAL is very limited, and allows for neither strategic operators nor knowledge modalities. Still, we can use it to verify concrete strategies if we carefully modify the input formula and the model. We will show how to do it in Sect. 7.

4   Use Case Scenario: vVote

Secure and verifiable voting is becoming more and more important for the democracy to function correctly. In this paper, we analyze the vVote implementation of Prêt à Voter which was used for remote voting and voting of handicapped persons in the Victorian elections in November 2014 [14]. The main idea of the Prêt à Voter protocol focuses on encoding the vote using a randomized candidate list. In this protocol the ballot consists of two parts: the randomized order of candidates (left part) and the list of empty checkboxes along with the number encoding the order of the candidates (right part). The voter casts her vote in the usual way, by placing a cross in the right hand column against the candidate of her choice. Then, she tears the ballot in two parts, destroys the left part, casts the right one, and takes a copy of it as her receipt. After the election her vote appears on the public Web Bulletin Board (WBB)[1] as the pair of the encoding number and the marked box, which can be compared with the receipt for verification. We look at the whole process, from the voter entering the polling station, to the verification of her vote on the Web Bulletin Board.

After entering the polling station, the Poll Worker (PW) authenticates the voter (using the method prescribed by the appropriate regulations), and sends a print request to the Print On Demand device (POD) specifying the district/region of the voter. If the authentication is valid (state *printing*) then the POD retrieves and prints an appropriate ballot for the voter, including a Serial Number (SN) and the district, with a signature from the Private Web Bulletin Board

---

[1] The WBB is an authenticated public broadcast channel with memory.

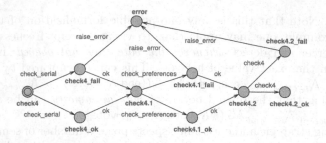

Fig. 2. Voter refinement: phase check4

(PWBB). The PWBB is a robust secure database which receives messages, performs basic validity checks, and returns signatures. After that, the voter may choose to check and confirm the ballot. This involves demanding a proof that the ballot is properly formed, i.e., that the permuted candidate list corresponds correctly to the cipher-texts on the public WBB for that serial number. If the ballot has a confirmation check, the voter returns to the printing step for a new ballot (transition from state *check1* to *printing*).

Having obtained and possibly checked her ballot (state *has_ballot*), the voter can scan it by showing the ballot bar code to the Electronic Ballot Marker (EBM). Then, she enters her vote (state *scanning*) via the EBM interface. The EBM is a computer that assists the user in filling in a Prêt à Voter ballot. The EBM prints on a separate sheet the voter's receipt with the following information: (i) the electoral district, (ii) the Serial Number, (iii) the voter's vote permuted appropriately to match the Prêt à Voter ballot, and (iv) a QR code with this data and the PWBB signature.

Further, the voter must check the printed vote against the printed candidate list. In particular, she checks that the district is correct and the Serial Number matches the one on the ballot form. If all is well done, she can optionally check the PWBB signature, which covers only the data visible to the voter. Note that, if either *check2* or *check3* fails, the vote is canceled using the cancellation protocol. If everything is OK, the voter validates the vote, shreds the candidate list, and leaves the polling station. Finally, the voter can check her vote on the WBB after the election closes. She only needs to check the SR and the order of her preference numbers.

5   Models

In this section we present the model of a simplified version of vVote, focusing on the steps that are important from the voter's perspective. We use UPPAAL as the modeling tool because of its flexible modeling language and user-friendly GUI.

5.1   Voter Model

The local model already presented in Fig. 1 captures the voter's actions from entering the polling station to casting her vote, going back home and verifying

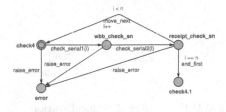 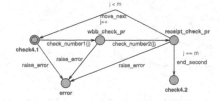

Fig. 3. Serial number check   **Fig. 4.** Preferences order check

her receipt on the Web Bulletin Board. As shown in the graph, some actions (in particular the additional checks) are optional for the voter. Furthermore, to simulate the human behavior we added some additional actions, not described in the protocol itself. For example the voter can skip even obligatory steps, like *check2*. This is especially important, as *check2* may be the most time-consuming action for the voter and many voters may skip it in the real life. To further simulate the real-life behavior of the voters, for each state we added a loop action labeled as *wait*, to allow the voter to wait in any state as long as she wants. We omit the loops from the graph for the clarity of presentation. After every check, the voter can signal an error, thus ending up in the *error* state. The state represents communication with the election authority, signaling that the voter could not cast her vote or a machine malfunction was detected.

5.2   Refinements of the Voter Model

The model shown in Fig. 1 is relatively abstract. For example, *check4* is shown as an atomic action, but in fact it requires that the voter compares data from the receipt and the WBB. In order to properly measure the complexity of the voter strategies, it is crucial to consider different levels of granularity.

Check4 Phase. Recall that this is the last phase in the protocol and it is optional. Here, the voter can check if the printed receipt matches her intended vote on the WBB. This includes checking that the serial numbers match (action *check_serial*), and that the printed preferences order match the one displayed on the WBB (action *check_preferences*). If both steps succeed, then the voter reaches state *check4_ok*. The refined model for this phase is presented in Fig. 2. Other phases, such as *check2*, can be refined in a similar way.

Serial Number Phase. In some cases the model shown in Fig. 2 may still be too general. For example, the length of the serial number may have impact on the level of difficulty faced by the voter. To capture this, we split the step into atomic actions: *check_serial1(i)* for checking the ith symbol on the WBB, and *check_serial2(i)* for checking the ith symbol on the receipt. The resulting model is shown in Fig. 3, where n is the length of the serial number.

Preferences Order Phase. Similarly to comparing the two serial numbers, the verification of the printed preferences can also be troublesome for the voter. In order to make sure that her receipt matches the entry on the WBB, the voter

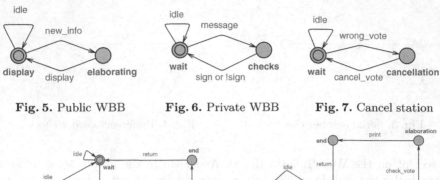

Fig. 5. Public WBB   **Fig. 6.** Private WBB   **Fig. 7.** Cancel station

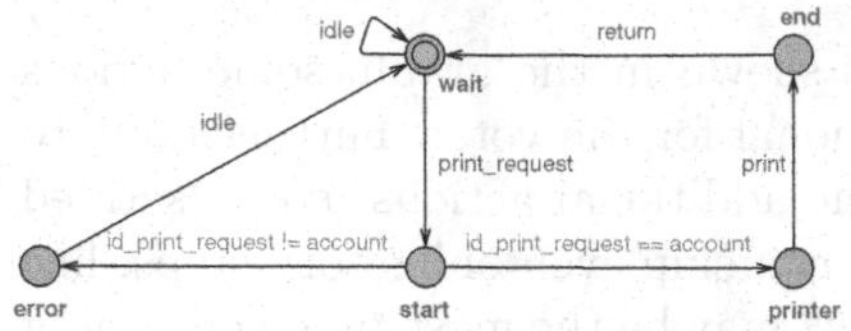

Fig. 8. Print-on-demand printer 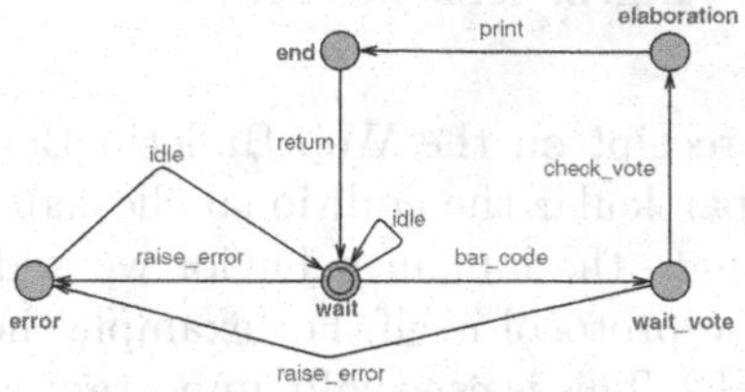   **Fig. 9.** Electronic Ballot Marker (EBM)

must check each number showing her preference. Actions *check_number*1(*i*) and *check_number*2(*i*) refer to checking a number on the WBB and on the receipt, respectively. This is shown in the local model in Fig. 4, where *m* is the number of candidates in the ballot.

5.3 Voting Infrastructure

The voter is not the only entity taking part in the election procedure. The election infrastructure and the electronic devices associated with it constitute a significant part of the procedure. Since there are several components involved in the voting process, we decided to model each component as a separate agent. The models of the Public WBB, Private WBB, the cancel station, the print-on-demand printer, and the EBM are shown in Figs. 5, 6, 7, 8 and 9.

5.4 Coercer Model

To model the coercer, we first need to determine his exact capabilities. Is he able to interact with the voter, or only with the system? Should he have full control over the network, like the Dolev-Yao attacker, or do we want the agent to represent implicit coercion, where the relatives or subordinates are forced to vote for a specified candidate? In this preliminary study, we assume a simple 1-state model of the coercer, with loops labeled by the following actions:

- *coerce*(*ca*): the coercer coerces the voter to vote for candidate *ca*;
- *modify_ballot*(*ca*): the coercer modifies the voter's ballot by setting a vote for *ca*;
- *request*: the coercer requests the receipt from the voter;
- *punish*: the coercer punishes the voter;

- *infect*: the coercer infects the voting machine with malicious code;
- *listen*: the coercer listens to the voter's vote on the voting machine;
- *replace(ca)*: the coercer replaces the voter's ballot with a vote for *ca*.

Some actions depend on each other. For example, *listen* and *replace* should be executed only after the *infect* has succeed, as the coercer needs some kind of access to the voting machine.

6 Strategies and Their Complexity

There are many possible objectives for the participants of a voting procedure. A voter's goal could be to just cast her vote, another one could be to make sure that her vote was correctly counted, and yet another one to verify the election results. The same goes for the coercer: he may just want to make his family vote in the "correct" way, or to change the outcome of the election. In order to define different objectives, we can use formulas of NatATL and look for appropriate natural strategies, as described in Sects. 2 and 3. More precisely, we can fix a subset of the participants and their objective with a formula of NatATL, find the smallest strategy that achieves the objective, and compute its size. The size of the strategy will be an indication of how hard it is to make sure that the objective is achieved.

An example goal that the voter may want to pursue is the verifiability of her vote. Given the model in Fig. 1, we can use the formula $\varphi_1 = \langle\langle v \rangle\rangle^{\leq k} \mathbf{F}(\text{check4\_ok} \lor \text{check4\_fail})$, as discussed in Sect. 3.

Note that it is essential to fix the granularity level of the modeling right. When shifting the level of abstraction, we obtain significantly different "measurements" of strategic complexity. This is why we proposed several variants of the voter model in Sect. 5. In this section, we will show how it affects the outcome of the analysis.

In the following we take another look at the previously defined models and try to list possible strategies for the participants.

6.1 Strategies for the Voter

In this section we focus on natural strategies for voter-verifiability.

Natural Strategy 1. *A strategy for the voter is:*

1. has_ballot $\rightsquigarrow$ *scan_ballot*
2. scanning $\rightsquigarrow$ *enter_vote*
3. voted $\rightsquigarrow$ *check2*
4. check2_ok $\lor$ check2_fail $\lor$ check_request $\rightsquigarrow$ *move_next*
5. vote_ok $\rightsquigarrow$ *shred_ballot*
6. shred $\rightsquigarrow$ *leave*
7. check4 $\rightsquigarrow$ *check4*
8. $\top \rightsquigarrow \star$.

Recall that the above is an ordered sequence of guarded commands. The first condition (guard) that evaluates to *true* determines the action of the voter. Thus, if the voter has the ballot and she has not scanned it (proposition has_ballot), she scans the ballot. If has_ballot is false and scanning is true then she enters her vote, and so on. If all the preconditions except ⊤ are false, then she executes an arbitrary available action (represented by the wildcard ⋆). For example, the voter will do *print_ballot* at the state *printing*, where the voter needs to wait while the Poll Worker identifies her and generates a new ballot.

In Natural Strategy 1, we have 8 guarded commands in which the command (4) costs 5 since in its condition there are five symbols (three atoms plus two disjunctions), while the other guarded commands cost 1, so the total complexity is $1 \cdot 7 + 5 \cdot 1 = 12$. So, the formula φ_1 is true with any k of 12 or more.

Next, we show a natural strategy with the additional guarded commands in case the voter wants to do the optional phases *check1* and *check3*, i.e., we want to satisfy the formula $\varphi_2 = \langle\langle v \rangle\rangle^{\leq k} \mathbf{F}(\text{checked1} \wedge \text{checked3} \wedge (\text{check4\_ok} \vee \text{check4\_fail}))$. In particular, φ_2 checks whether there exist a natural strategy for the voter such that sooner or later she does *check1*, *check3*, and verifies her vote. Note that, apart from the standard propositions like *check1*, we also add their persistent versions like *checked1* designed in such a way that once *check1* gets true, *checked1* also becomes true and remains true forever.

Natural Strategy 2. *A strategy for the voter that considers the optional phases check1 and check3 is:*

1. has_ballot ∧ counter == 0 ⤳ *check_ballot*
2. has_ballot ⤳ *scan_ballot*
3. scanning ⤳ *enter_vote*
4. voted ⤳ *check2*
5. check2_ok ∨ check2_fail ⤳ *check3*
6. check1 ∨ check3 ∨ check_request ⤳ *move_next*
7. vote_ok ⤳ *shred_ballot*
8. shred ⤳ *leave*
9. check4 ⤳ *check4*
10. ⊤ ⤳ ⋆.

In Natural Strategy 2, we introduce the verification of *check1* and *check3*. To do this we add two new guarded commands (5) and (6), and update clause (1) by adding a control on a counter to determine if *check1* is done or not. This gives the total complexity of $1 \cdot 7 + 3 \cdot 2 + 5 \cdot 1 = 18$. Thus, the formula φ_2 is true for any $k \geq 18$.

An important aspect to evaluate in this subject concerns the detailed analysis of *check4*. Some interesting questions on this analysis could be: how does the voter perform *check4*? How does she compare the printed preferences with the information on the public WWB? These questions open up several scenarios both from a strategic point of view and for the model to be used. From the strategic point of view, we can consider a refinement of Natural Strategy 1, in which the action *check4* is evaluated as something of atomic. If we consider that the *check4* includes: comparing preferences with the information in the public WWB and checking the serial number, we can already divide the single action into two different actions for each of the checks to be performed. So, given the model in Fig. 2, to verify that the voter does each step of *check*4, we need to provide a formula that verifies atoms check4_ok, check4.1_ok, and check4.2_ok. To do this in NatATL, we use the formula $\varphi_3 = \langle\!\langle v \rangle\!\rangle^{\leq k} \mathbf{F}((\text{checked4\_ok} \wedge \text{checked4.1\_ok} \wedge \text{checked4.2\_ok}) \vee \text{check4\_fail} \vee \text{check4.1\_fail} \vee \text{check4.2\_fail})$. To achieve this, we refine the previous natural strategy for the voter, as follows.

Natural Strategy 3. *A strategy for the voter that works in the refined model of phase check4 is:*

1. has_ballot $\rightsquigarrow$ *scan_ballot*
2. scanning $\rightsquigarrow$ *enter_vote*
3. voted $\rightsquigarrow$ *check2*
4. check2_ok $\vee$ check2_fail $\vee$ check_request $\rightsquigarrow$ *move_next*
5. vote_ok $\rightsquigarrow$ *shred_ballot*
6. shred $\rightsquigarrow$ *leave*
7. check4 $\rightsquigarrow$ *check_serial*
8. check4_ok $\rightsquigarrow$ *ok*
9. check4.1 $\rightsquigarrow$ *check_preferences*
10. check4.1_ok $\rightsquigarrow$ *ok*
11. check4.2 $\rightsquigarrow$ *check4*
12. $\top \rightsquigarrow \star$.

In Natural Strategy 3, we have 12 guarded commands in which all the conditions are defined with a single atom but (4) in which there is a disjunction of three atoms. So, the total complexity is $1 \cdot 11 + 5 \cdot 1 = 16$. So, φ_3 is true for any $k \geq 16$; one can use Natural Strategy 3 to demonstrate that.

6.2   Counting Other Kinds of Resources

So far, we have measured the effort of the voter by how complex strategies she must execute. This helps to estimate the mental difficulty related, e.g., to voter-verifiability. However, this is not the only source of effort that the voter has to invest. Verifying one's vote might require money (for example, if the voter needs to buy special software or a dedicated device), computational power, and, most of all, time. Here, we briefly concentrate on the latter factor.

For a voter's task expressed by the NatATL formula $\langle\!\langle v \rangle\!\rangle^{\leq k} \mathbf{F} \varphi$ and a natural strategy s_v for the voter, we can estimate the time spent on the task by the number of transitions necessary to reach φ. That is, we take all the paths in $out(q, s_v)$, where q is the initial state of the procedure. On each path, φ must occur at some point. We look for the path where the first occurrence of φ happens *latest*, and count the number of steps to φ on that path. We will demonstrate how it works on the goals and strategies presented in Sect. 6.1.

For example, for Natural Strategy 3, starting from the initial state, the voter needs of $10 + 5 = 15$ steps to achieve (checked4_ok $\wedge$ checked4.1_ok $\wedge$

checked4.2_ok) ∨ check4_fail ∨ check4.1_fail ∨ check4.2_fail in the worst case. More precisely, 10 steps are needed to achieve *check*4 in the local model shown in Fig. 1, and 5 more steps to reach check4.2_ok ∨ check4.2_fail in the refinement of the final section of the procedure (see Fig. 2).

Similarly, the voter executing Natural Strategy 1 needs 11 steps to achieve the state check4_fail or the state check4_ok. Finally, Natural Strategy 2 requires 15 steps to conclude the verification of the voter's vote.

6.3   Natural Strategies for Coalitions

Some properties, such as receipt-freeness, refer to the joint abilities of the voter and the coercer (see Sect. 3). Unfortunately, receipt-freeness is underpinned by strategic-epistemic reasoning – something that we want to avoid here. Instead, we consider a simpler property stating that "the coercer can obtain the receipt of the voter's vote if the voter cooperates with him." This can be formalized as:

$$\varphi_4 = \langle\!\langle c, v \rangle\!\rangle^{\leq k} F \text{ has\_receipt}.$$

The natural strategies for the coalition are presented below.

Natural Strategy 4 (Coalitional strategy, the voter's part)

1. has_ballot ⤳ *scan_ballot*
2. scanning ⤳ *enter_vote*
3. voted ⤳ *check*2
4. check2_ok ∨ check2_fail ⤳ *move_next*
5. vote_ok ⤳ *shred_ballot*
6. shred ⤳ *leave*
7. check_request ⤳ *share*
8. ⊤ ⤳ ⋆.

Natural Strategy 5 (Coalitional strategy, the coercer's part)

1. ⊤ ⤳ *request*

In Natural Strategy 4, we have 8 guarded commands in which all the conditions are defined with a single atom but (4) in which there is disjunction of two atoms. Thus, the total complexity is $1 \cdot 7 + 3 \cdot 1 = 10$. Moreover, Natural Strategy 5 for the coercer has complexity 1 since it has one guarded command with a single symbol. So, φ_4 is true for any $k \geq 11$.

7   Automated Verification of Strategies

In this section we explain how the model checking functionality of UPPAAL can be used for an automated verification of the strategies presented in Sect. 6. To verify selected formulas and the corresponding natural strategies, we need to modify several things, namely: *(i)* the formula, *(ii)* the natural strategy, and finally *(iii)* the model. We explain the modifications step by step.

Formula. To specify the required properties for the protocol, we have used a variant of strategic logic. Unfortunately, UPPAAL supports neither NatATL nor ATL, but only a fragment of the branching-time temporal logic CTL. Thus, we cannot use UPPAAL to model-check the formulas of Sect. 6. What we can do, however, is to verify if *a given natural strategy achieves a given goal.* To this end, we replace the strategic operator $\langle\!\langle A \rangle\!\rangle^{\leq k}$ in the formula with the universal path quantifier A. For example, instead of formula $\varphi_1 \equiv \langle\!\langle v \rangle\!\rangle F\,(\text{check4\_ok} \vee \text{check4\_fail})$ we use $\varphi_1' = \text{AF}\,(\text{check4\_ok} \vee \text{check4\_fail})$. Furthermore, we "prune" the model according to the given strategy, see below for the details.

Natural Strategy. In order to efficiently merge the natural strategy with the model, the strategy should be modified so that all the guard conditions are mutually exclusive. To this end, we go through the preconditions from top to bottom, and refine them by adding the negated preconditions from all the previous guardeds. For example, Natural Strategy 1 becomes:

1. has_ballot $\leadsto$ *scan_ballot*
2. $\neg$has_ballot $\wedge$ scanning $\leadsto$ *enter_vote*
3. $\neg$has_ballot $\wedge$ $\neg$scanning $\wedge$ voted $\leadsto$ *check2*
4. $\neg$has_ballot $\wedge$ $\neg$scanning $\wedge$ $\neg$voted $\wedge$ (check2_ok $\vee$ check2_fail $\vee$ check_request) $\leadsto$ *move_next*
5. $\neg$has_ballot $\wedge$ $\neg$scanning $\wedge$ $\neg$voted $\wedge$ $\neg$(check2_ok $\vee$ check2_fail $\vee$ check_request) $\wedge$ vote_ok $\leadsto$ *shred_ballot*
6. $\neg$has_ballot $\wedge$ $\neg$scanning $\wedge$ $\neg$voted $\wedge$ $\neg$(check2_ok $\vee$ check2_fail $\vee$ check_request) $\wedge$ $\neg$vote_ok $\wedge$ shred $\leadsto$ *leave*
7. $\neg$has_ballot $\wedge$ $\neg$scanning $\wedge$ $\neg$voted $\wedge$ $\neg$(check2_ok $\vee$ check2_fail $\vee$ check_request) $\wedge$ $\neg$vote_ok $\wedge$ $\neg$shred $\wedge$ check4 $\leadsto$ *check4*
8. $\top \leadsto \star$.

Model. To verify the selected strategy of the voter, we merge it with the voter model by adding the guard conditions from the strategy to the preconditions of the corresponding local transitions in the model. Thus, we effectively remove all transitions that are not in accordance with the strategy. In this way, only the paths that are consistent with the strategy will be considered by the model-checker.

Levels of Granularity. As we showed in Sect. 5, it is often important to have variants of the model for different levels of abstraction. To handle those in UPPAAL, we have used synchronizations edges. For example, to have a more detailed version of the phase *check4*, we added synchronization edges in the voter model (Fig. 1) and in the *check4* model (Fig. 2). Then, when going through the *check4* phase in the voter model, UPPAAL will proceed to the more detailed submodel, and come back after getting to its final state.

Running the Verification. We have modified the models, formulas, and strategies from Sects. 5 and 6 following the above steps. Then, we used UPPAAL to verify that Natural Strategies 1–5 indeed enforce the prescribed properties. The tool reported that each formula holds in the corresponding model. The execution time was always at most a few seconds.

8 Conclusions

In the analysis of a voting protocols it is important to make sure that the voter has a strategy to use the functionality of the protocol. That is, she has a strategy to fill in and cast her ballot, verify her vote on the bulletin board, etc. However, this is not enough: it is also essential to see how hard that strategy is. In this paper, we propose a methodology that can be used to this end. One can assume a natural representation of the voter's strategy, and measure its complexity as the size of the representation.

We mainly focus on one aspect of the voter's effort, namely the mental effort needed to produce, memorize, and execute the required actions. We also indicate that there are other important factors, such as the time needed to execute the strategy or the financial cost of the strategy. This may lead to trade-offs where optimizing the costs with respect to one resource leads to higher costs in terms of another resource. Moreover, resources can vary in their importance for different agents. For example, time may be more important for the voter, while money is probably more relevant when we analyze the strategy of the coercer. We leave a closer study of such trade-offs for future work.

An interesting extension would be to further analyze the parts of the protocol where the voter compares two numbers, tables, etc. As the voter is a human being, it is natural for her to make a mistake. Furthermore, the probability of making a mistake at each step can be added to the model to analyze the overall probability of successfully comparing two data sets by the voter.

Finally, we point out that the methodology proposed in this paper can be applied outside of the e-voting domain. For example, one can use it to study the usability of policies for social distancing in the current epidemic situation, and whether they are likely to obtain the expected results.

Acknowledgements. The authors thank the anonymous reviewers for their valuable comments. W. Jamroga and D. Kurpiewski acknowledge the support of the National Centre for Research and Development, Poland (NCBR), and the Luxembourg National Research Fund (FNR), under the PolLux/FNR-CORE projects VoteVerif (POLLUX-IV/1/2016) and STV (POLLUX-VII/1/2019).

References

1. Ågotnes, T., Goranko, V., Jamroga, W., Wooldridge, M.: Knowledge and ability. In: Handbook of Epistemic Logic, pp. 543–589 (2015)
2. Alur, R., Henzinger, T.A., Kupferman, O.: Alternating-time temporal logic. J. ACM **49**, 672–713 (2002)
3. Basin, D., Gersbach, H., Mamageishvili, A., Schmid, L., Tejada, O.: Election security and economics: it's all about eve. In: Krimmer, R., Volkamer, M., Braun Binder, N., Kersting, N., Pereira, O., Schürmann, C. (eds.) E-Vote-ID 2017. LNCS, vol. 10615, pp. 1–20. Springer, Cham (2017). https://doi.org/10.1007/978-3-319-68687-5_1
4. Basin, D.A., Radomirovic, S., Schmid, L.: Modeling human errors in security protocols. In: CSF, pp. 325–340 (2016)

5. Behrmann, G., David, A., Larsen, K.G.: A tutorial on UPPAAL. In: Bernardo, M., Corradini, F. (eds.) SFM-RT 2004. LNCS, vol. 3185, pp. 200–236. Springer, Heidelberg (2004). https://doi.org/10.1007/978-3-540-30080-9_7
6. Bella, G., Curzon, P., Giustolisi, R., Lenzini, G.: A socio-technical methodology for the security and privacy analysis of services. In: COMPSAC, pp. 401–406 (2014)
7. Bella, G., Curzon, P., Lenzini, G.: Service security and privacy as a socio-technical problem. J. Comput. Secur. **23**(5), 563–585 (2015)
8. Benaloh, J., Tuinstra, D.: Receipt-free secret-ballot elections. In: ACM symposium on Theory of Computing, pp. 544–553 (1994)
9. Bourne, L.E.: Knowing and using concepts. Psychol. Rev. **77**, 546–556 (1970)
10. Buldas, A., Mägi, T.: Practical security analysis of E-voting systems. In: Miyaji, A., Kikuchi, H., Rannenberg, K. (eds.) IWSEC 2007. LNCS, vol. 4752, pp. 320–335. Springer, Heidelberg (2007). https://doi.org/10.1007/978-3-540-75651-4_22
11. Carlos, M.C., Martina, J.E., Price, G., Custódio, R.F.: A proposed framework for analysing security ceremonies. In: SECRYPT, pp. 440–445 (2012)
12. Chatterjee, K., Henzinger, T.A., Piterman, N.: Strategy Logic. Inf. Comput. **208**(6), 677–693 (2010)
13. Cortier, V., Galindo, D., Küsters, R., Müller, J., Truderung, T.: SoK: verifiability notions for e-voting protocols. In: IEEE Symposium on Security and Privacy, pp. 779–798 (2016)
14. Culnane, C., Ryan, P.Y.A., Schneider, S.A., Teague, V.: vVote: a verifiable voting system. ACM Trans. Inf. Syst. Secur. **18**(1), 3:1-3:30 (2015)
15. Culnane, C., Teague, V.: Strategies for voter-initiated election audits. In: Zhu, Q., Alpcan, T., Panaousis, E., Tambe, M., Casey, W. (eds.) GameSec 2016. LNCS, vol. 9996, pp. 235–247. Springer, Cham (2016). https://doi.org/10.1007/978-3-319-47413-7_14
16. David, N., et al.: Modelling social-technical attacks with timed automata. In: MIST, pp. 21–28 (2015)
17. Davis, E., Marcus, G.: Commonsense reasoning. Commun. ACM **58**(9), 92–103 (2015)
18. Delaune, S., Kremer, S., Ryan, M.: Coercion-resistance and receipt-freeness in electronic voting. In: CSF, 12-pp (2006)
19. Dreier, J., Lafourcade, P., Lakhnech, Y.: A formal taxonomy of privacy in voting protocols. In: ICC, pp. 6710–6715 (2012)
20. Fagin, R., Halpern, J.Y., Moses, Y., Vardi, M.Y.: Reasoning about Knowledge. MIT Press, Cambridge (1995)
21. Feldman, J.: Minimization of Boolean complexity in human concept learning. Nature **407**, 630–633 (2000)
22. Ghallab, M., Nau, D., Traverso, P.: Automated Planning: Theory and Practice. Morgan Kaufmann, San Francisco (2004)
23. Hunker, J., Probst, C.W.: Insiders and insider threats - an overview of definitions and mitigation techniques. J. Wirel. Mob. Networks Ubiquitous Comput. Dependable Appl. **2**(1), 4–27 (2011)
24. Jamroga, W., Knapik, M., Kurpiewski, D.: Model checking the SELENE E-voting protocol in multi-agent logics. In: Krimmer, R., Volkamer, M., Cortier, V., Goré, R., Hapsara, M., Serdült, U., Duenas-Cid, D. (eds.) E-Vote-ID 2018. LNCS, vol. 11143, pp. 100–116. Springer, Cham (2018). https://doi.org/10.1007/978-3-030-00419-4_7
25. Jamroga, W., Malvone, V., Murano, A.: Reasoning about natural strategic ability. In: AAMAS, pp. 714–722 (2017)

26. Jamroga, W., Malvone, V., Murano, A.: Natural strategic ability. Artif. Intell. **277** (2019)
27. Jamroga, W., Malvone, V., Murano, A.: A.: Natural strategic ability under imperfect information. In: AAMAS, pp. 962–970 (2019)
28. Jamroga, W., Tabatabaei, M.: Preventing coercion in E-voting: be open and commit. In: Krimmer, R., Volkamer, M., Barrat, J., Benaloh, J., Goodman, N., Ryan, P.Y.A., Teague, V. (eds.) E-Vote-ID 2016. LNCS, vol. 10141, pp. 1–17. Springer, Cham (2017). https://doi.org/10.1007/978-3-319-52240-1_1
29. Jamroga, W., van der Hoek, W.: Agents that know how to play. Fund. Inform. **63**(2–3), 185–219 (2004)
30. Juels, A., Catalano, D., Jakobsson, M.: Coercion-resistant electronic elections. In: ACM Workshop on Privacy in the Electronic Society, pp. 61–70 (2005)
31. Küsters, R., Truderung, T., Vogt, A.: A game-based definition of coercion-resistance and its applications. In: IEEE Computer Security Foundations Symposium, pp. 122–136 (2010)
32. Martimiano, T., Dos Santos, E., Olembo, M., Martina, J.E.: Ceremony analysis meets verifiable voting: individual verifiability in Helios. In: SECURWARE, pp. 169–183 (2015)
33. Martimiano, T., Martina, J.E.: Threat modelling service security as a security ceremony. In: ARES, pp. 195–204 (2016)
34. Mogavero, F., Murano, A., Perelli, G., Vardi, M.Y.: Reasoning about strategies: on the model-checking problem. ACM Trans. Comput. Log. **15**(4), 1–42 (2014)
35. Okamoto, T.: Receipt-free electronic voting schemes for large scale elections. In: Christianson, B., Crispo, B., Lomas, M., Roe, M. (eds.) Security Protocols 1997. LNCS, vol. 1361, pp. 25–35. Springer, Heidelberg (1998). https://doi.org/10.1007/BFb0028157
36. P. Y. A. Ryan. The computer ate my vote. In: Boca, P., Bowen, J., Siddiqi, J. (eds.) Formal Methods: State of the Art and New Directions, pp. 147–184. Springer, London (2010). https://doi.org/10.1007/978-1-84882-736-3_5
37. Ryan, P.Y.A., Schneider, S.A., Teague, V.: End-to-end verifiability in voting systems, from theory to practice. IEEE Secur. Privacy **13**(3), 59–62 (2015)
38. Santos, F.P.: Dynamics of reputation and the self-organization of cooperation. Ph.D. thesis, University of Lisbon (2018)
39. Santos, F.P., Santos, F.C., Pacheco, J.M.: Social norm complexity and past reputations in the evolution of cooperation. Nature **555**, 242–245 (2018)
40. Shoham, Y., Leyton-Brown, K.: Multiagent Systems - Algorithmic, Game-Theoretic, and Logical Foundations. Cambridge University Press, New York (2009)
41. Tabatabaei, M., Jamroga, W., Peter, Ryan, Y.A.: Expressing receipt-freeness and coercion-resistance in logics of strategic ability: preliminary attempt. In: PrAISe@ECAI 2016, pp. 1:1–1:8 (2016)
42. Verified Voting. Policy on direct recording electronic voting machines and ballot marking devices (2019)

A Study of Targeted Telephone Scams Involving Live Attackers

Ian G. Harris[1]($\boxtimes$), Ali Derakhshan[1], and Marcel Carlsson[2]

[1] University of California Irvine, Irvine, CA 92697, USA
harris@ics.uci.edu, aderakh1@uci.edu
[2] Lootcore, Kristianstad, Sweden
mc@lootcore.com

Abstract. We present the results of a research study in which participants were subjected to social engineering attacks via telephone, *telephone scams*, in order to determine the features of scams which people are most susceptible to. The study has involved 186 university participants who were attacked with one of 27 different attack scripts which span different independent variables including the pretext used and the method of elicitation. In order to ensure informed consent, each participant was warned that they would receive a scam phone call within 3 months. One independent variable used is the time between the warning and launching the scam. In spite of this warning, a large fraction of participants were still deceived by the scam.

A limitation to research in the study of telephone scams is the lack of a dataset of real phone scams for examination. Each phone call in our study was recorded and we present the dataset of these recordings, and their transcripts. To our knowledge, there is no similar publicly-available dataset or phone scams. We hope that our dataset will support future research in phone scams and their detection.

Keywords: Social engineering · Telephone scams · Attack dataset

1 Introduction

Social engineering attacks, or scams, describe the psychological manipulation of people to convince them to do something that they should not do [8,15]. Social engineers pretend to be some trustworthy entity, or some entity with authority over the victim. Social engineering attacks can be delivered in many ways but electronic communications, such as email or text message are common platforms. Email phishing has been shown to be an effective attack over the years, deceiving a broad range of people [11]. Attackers often gain personal information that affects the victims' personal lives, financial wellbeing, and work environment. Phishing, in all of its forms, is very popular in real attacks. The Verizon 2019 Data Breach Investigations Report [26] states that 32% of all breaches included phishing and 78% of all cyber-espionage which involved state-affiliated actors.

© Springer Nature Switzerland AG 2021
T. Groß and L. Viganò (Eds.): STAST 2020, LNCS 12812, pp. 63–82, 2021.
https://doi.org/10.1007/978-3-030-79318-0_4

A growing problem is social engineering attacks launched over the phone, or *telephone scams*. Telephone-based attacks can be more effective that email-based attacks in part because the victim is involved in a live conversation, so they feel pressured to respond quickly, without having time to think as would be the case with emails. The sheer volume of phone scams has greatly increased recently. First Orion, a call blocking technology company, estimates that more than 29% of all cellphone calls in 2018 were scams, and expects that almost half of cellphone calls in 2019 will have been scams [24]. The financial losses associated with phone scams are significant. There is a wide variety of common phone scams including the Technical Support scam which Microsoft reports targeted over 3.3 million people in 2015 and cost those people $1.5 million [14]. Nearly 70% of frauds reported to the Federal Trade Commission in 2017 where perpetrated by phone, while only 9% were conducted by email during the same period [17]. The 2019 U.S. Spam & Scam Report from Truecaller, a caller ID and spam blocking company, reveals that Americans lost $10.5 billion to phone scams in the 12 month period before the report was released in April 2019 [14].

The importance of phone scams motivates the need to understand what aspects of phone scams cause people to be convinced by them, so that defense approaches may be developed. Many empirical studies have been performed to understand phishing email scams and their ability to convince victims [2,6,7,11]. However, telephone scams are different from phishing emails in their application and effect. Telephone conversations are real-time, unlike emails, so the victim feels time pressure to respond. Telephone scams can also involve direct human-to-human interaction, which has a different emotional impact on a victim as compared to the receipt of an email. A study of user responses to telephone scams has been presented [25] which begins to shed light on critical aspects of scams, such as the importance of caller ID. However, the study presented in [25] uses only pre-recorded attack calls which have a different impact than calls from live attackers. There are also other aspects of telephone scams which need to be understood, such as the sensitivity of users to different items of information which an attacker may ask them to reveal.

In order to perform research to help protect against telephone scams, researchers need access to datasets of realistic telephone scams which can be studied, and used for training and evaluation of detection approaches. Several large datasets of phishing emails are publicly available [20–22], but similar datasets of telephone scams are not available. As a result, there is a large body of previous work on the detection of phishing emails, but very little on the detection of telephone scams [3]. It is difficult to build a dataset of telephone scams due to the legal need for consent of both communicating parties in order to record a telephone call, as is required in most states in the US.

1.1 Social Engineering Study

This paper presents the results of an empirical study on the susceptibility of people to telephone scams. We created a set of 27 different *attack scripts* which were used to scam 186 participants. The attack scripts varied over several different independent variables including the pretext used and the information requested by the attacker. We present results to show the impact of each independent variable on the success of the attack.

Targeting of the Attack. We want to understand the impact of three different aspects of social engineering attacks on the success of the attack. We define the **targeting** of an attack as degree to which the attack is personalized to appeal to a subset of the population. An attack which can be applied to a wide range of people is not well targeted, such as an IRS scam which is generically applicable to any adult in the US who interacts with the IRS. An attack which is targeted to a medium degree would be one in which a caller pretends to be from the IT office of a particular company. Such an attack is targeted towards a smaller set of people, those who work at the company in question. A highly targeted attack might be focus on a single individual by referencing personal information which has been gathered using open-source intelligence techniques.

Targeting is used by attackers because it generally improves the effectiveness of the attack, but the attacker may mis-target an attack because she does not have full information about the target. For example, an attacker may assume that people who use a particular app (i.e. tik tok) are generally young, so an attack against users of the app might be designed to appeal to young people. However, not all users of the app are young, so an attack is mis-targeted when it is launched against a user of the app who is old. To formalize the concept of attack targeting, we define the set P to be the set of people whom the attack campaign is made to appeal to, and the set Q to be the set of people who are actually attacked. We refer to the *targeting accuracy*, a, of an attack as follows, $a = \frac{|P \cap Q|}{|Q|}$. An attacker with limited knowledge of the victims is forced to choose a trade-off between increasing the number of people attacked but reducing targeting accuracy because the attack may not appeal to victims.

We explored the relationship between the targeting accuracy of the attack and the success of the attack. We consider the following hypotheses:

- **Alternative Hypothesis.** $H_{1,1}$: The targeting accuracy of the attack, a, impacts the success rate of the attack.
- **Null Hypothesis.** $H_{0,1}$: The targeting accuracy of the attack has no impact on the success rate of the attack.

Sensitivity of Information. We are investigating attacks in which the attacker attempts to gain information from the victim and we want to understand the impact that the choice of information has on the success of the attack. Different types of information have different protection requirements from the perspective of the victim. An email address may not need to be hidden, especially if your email is already publicly available. However, the cost of revealing a social security number is high. We expect that the success of a social engineering attack will depend on the type of information requested.

We define an independent variable *information goal* which describes the private information requested during an attack. We consider the following hypotheses:

- **Alternative Hypothesis.** $H_{1,2}$: The independent variable *information goal* impacts the success rate of the attack.
- **Null Hypothesis.** $H_{0,2}$: The independent variable *information goal* has no impact on the success rate of the attack.

Attack Awareness over Time. A common defense against social engineering attacks is the use of "awareness training" to prepare employees to protect themselves [23]. However, the effectiveness of this type of training is not clear because people may easily forget their training over time. As part of our study, we notify participants that they will be attacked as part of the study, so they have complete awareness that the attack will come. However, we call them between 1 and 3 months after joining the study. We expect that individuals may lose their attack awareness over time, so the success rate of an attack will depend on the *attack delay*, the time between when an individual is made aware of a potential attack and the when an attack occurs. We consider the following hypotheses:

- **Alternative Hypothesis.** $H_{1,3}$: The independent variable *attack delay* impacts the success rate of the attack.
- **Null Hypothesis.** $H_{0,3}$: The independent variable *attack delay* has no impact on the success rate of the attack.

1.2 Social Engineering Dataset

We additionally present the recordings of the 186 attack phone calls, and their transcripts, as a publicly-available dataset for use by researchers studying telephone scams. Each recording was made with the explicit permission of the participant. We hope that this dataset can be used by others as examples of both successful and unsuccessful social engineering attacks. Although each call is based on one of only 27 attack scripts, there are significant variations between calls based on the unpredictable responses of the victims. We provide the audio files of the phone calls in addition to transcripts so that researchers can examine prosodic content of the calls.

2 Telephone vs. Email Scams

This study specifically focuses on telephone scams rather than email phishing scams. Many studies have been performed using phishing emails, and datasets of phishing emails have been compiled. However, these studies and datasets do not adequately represent the properties of telephone-based attacks. Phishing studies have the following limitations in representing telephone scams.

- **Communication Metadata** - Emails contain significant metadata produced as part of the communication protocols used (i.e. headers, footers, embedded URL links) which can be used to detect phishing. Unfortunately, much of this information is different for texting and telephone communication, and entirely absent for in-person communication. This problem is most apparent for the problem of authenticating the source of a communication. Many phishing detection approaches achieve high precision and accuracy by analyzing email metadata to determine that the actual source is not the same as the stated source. These approaches are not applicable to non-email communications however. The availability of non-email social engineering attacks will enable researchers to study the detection of a broader range of attacks.
- **One-way, Context-free Communication** - Phishing emails found in existing databases all show a single communication from an attacker to a victim. They do not show conversations between the attacker and the victim. In most cases of phishing attacks, there is no conversation and the entire attack is composed of a single email. Even in cases of phishing attacks which lead to a conversation between the attacker and victim, the phishing emails found in existing databases are individual with no context given. Social engineering attacks launched via texting, phone, or in-person almost always involve a conversation between the attacker and the victim. The context of the entire sequence of communications can contain information essential to identifying an attack. An examples of the importance of context is the use of dialog designed to alter the victim's mood (i.e. urgency, flirtation, etc.). A mood change early in the conversation can change the victim's response to a request for private data later in the conversation.
- **Text-based vs. Oral** - Text-based communication depends only on text to transfer information, while verbal communication can use properties of the voice, prosody, to transfer information. As a result, people have developed different approaches for encoding information in text as compared to voice. A simple example is a sense of irony which can be captured in the tone of voice during an oral conversation, but might be captured using an emoji in a text-based conversation.

3   Experimental Procedure

We performed a set of experiments to determine the effectiveness of a variety of telephone-based social engineering attacks. Each participant received a scam phone call within 3 months of joining the study. Each scam phone call requested a single piece of personally identifying information (PII). A scam phone call is considered a success if the PII data was provided, and it is considered a failure otherwise. A call is considered a failure if the participant hangs up before he/she has the opportunity to provide an answer. A call is also considered a failure if the participant asks questions which force the attacker to diverge from the script in a significant way. A divergence from the script is acceptable if the participant explicitly asks for assistance in providing the requested private data, such as,

"How do I find my IP address?". If the participant does not answer the phone then he/she is called again up to five times during the next 5 business days in order to establish contact. If the participant does not answer the phone after 5 call attempts then the participant is dropped from the study and their results are not included in the study.

The main difficulty in designing this experiment is the inherent conflict between the two primary goals of *accuracy* and *ethicality* [12]. In order for the experiment to accurately determine the effectiveness of an attack, deception is required to apply the attack in a realistic fashion against an unsuspecting participant. However, in order for an experiment to be ethical, deception of the participants must be well justified in terms of the needs of the experiment and the benefits of the research [19]. In designing these experiments we have used the advice of the Ethics Feedback Panel for Networking and Security (http://www.ethicalresearch.org/efp/netsec/) which provided us with several ideas on achieving accuracy while maintaining ethicality.

The procedural steps are presented here.

1. **Attract Voluntary Participants**: We advertised for participants in the following ways: posters on campus, announcements in classes, announcements on Facebook pages of campus student groups. The target population was primarily campus students and financial compensation of a $15 Amazon gift card was offered for participation.
2. **Obtaining Informed Consent**: We informed the participants of the deceptive nature of the experiments and we obtained their consent before launching the attack. Specifically, subjects were advised that we would attempt to deceive them and that phone calls would be recorded for analysis. We also advised them that the contents of the phone calls would be edited for PII and then published.
3. **Launch the Attack**: At some point within the three month period after the subject joins the study, we launched the attack. Attacks were conducted via telephone and each attack was recorded.
4. **Debriefing**: Immediately after the attack has been concluded, while the participant is still on the phone, the participant was informed that the preceding conversation was actually an attack conducted as part of the study. This occurred whether the attack was successful or not. In cases where the participant hung up the phone before the completion of the attack, the student was later contacted via email for debriefing.

3.1   Ethical and Legal Concerns

A number of issues arose which were addressed in order to gain IRB approval for the study, and which impact the validity of the results. We have considered these issues and we have structured the study to ensure that it is legal and ethical, while still producing the desired result of evaluating the effectiveness of a set of synthesized social engineering attacks.

Legal. The use of deception as part of these experiments requires that we consider state and federal laws prohibiting such deception. The first set of laws which impact our study are generally referred to as *wiretap* laws which define when it is illegal to record communications. Federal wiretap laws are "one-party consent" laws which allow communication to be recorded if a single party has given consent to the recording. Our study is at no risk of violating federal wiretap laws since our student assistants who launch the attacks are clearly giving consent for recording the communication. Many states however, including the state in which the study was conducted, have stronger "two-party consent" laws which require both parties involved in a communication to consent to the recording. Our study is also at no risk of violating these laws because we received informed consent of each subject when they first joined the study.

The pretexting component of a social engineering attack includes the act of "impersonation" as a tool to gain the trust of the subject. We are aware that federal laws prohibit the impersonation of any government worker or officer. We have only used pretexts involving campus officials and the campus IRB has explicitly given us permission to do so.

Protecting Participants from Harm. There is a risk of two types of harm to the participants of this study.

- **Material Harm:** This describes the possibility of the participant suffering harm in a physical or financial sense. Physical harm is not likely but the participant may reveal information which could enable theft, such as a social security number or a bank account password. The participant might also reveal sensitive private information which could be used by a malicious actor to perform blackmail against the participant.
- **Psychological Harm:** This describes the emotional distress which the participant might suffer from being deceived.

The risk of psychological harm was considered by our IRB to be very low since participants are immediately debriefed at the end of the conversation. In order to protect private participant data which is learned during an attack, we delete all PII from each recording immediately after the completion of the phone call. Each item of PII is replaced in the audio file with 440 Hz tone of equal duration, completely overwriting the PII data in the audio file.

Subject Attack Awareness. It is essential to inform each subject of the nature of the social engineering attacks when they enter the study, but the disadvantage of informing the participants is that it may increase their attack awareness and skew their responses. There is a large body of evidence [5,10] showing that the rate at which information is forgotten is exponential in time. As a result, we expect that the subject's attack awareness will degrade quickly after they have given informed consent. At the beginning of the experiment, the subjects were informed that the attack may occur anytime within the following three months. We varied the time period between when the participant joined the study and when the participant was called in order to explore how the delay impacts the likelihood of the attack being successful.

4   Attack Scripts

Based on previous work studying the content of social engineering attacks [9,16], we describe the key parts of an attack.

- **Pretext.** The act of *pretexting* is the creation of a scenario to persuade the target to either provide the desired information, or perform the desired action. We define the pretext of the attack as the communication which is used by the attacker to present the pretext to the target. The context of the pretext will define a false identity for the attacker which is trusted by the target to some degree. The pretext may be as simple as a false introduction such as, "Hi, I am Joe from the bank", but it may also include a detailed description of a false situation which would justify the communication attempt from the attacker's false identity. For example, the pretext might be, "Hi, I am Joe from the bank and we have detected strange activity on your account. We will need to verify your account information before we can fix the problem". This pretext defines a false, trusted identity, and justifies requests for account information.
- **Elicitation.** Elicitation is the process of changing the emotional state of the victim to one in which the victim is more likely to provide information. This is generally done by either building a rapport with the victim to make the target comfortable, or by threatening the victim to make the victim afraid of some negative consequence. An attacker might build a rapport by asking for assistance, such as "I need your help to resolve a problem with our database". An attacker might cause fear by making a threat, such as, "We will have to unregister you from your classes unless you resolve this issue immediately".
- **Information Goal.** The culmination of the social engineering attack is to request private information, such as, "Please provide your social security number to verify your identity".

4.1   Structure of a Script

Each script describes the statements that the caller must make during an attack, and the sequence in which the statements must be made. Each script is a sequence of the following 4 steps.

1. Pretext
2. Name Verification
3. Elicitation
4. Information Goal.

The *Name Verification* step is a request to verify the name of the caller: "Am I speaking to <first name>, <last name>?". This is required to ensure that the caller is speaking to the participant who has given consent. Aside from Name Verification, each attack script is built from one Pretext, one Elicitation, and one Information Goal. We used 3 possible Pretexts, and for each Pretext we used 3 Elicitations and 3 Information Goals. The scripts are generated as the cross-product of these three sets, so there are 27 scripts in total.

Pretexts. We use the following three pretexts which are all targeted towards campus students.

- Pretext 1: Registrar's Office - "Hi, I'm Jim/Jane from the XXX Registrar's Office and I have a couple of questions about your course registration."
- Pretext 2: Transportation Services (parking) - "Hi, I'm Jim/Jane from XXX Transportation Services."
- Pretext 3: Office of Information Technology (OIT) - "Hi, my name is Jane/Jim and I am with the XXX Office of Information Technologies."

These three pretexts vary in terms of the accuracy of targeting. Notice that pretext 1 and pretext 3 both apply to all students, but pretext 2 only applies to a student who owns or has access to a car. Since our study involves the community of all students at our school, pretext 2 is targeted with lower accuracy than 1 and 3 because pretext 2 is not applicable to all victims of the attack.

Elicitations. For each pretext, we use three elicitations which make sense with the pretext. Almost all elicitations are meant to either induce fear in the victim, or build a rapport by asking the victim for help. The elicitations used for each pretext are shown here.

- Registrar's Office
  - Elicitation 1.1: "OK, thanks. We believe that our registration system has been hacked so we need to verify your course registration. You are currently registered for ICS 155 in Spring quarter, is that correct?"
  - Elicitation 1.2: "Great. We received a phone call from a person claiming to be you, who requested that you be dropped from all of your courses. We need to verify that request."
  - Elicitation 1.3: "OK thanks a lot."
- Transportation Services
  - Elicitation 2.1: "OK, thanks. We believe that our computer system has been hacked and some of our information on you might have been altered. We need to verify some of your information, if you have a minute to do it right now."
  - Elicitation 2.2: "Alright. Our parking database seems to have multiple records associated with your name. One record says that you own one car and no pending citations, while the other record says that you have 10 pending citations. We need to get some information from you to resolve the inconsistency."

- Elicitation 2.3: "Thank you. At this point your citation is overdue by 3 months."
- Office of Information Technology
  - Elicitation 3.1: "OK, thanks. It looks like your computer is infected by a virus of some kind and it is attempting to infect other computers whenever you connect to the campus network."
  - Elicitation 3.2: "Thanks. We have detected multiple attacks on the OIT servers which seem to originate from IP addresses which you were using at the time."
  - Elicitation 3.3: "Thanks. Someone has just attempted to setup a new campus account using your name. This may not be a problem. It may be that another campus member has the same name as you do, but we need to be certain."

Information Goals. Across all attack scripts, we use a total of 6 information goals: Postal Address, Social Security Number, Email Address, Driver's License Number, License Plate Number, and IP Address. Each information goal is a data considered to be personally identifying information (PII) by our institutional review board (IRB), but they are expected to have different levels of sensitivity from the participant's perspective. For each pretext, we use three information goals which make sense with the pretext.

- Registrar's Office
  - Goal 1.1: Postal Address, "Can you give me your postal address for verification purposes?"
  - Goal 1.2: Social Security Number, "Please give me your social security number for verification purposes."
  - Goal 1.3: Email Address, "Can you give me your email address for verification purposes?"
- Transportation Services
  - Goal 2.1: Driver's License Number, "Please give me your driver's license number so that I can verify your record."
  - Goal 2.2: License Plate Number, "Can you give me your license plate number so that I can verify your record?"
  - Goal 2.3: Social Security Number, "Please give me your social security number so that I can verify your record."
- Office of Information Technology
  - Goal 3.1: Email Address, "Can you give me your email address for verification purposes?"
  - Goal 3.2: IP Address, "Please give me your computer's IP address for verification purposes."
  - Goal 3.3: Social Security Number, "Can you give me your social security number for verification purposes?"

4.2   Controlled and Uncontrolled Variables

Controlled variables are those independent variables which are held constant throughout the experiment so that their value does not obscure the causal relationships which we seek to identify between the other independent variables and the success rate of the attacks. The main controlled variables in our experiment are the *source phone number* used to place the attack phone calls, and the *accent* of the callers.

All attacks were made from a legitimate campus phone number which would appear on the caller ID of the victim with the same area code and three-digit prefix as any other campus number. The number used was not the actual number of the campus offices used as pretexts, but it is safe to assume that in most cases, just the area code and three-digit prefix were sufficient to convince many participants that the call was from an official campus source. We used a real campus phone number to simulate the process of spoofing a caller ID which is most often done by real attackers to enhance the believability of the attack. All of the callers were American and had neutral accents.

Uncontrolled variables are those which might have an impact on the results but were not explicitly controlled as part of the experiment. The main uncontrolled variable was the *gender* of the caller. Of the total 186 phone calls, 60 were made by a man and the remaining 126 were made by two women. The calls made by men and women were well distributed across the set of 27 attack scripts, but most of the calls were made by women.

5   Study Results

A total of 234 people joined the study and 48 of those, 20.5%, were dropped from the study because they did not pick up their phone after 5 phone call attempts during a week. A total of 186 attacks were completed, and of those, 58 were successful, so 31.18% of calls were successful, overall. On average, 6.89 calls were made using each script, and the standard deviation of the number of calls per script is 2.64.

5.1   Demographics of the Participants

The participants were undergraduate students at the University of California Irvine. Figure 1 shows the age distribution of the participants whose average age is 19.46 years old. Figure 2 shows the distribution of the participants according to the school at the university which contains their major. It is clear that the participants are most concentrated in "ICS" which stands for Information and Computer Science. Note that the sum of all numbers in the table is greater than the 186 participants who completed the study because students with double majors are counted twice if their two majors are in different schools.

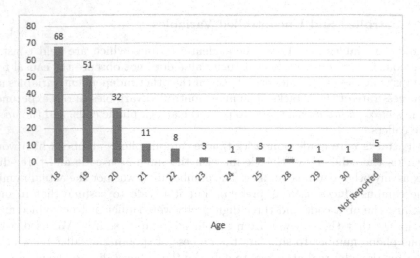

Fig. 1. Age distribution of participants

5.2 Success Rates

To gain insight into what attack features are correlated with success rate, we examine the success rates for different values of the independent variables.

Table 1. Success rate according to pretext

Pretext	Calls	Succ.	Succ. rate
Registrar's	85	37	43.53%
Transportation	50	3	6.00%
OIT	51	18	35.29%
Total	186	58	31.18%

Table 1 shows the success rate according to the pretext used. Each row, other than the first and last, shows the results for one pretext. The columns show the name of the pretext (**Pretext**), the number of attacks made using that pretext (**Calls**), the number of successful attacks (**Succ**), and the success rate (**Succ. Rate**). It is clear from these results that the Transportation pretext resulted in a lower success rate than the other two. This is probably because some students do not own cars, while almost all students will be registered for classes and have a computer account through the Office of Information Technology (OIT). By questioning during debriefing we found that only 62% of subjects who were scammed using the Transportation pretext owned or had access to cars.

Table 2 shows the success rate according to the information goal. It is clear from the table that victims have some understanding of the sensitivity of information. For example, email address was provided 75% of the time because it

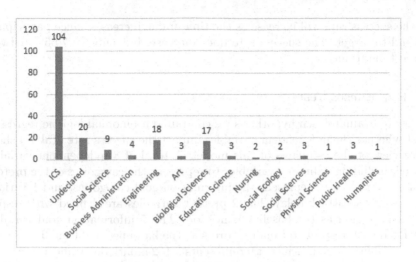

Fig. 2. Major distribution of participants

Table 2. Success rate according to information goal

Info. goal	Calls	Succ.	Succ. rate
Postal Address	33	17	51.56%
Soc. Security	58	1	1.72%
Email Address	44	33	75.00%
Driver's License	17	0	0.00%
License Plate	16	3	18.75%
IP Address	18	4	22.22%

is usually easy to determine a student's email address by searching the public campus database. The success rates for Driver's License and License Plate Number are likely to be artificially low because they were only associated with the Transportation pretext, whose success rate is low as shown in Table 1.

Table 3. Success rate according to time frame

Attack delay	Calls	Succ.	Succ. rate
1–2 months	87	26	29.88%
2–3 months	99	32	32.32%

Table 3 shows the success rate according to the time frame, the time between when a participant joined the study and when he/she was attacked. When joining the study, participants are informed that they will be attacked, so it is expected that the success rate will increase as the time frame increases, since participants will tend to forget. The success rate does increase, but only by 7.55% between the two time frames.

5.3   Hypotheses Tests

In order to evaluate each hypothesis we computed a binomial logistic regression to test whether the independent variables impact the success rate. Table 4 shows an overview of the estimates of this model. A total of 8 independent variables are used, including 2 dummy variables to represent the categories of the pretext, 5 dummy variables to represent the information goal categories, and 1 variable to represent the attack delay. The 2 pretext variables are defined with respect to Transportation as the baseline condition. The 5 information goal variables are defined with respect to Email Address as the baseline condition. The Attack Delay variable is coded such that 0 represents a 1–2 month delay and 1 represents a 2–3 month delay. The Registrar's and OIT pretexts are considered to have high targeting accuracy since all students register for classes and all students have computer accounts. The Transportation pretext, which is the baseline condition, has low targeting accuracy since only 62% of the victims of the Transportation pretext actually owned or had access to cars.

Table 4. Logisitic regression

Independent variable	β	SE	z value	p value
Registrar's	1.0987	0.477	2.303	0.021
OIT	1.4079	0.684	2.058	0.040
Postal Address	−1.3126	0.559	−2.346	0.019
Social Security	−5.1515	1.111	−4.638	0.000
Driver's License	−3.8505	1.703	−2.260	0.024
License Plate	−1.5787	0.706	−2.237	0.025
IP Address	−2.6593	0.824	−3.228	0.001
Attack Delay	0.0196	0.434	0.045	0.964

- $H_{1,1}$: There was a statistically significant positive impact of using the high targeting accuracy pretexts Registrar's ($z = -2.303$, $p = 0.021$, OR = 3.00, 95% CI [1.18, 7.64]) and OIT ($z = -2.058$, $p = 0.040$, OR = 4.09, 95% CI [1.07, 15.63]). Based on these results, we can reject the null hypothesis $H_{0,1}$ and accept the alternate hypothesis $H_{1,1}$.
- $H_{1,2}$: The logistic regression produces the following statistics for each information goal.
  - Postal Address, $z = -2.346$, $p = 0.019$, OR = 0.27, 95% CI [0.09, 0.81]
  - Social Security, $z = -4.638$, $p = 0.000$, OR = 0.01, 95% CI [0.00, 0.05]
  - Driver's License, $z = -2.260$, $p = 0.024$, OR = 0.02, 95% CI [0.00, 0.60]

- License Plate, $z = -2.237$, $p = 0.025$, OR $= 0.21$, 95% CI [0.05, 0.82]
- IP Address, $z = -3.228$, $p = 0.001$, OR $= 0.07$, 95% CI [0.01, 0.35].

All of information goals have a statistically significant negative impact on success as compared to the baseline Email Address. There is also clearly a wide range of odds ratios between 1.0 (for the Email Address information goal itself) down to 0.01. Based on these results we can reject the null hypothesis $H_{0,2}$ and accept the alternate hypothesis $H_{1,2}$.

- $H_{1,3}$: The logistic regression for the Attack Delay variable shows that the CI of the odds ratio contains 1.0 ($z = 0.045$, $p = 0.964$, OR $= 1.02$, 95% CI [0.44, 2.39]). Although the overall success rate is high, 31.18%, in spite of the fact that participants were made aware of future attacks, there is no indication that their awareness decreased over time. We cannot reject the null hypothesis $H_{0,3}$.

6 Discussion and Limitations

A surprising result was the fact that the attack delay seems to have no impact on the success rate. We assumed that the success rate would increase as participants forgot their "training". However, it is still possible that the time scales that we examined were too large to see the effect. It is entirely possible that an attack delay of a single day, for instance, would be small enough that the study instructions would still be fresh in the minds of the participants.

There were several possible confounding variables which were not controlled for in the experiment. The gender of the participants was not recorded and that may have impacted susceptibility to scams. The manner in which the scams were delivered, the prosody, was not controlled for. Each caller was trained to follow each script when delivering a scam, but it is possible that the manner of speech has an impact on the success rate.

To consider the ecological validity of the experiment, we need to define what the "setting" of the experiment is so that we can consider whether or not the results would generalize to a different setting. One aspect of the setting would be the age of the participants, whose average was 19.46 years. This is quite young and it is reasonable to expect that older people would respond differently to a telephone scam. Another aspect of the setting is the fact that it was college-oriented. The participants were all college students, and the pretexts were all related to college. It is reasonable to assume that college student's reactions to scams might be different than those of people with a non-college background. A further constraint on the participants is that they were all students of a single college, the University of California Irvine. Aspects of the culture specific to UCI could affect the results of the study.

7 Telephone Scam Dataset

We present a dataset comprised of recordings and transcripts of all of the attacks made as part of this study, as well as associated metadata. The repository for the dataset can be found at https://gitlab.com/beatscams/study-on-scam-calls.

The main content of the dataset is contained in two directories, the **audio recordings** directory which contains all of the audio recordings, and the

transcripts directory which contains all of the transcripts of the audio recordings. Each recording in the audio recordings directory is an mp3 (".mp3" suffix) file whose name is the number of the associated study participant. Participants were anonymously numbered as they entered the study. Each transcript in the transcripts directory is a Microsoft Word file (".docx" suffix) file whose name is also the number of the associated study participant. Each line in the transcript file is annotated with a time stamp which indicates the start time of the line in the corresponding audio recording. All of the files in the audio recordings directory have been anonymized by replacing PII with 440 Hz tone. All of the files in the transcripts have been anonymized as well.

The repository also contains several files containing metadata associated with each phone call. The metadata is contained in three files, the **CallInfo** spreadsheet, the **ScriptInfo** spreadsheet, and the **ScriptText** file. The **Call-Info** spreadsheet contains one record for each phone call and each record contains the following fields: *Call Number*, *Script Number*, *Time Frame*, and *Success?*. The *Call Number* is the number of the associated participant and the *Script Number* is the number of the script used in the call. The *Time Frame* indicates the time between when the participant joined the frame and when he/she was called. There are two possible values for this field: "0" indicates a time frame between 2 and 3 months, and "1" indicates a time frame between 1 and 2 months. The *Success?* field indicates that the attack either failed ("0") or succeeded ("1").

The **ScriptInfo** spreadsheet describes the contents of each of the 27 scripts used. Each row of the spreadsheet contains a record describing one attack script. Each record contains the following fields: *Script Number*, *Pretext Number*, *Elicitation Number*, and *Information Goal Number*. The *Script Number* is the number of the script, and the remaining fields are the numbers of the Pretext, Elicitation, and Information Goal.

The **ScriptText** file is a Microsoft Word (".docx") document containing a list which associates the Pretext, Elicitation, and Information Goal Numbers with their associated text. This information is the same as the information presented in Sect. 4.1 of this paper.

7.1 Transcript Examples

Although all of the recordings and transcripts are based on a set of only 27 attack scripts, the responses of the victims cannot be fully predicted. Due to the range of victim responses and the variations from the script which they result in, reveal interesting aspects of effectiveness of the scam and the victim's mindset.

The transcript shown in Fig. 3 is a case where the Information Goal, a request for license plate number, did not match this participant since he did not have a car. We used the debriefing to identify the subset of participants who were scammed with the Transportation pretext and did not have access to a car.

Another example transcript is shown in Fig. 4 in which the victim is asked for his IP address. The victim is clearly suspicious based on the question, "So what do you need my IP address for again?" on the highlighted line. In spite of that, the victim proceeds to provide the information later in the conversation.

Victim: [0:16] Hello?
Attacker: [0:17] Hi, I'm Jane from UCI Transportation Services. Am I speaking to
[censored]?
Victim: [0:26] Sure! Yeah.
Attacker: [0:28] Okay—
Victim: [0:29] This is him. [indistinguishable]
Attacker: [0:30] Okay, thanks. We believe that our computer system has been
hacked and some of our information on you might have been altered. We need
to verify some of your information if you have a minute to do it right now.
Victim: [0:41] What kind of information?
Attacker: [0:43] Can you give me your license plate number so that I can verify
your record.
Victim: [0:47] Oh, I-I'm too poor to have a car actually so I don't have one.
Attacker: [0:50] [small laugh]

Fig. 3. Information goal is not applicable

Victim: [0:00] Hello?
Attacker: [0:01] Hi, I'm Jane and I'm with the UCI Office of Information Technologies. Am I speaking to [Censored]?
Victim: [0:08] Yes.
Attacker: [0:09] Ok thanks. It looks like your computer is infected by a virus of some kind and it's attempting to infect other computers
whenever you connect to the campus network.
Victim: [0:18] My computer?
Attacker: [0:19] Yes. Yeah so, so then um can you please give me your computer's IP address for verification purposes.
Victim: [0:30] Alright, I have a Mac book, don't know how it'd get a virus.
Attacker: [0:35] Um, say that again?
Victim: [0:37] I have a Mac book.
Attacker: [0:39] Uh yes, um did you need help looking for your IP address?
Victim: [0:44] No, I'll look, just give me a second.
Attacker: [0:47] Okay.
Victim: [1:30] Hello?
Attacker: [1:31] Yes.
Victim: [1:36] Give me one second, let me find my laptop.
Attacker: [1:39] Okay, no problem.
Victim: [2:40] So what do you need my IP address for again?
Attacker: [2:43] Um for verification purposes.
Victim: [2:48] Okay. [3:14] IP address is in settings right?

Fig. 4. Victim is suspicious

8   Related Work

8.1   Social Engineering Studies

Many studies have been performed in which participant susceptibility is evaluated by evaluating their reaction to receiving a phishing email. Phishing email studies have either asked participants to click on a link or to provide sensitive information, but studies vary in other aspects of the content of the email, such as the pretext used. One study involved a professor sending phishing emails to students in his class requesting their username and password [7]. This attack had a high success rate, 41%, likely in part because the email source was a trusted person, the professor of the course. Several phishing email studies use a trusted email source such as a member of the IT department [2] or a friend identified using open source intelligence [11]. The effectiveness of web browser warning messages has been studied by observing the success rate of phishing emails in the presence of a warning message [6].

Researchers have presented results of full penetration tests against industrial partners which involve phishing emails but also other attack vectors including in-person attacks [18] postal mails [28], and phone calls [1, 28]. Another attack vector which has been explored is the use of QR codes which represent links to phishing websites [27].

Rather than launch attacks, some studies have instead asked subjects to judge the veracity of websites [1,4] and emails [13] to identify phishing.

Telephone-based scams have been used in several studies. In [28], student-actors were hired to perform comprehensive attacks which included telephone calls, postal letters, and phishing emails. The contents of the phone calls were not revealed, except to list general classes of pretexts and to say that a "range of persuasive techniques" were used. The attacks in this study used a combination of methods, so there is no way to identify the impact of the telephone calls separately from the other approaches used.

The use of telephone-based scams is described in case study involving employees of a bank [1]. Again, detailed contents of the phone calls are not presented. The authors state that attackers "conducted friendly conversations" with participants before asking for internet banking credentials. Examples of elicitations are given including checking privileges and accessibility and checking account integrity.

A recent study on telephone-based scams involved 3000 subjects, 10 different social engineering attack versions, based on 4 attack scripts [25]. The attack scripts were recorded and an autodialer was used to call the participants. The participants were university staff and faculty who were unaware of the study and whose phone numbers were chosen randomly from the university's internal phone directory. Several variables were evaluated including caller gender, accent, and caller ID shown.

8.2   Social Engineering Attack Datasets

Many datasets of phishing emails have been made publicly available for study [20–22]. Collectively, these datasets contain well over 100,000 scam emails of various types which have been contributed. To our knowledge, there does not exist a similar dataset containing telephone scams. One likely reason for this is that the laws in many states prevent the recording of telephone calls without prior consent from both parties involved in the call.

9   Conclusion

We present the results of a study on the effectiveness of telephone scams, and we present a dataset containing the recordings and transcripts of these scams. Telephone scams are under-explored as compared to phishing emails and websites, yet the occurrence of telephone scams is on the rise. Our study explores variables which have not been explored in previous work on telephone scams, including the importance of the pretext, the information goal, and the awareness of the victims. Our study also investigates the effectiveness scams involving live attackers rather than pre-recorded messages. To our knowledge, our dataset of telephone scam recordings is the first of its kind to be made publicly available.

Acknowledgements. This material is based upon work supported by the National Science Foundation under Grant No. 1813858. This research was also supported by a generous gift from the Herman P. & Sophia Taubman Foundation.

References

1. Aburrous, M.R., Hossain, M.A., Dahal, K.P., Thabtah, F.A.: Experimental case studies for investigating e-banking phishing techniques and attack strategies. Cogn. Comput. **2**, 242–253 (2010)
2. Bakhshi, T., Papadaki, M., Furnell, S.: A practical assessment of social engineering vulnerabilities. In: HAISA (2008)
3. Das, A., Baki, S., El. Aassal, A., Verma, R., Dunbar, A.: SoK: a comprehensive reexamination of phishing research from the security perspective. IEEE Commun. Surv. Tutor. **22**, 671–708 (2019)
4. Dhamija, R., Tygar, J.D., Hearst, M.: Why phishing works. In: Proceedings of the SIGCHI Conference on Human Factors in Computing Systems (2006)
5. Ebbinghaus, H.: Memory: A Contribution to Experimental Psychology. Teachers College, Columbia University, New York (1913)
6. Egelman, S., Cranor, L.F., Hong, J.: You've been warned: an empirical study of the effectiveness of web browser phishing warnings. In: Proceedings of the SIGCHI Conference on Human Factors in Computing Systems (2008)
7. Greening, T.: Ask and ye shall receive: a study in "social engineering". SIGSAC Rev. **14**(2), 8–14 (1996)
8. Hadnagy, C., Wilson, P.: Social Engineering: The Art of Human Hacking. Wiley, Hoboken (2010)
9. Hadnagy, C.: Social Engineering The Art of Human Hacking. Wiley, Hoboken (2011)
10. Roediger III, H.L., Karpicke, J.D.: The power of testing memory: basic research and implications for educational practice. Perspect. Psychol. Sci. **1**(3), 181–210 (2006)
11. Jagatic, T.N., Johnson, N.A., Jakobsson, M., Menczer, F.: Social phishing. Commun. ACM **50**(10), 94–100 (2007)
12. Jakobsson, M., Johnson, N., Finn, P.: Why and how to perform fraud experiments. IEEE Secur. Privacy **6**(2), 66–68 (2008)
13. Karakasiliotis, A., Furnell, S.M., Papadaki, M.: Assessing end-user awareness of social engineering and phishing. In: Australian Information Warfare and Security Conference (2006)
14. Kok, K.F.: 2019 U.S. spam & scam report. Truecaller Insights, April 2019. https://truecaller.blog/2019/04/17/truecaller-insights-2019-us-spam-phone-scam-report/. Accessed 17 Feb 2020
15. Mitnick, K., Simon, W.: The Art of Intrusion: The Real Stories Behind the Exploits of Hackers, Intruders and Deceivers. Wiley, Hoboken (2009)
16. Mitnick, K.: The Art of Deception. Wiley, New York (2003)
17. Olson, E.: When answering the phone exposes you to fraud. New York Times, December 2018. https://www.nytimes.com/2018/12/07/business/fraud-robocalls-spoofing.html. Accessed 11 June 2020
18. Orgill, G.L., Romney, G.W., Bailey, M.G., Orgill, P.M.: The urgency for effective user privacy-education to counter social engineering attacks on secure computer systems. In: Proceedings of the 5th Conference on Information Technology Education (2004)

19. Ethical principles of psychologists and code of conduct, June 2010
20. Scamalot. http://scamalot.com. Accessed 11 Oct 2017
21. Scamdex. www.scamdex.com. Accessed 11 Oct 2017
22. Scamwarners. scamwarners.com. Accessed 11 Oct 2017
23. Scheeres, J.: Establishing the human firewall: reducing an individual's vulnerability to social engineering attacks. Biblioscholar (2012)
24. Shaban, H.: Nearly half of cellphone calls will be scams by 2019, report says. The Washington Post, September 2018. https://www.washingtonpost.com/technology/2018/09/19/nearly-half-cellphone-calls-will-be-scams-by-report-says/. Accessed 17 Feb 2020
25. Tu, H., Doupé, A., Zhao, Z., Ahn, G.J.: Users really do answer telephone scams. In: Proceedings of the 28th USENIX Conference on Security Symposium (2019)
26. Verizon: 2019 data breach investigations report (2019). https://enterprise.verizon.com/resources/reports/dbir/
27. Vidas, T., Owusu, E., Wang, S., Zeng, C., Cranor, L.F., Christin, N.: QRishing: the susceptibility of smartphone users to QR code phishing attacks. In: Adams, A.A., Brenner, M., Smith, M. (eds.) FC 2013. LNCS, vol. 7862, pp. 52–69. Springer, Heidelberg (2013). https://doi.org/10.1007/978-3-642-41320-9_4
28. Workman, M.: A test of interventions for security threats from social engineering. Inf. Manag. Comput. Security **16**, 463–483 (2008)

Smart Environments

User Privacy Concerns and Preferences in Smart Buildings

Scott Harper, Maryam Mehrnezhad, and John C. Mace[✉]

School of Computing, Newcastle University, Newcastle upon Tyne, UK
{s.harper,maryam.mehrnezhad,john.mace}@ncl.ac.uk

Abstract. Smart buildings are socio-technical systems that bring together building systems, IoT technology and occupants. A multitude of embedded sensors continually collect and share building data on a large scale which is used to understand and streamline daily operations. Much of this data is highly influenced by the presence of building occupants and could be used to monitor and track their location and activities. The combination of open accessibility to smart building data and stringent data protection legislation such as the GDPR makes the privacy of smart building occupants a concern. Until now, little if any research exists on occupant privacy in work-based or commercial smart buildings. This paper begins to address this gap by reporting on a study conducted amongst occupants of a state-of-the-art commercial smart building to understand their privacy concerns and preferences. Our results show that the majority of the occupants are not familiar with the types of data being collected, that it is subtly related to them, nor the privacy risks associated with it. When we informed occupants about this data and the risks, they became more concerned and called for more transparency in the data collection process. The occupants were also largely averse to open accessibility of the collected data.

Keywords: Socio-technical systems · Internet of Things · User study · User privacy · Smart building

1 Introduction

Online services are diversifying at a high speed from traditional websites to smart devices and infrastructures whose sensors enable diverse large scale (and potentially personal) data generation including data about people, their activities and environments. Although the sensitivity of certain smart systems such as medical wearables is more intuitively visible, the risk of sharing data in other systems might not be immediately perceived. As an example, the sensor data coming from a smart building office (light, CO_2 level, etc.) can easily compromise the occupant's privacy [18,24]. Ambient and motion sensor data is not typically protected in such systems and is freely available to developers [16]. Research has shown sensor APIs are accessed in 3695 of Alexa's top 100K websites, 63% of whom also engage in browser fingerprinting [9]. In addition, user

© Springer Nature Switzerland AG 2021
T. Groß and L. Viganò (Eds.): STAST 2020, LNCS 12812, pp. 85–106, 2021.
https://doi.org/10.1007/978-3-030-79318-0_5

tracking is spreading from PC browsers to mobile browsers and apps [15], smart home devices [31], and potentially other IoT devices. In terms of infrastructure, research exists into smart home privacy [4] and occupant privacy concerns [34] as well as privacy studies on smart cities [26,30]. Until now however, there is little if any research on occupant privacy in work-based or commercial smart buildings [21].

This new research area is critical for several reasons: (1) occupant-centric data is processed on a large scale which may present a risk to privacy [14,22]; (2) seemingly anonymous IoT data such as CO_2 can be aggregated and used to monitor and track occupancy [5,10,27]; (3) a commission of 122 global privacy and data protection authorities stated IoT data should be treated as personal data [12]; (4) data may be openly published [14] or openly accessible via IoT search engines (e.g. shodan.io and censys.io); (5) the violation of stringent privacy and data protection laws such as the EU General Data Protection Regulation (GDPR) can result in large financial fines [7,19]; (6) compelling industry reports and blogs are stating how the GDPR could or should apply to smart buildings [29,32,35]; (7) several organisations had to scrap workplace surveillance mechanisms once staff and their trade unions became aware of them [6,33]; (8) the number of commercial smart buildings is set to increase rapidly with a market value predicted to be over $160 Billion US by 2026 [2].

We aim to address the research gap by designing and conducting a user study of occupants' privacy concerns and preferences within a commercial smart building setting. To the best of our knowledge, this paper is the first user study concerning users' views and preferences in a smart building used as their workplace. Our study is conducted via an online questionnaire within a state-of-the-art smart building. Designed as a Building-as-a-Lab, over 1 million data points on average are collected per day, much of which is stored and openly published for research purposes. The questionnaire included 5 sections: (i) background information, (ii) privacy views, (iii) views of smart building data collection, (iv) user concerns, and after providing some information about smart building sensors and risks, (v) revisited concerns. It was completed by 81 participants, who are all occupants or visitors of the USB. Our results demonstrate that:

- **Knowledge:** There is a lack of knowledge among the participants in terms of the data collection and how it is used. For example, when we presented our participants with a list of real sensors in the building and dummy ones, they could not differentiate between them.
- **Concerns:** There is a shared concern regarding the privacy of the data collected and how this data may be used, especially for certain sensors presented to them e.g. Occupancy and beyond it (e.g. smart card data and cameras).
- **Preferences:** There is a desire among smart building occupants for more transparency about the data collection processes, and consent and/or opt-out mechanisms.

In the rest of the paper, we explain our methodology in Sect. 2, and present our results in Sect. 3. We discuss our findings and provide recommendations for improving user privacy in Sect. 4, and conclude our paper in Sect. 5.

2   Methodology

We have conducted an online user study. Here we explain our user study design and its structure, as well as its distribution among our participants.

2.1   Survey Design

We have designed the questions of our study based on the set of tools and techniques suggested for measuring privacy concerns in [23] and [25]. We have tailored our questionnaire according to the characteristics of a smart building. For this, we used some of the ideas previously adopted in the context of smart homes [1,20,28,34] and mobile sensors [8,17]. We have included experts from various backgrounds (security, privacy, and law researchers, admin and building management staff, and partners from the smart infrastructure industry) in the design process of this questionnaire through their feedback on its sections and questions.

2.2   Questionnaire Structure

In order to find out about the users' concerns towards data collection within the smart building and how this data is used, a questionnaire was created and distributed. The aim of this questionnaire was to both find out how aware the participants are of the data collection and its use, as well as any concerns they have regarding this. Here we present an overview of our questionnaire. Please see the complete questionnaire in Appendix A.

Section 1: Background Information: This section just gathers some basic, non-sensitive demographic information about the user.

Section 2: Views on Privacy: This section involves questions on user concerns about personal information and data collection in general.

Section 3: Awareness of Data Collection and Access: This is to find out what types of environmental data the participant thinks are collected, how the collected data is used and who they think can access the data.

Section 4: Smart Building Privacy Concerns: This looks at the possible concerns of the user regarding the building sensors including data collection, usage, and sharing. Participants are also asked whether they believe the data is secure and if they would deny access to certain pieces of data. It ends with open answer questions about any additional concerns and comments.

Information Page: Next, the participants are informed about the smart building and its data usage e.g. operational and research. The information was gathered from university and architect publicity materials, USB data researchers, and our own USB research (e.g. [13,14]).

Section 5: Smart Building Privacy Concerns (Revisited): This section is largely a repeat of Sect. 4 for the participant to answer after reading about the building. This repetition was done to see if people would change their opinions after being informed more about the building.

2.3   Case Study

When designing our questions, we tailored them according to the sensors and features of a smart building, the USB (Urban Sciences Building) which is currently used by the participants of this study as their workplace. The USB has been designed for a variety of activities including teaching, laboratory research, events, and the testing of real-time smart technologies for urban sustainability. On average, the building houses approximately 1,200 students, 55 academic staff and 120 post-doctoral researchers as well as regular visitors from across academia, industry and government. Large parts of the USB are also accessible to the general public. The core functionality of the USB is comparable to other smart buildings however its Building-as-a-Lab design means over 4000 digital sensors have been integrated into open spaces and the building structure itself making it one of the most densely monitored buildings in the world. For details of this building please see the Information page in the Appendix, and/or visit its website (https://www.ncl.ac.uk/computing/about/usb/). The key types of workspace environmental data available are: CO_2, Temperature, Humidity, Brightness, and Occupancy. In order to be able to evaluate our participants' knowledge, concern, and preferences more accurately, when presenting them with a list of sensors embedded in the USB, we included a few dummy options. These sensors include: Sound level and Air pressure. Please note that while our case study smart building (USB) does not collect data via these dummy sensors, they might be embedded in other smart buildings or be added in the future. Hence, including them in our list is sensible.

2.4   Questionnaire Distribution

The questionnaire was created using 'onlinesurveys'[1] as it allowed for the easy creation and distribution of the questionnaire. As well as this, the university has a subscription with the service, allowing for the questionnaire to stay up longer without financial cost. Once created and live, the questionnaire was distributed to both staff and students that use the USB via the university email service. 81 participants took part in this questionnaire during April and May 2020. A large majority (67.9%) of the participants go into the smart building 4–5 days a week, with another 24.7% going in 2–3 days a week. Our participants included 33 students (undergraduate and postgraduate), 45 staff (academic and support), and 3 visitors, aged between 20 to over 60 years old. It took about 15 minutes on average to complete the questionnaire.

2.5   Analysis Methods

Our method is processing the collected data in order to report our results is a mix of quantitative and qualitative analysis. The results for most of the questions are presented by stacked bar figures where the number of the answers to each category is counted. For some of our questions with free-text style, we

---

[1] https://www.onlinesurveys.ac.uk/.

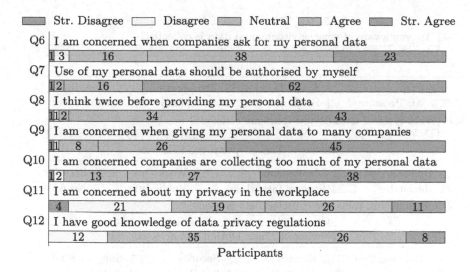

Fig. 1. Participant views on data privacy

run thematic analysis to report our results. We take an inductive approach and allow the data to determine our themes. Two independent researchers (one of the paper's authors and an independent researcher) perform coding and extract the key themes. These themes are reviewed by both researchers and the results are reported, accordingly.

2.6 Ethics

This research includes collecting data from users and had full approval from Newcastle University's Ethics Committee before the research commenced. In addition to having undergone independent ethical review, we designed our user studies to address pillars of responsible research in computer science (Menlo Report) [3]: respect for persons, beneficence, justice, and respect for law and public interest. Participation in this study was completely voluntary and anonymous.

3 Evaluation

In this Section, we present the results of our user studies by providing statistics on the answers given by the participants as well as thematic analysis of the open-text questions.

3.1 Results

View on General Privacy (Qs 6–12): As it can be seen in Fig. 1, the majority of our participants are fairly concerned with their personal data being collected

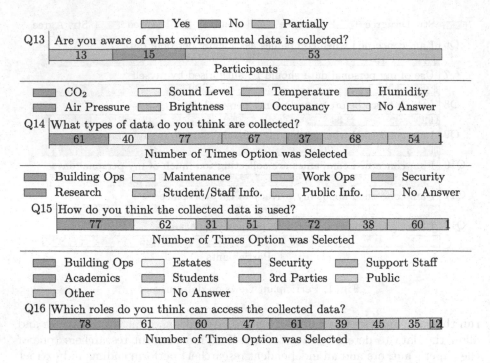

Fig. 2. Participant awareness of data collection and data access in the USB

and used. Most of our participants were concerned when companies ask for personal information and would sometimes think twice before giving consent. They also believed that companies generally collect too much data about them. When it came to privacy concern in the workplace and knowledge about data privacy regulations, the answers were more scattered across categories. Yet, more participants were concerned and knowledgeable at the same time than those with no concern and knowledge.

Awareness of Data Collection (Qs 13–16): The majority of participants selected that they partially knew what environmental data is collected in the USB. This suggests that while they know some sort of data collection is happening in the building, they are not confident about the process and its details.

Regarding what sensors they thought were present in the building, the majority of our participants chose most of the listed sensors (including the dummy ones). With not too much of a gap from Brightness, Humidity, CO_2 and Occupancy, Temperature was the most selected sensor. The least selected options were the two dummy sensors Sound Level and then Air pressure, respectively.

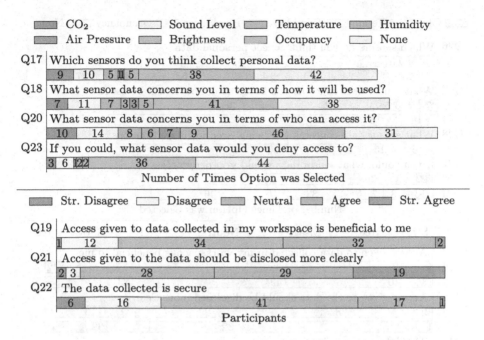

Fig. 3. Participant privacy concerns before being informed about USB data collection and data access.

Yet, around half of our participants thought such sensors exist in the building. This reconfirms that our participants can only guess what type of data may be collected by a smart building, but they don't have proper knowledge on the actual sensor collection in their work environment.

For how the data is used, Building Operation was chosen the most times, followed by Research, Maintenance, Public Information, Security, Student/Staff Information and then Work-based Operations respectively. Concerning the roles that can access the data, Building Operations Management was selected more than any other option. This was followed by Estates Support Service, Academics, Security, Professional Support, External Third Parties, Students, Public and then Other respectively.

Privacy Concerns of Sensors (Qs 17–18, 20, and 23): As it can be seen in Fig. 3 (top), the participants were mostly concerned about the occupancy data which they thought revealed personal data and would deny access to it. Sound level, CO_2, Temperature, Brightness, Air pressure and Humidity come respectively with a significant gap after Occupancy.

Views on Sensor Data Collection Process (Qs 19, 21–22): In Fig. 3 (bottom), it can be seen that participants were mostly neutral or agreed that access given to data collected in their workspace was beneficial to them and that the data is collected securely. At the same time, they mostly believed that access to

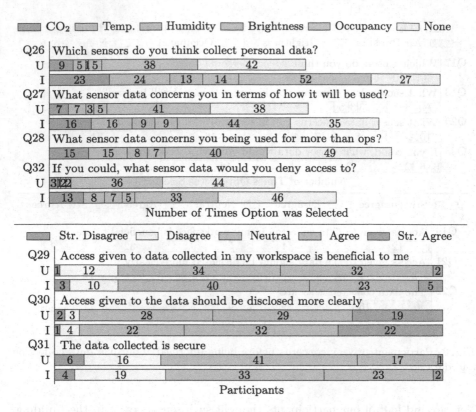

Fig. 4. Comparison of participant privacy concerns before and after being informed of USB data collection and data access (uninformed [U] and informed [I] respectively).

the data should be disclosed more clearly. In the next section, we discuss reasons that may be behind these statements.

Privacy Concerns of Sensors - Revisited (Qs 26–28, and 32): Recall that at this stage of our study, we presented our participants with an Information Page including data collection and data access processes in the USB, and potential privacy issues. It can be seen from Fig. 4 (top) there is an increase in concerns about the CO2, Temperature, Humidity and Brightness data. Concerns about Occupancy data remain relatively high. There is also a clear increase in the number of the sensors that our participants said would deny access to.

Views on Data Collection Process - Revisited (Qs 29–31): In Fig. 4 (bottom), it can be seen that, overall, less participants agreed that access given to data collected in their workspace was beneficial to them. More participants agreed that access to the data should be disclosed more clearly while less participants were neutral about the data collection being secure, but instead either agreed or disagreed.

Data Control Preferences (Q35): As it can be seen in Fig. 5, the participants have more or less equal preference towards the ability to control (i) what is collected in their workspace (ii) who can have access to it (iii) controlling what the data is used for and (iv) deciding what data is sensitive. Participants had a lesser preference for controlling when the data could be accessed. This suggests that a wide range of features and options can be included in a system which can enable the building occupants to have control over their data (e.g. a privacy dashboard).

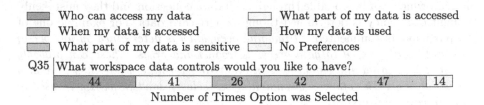

Fig. 5. Participant workspace data control preferences for the USB.

3.2 Thematic Analysis

Through our analysis, we identified a few common themes in the free-text questions answered by our participants. Here we present them for each question.

Personal Data (Q17.a): In Q17, we asked our participants to choose the sensors that they thought would collect personal data. In a follow-up question (Q17.a), we asked them to tell us why. Except for one, all the participants who chose at least one sensor in the previous question (38 participants) expressed their reasons as the following:

Monitoring and tracking at work: Almost all of these participants (37) believed that one or some of these sensors would enable work monitoring, including their presence, identity, location around the building, work patterns, etc., and specially at personal office level. For example, one participant commented: *"occupancy can be interpreted to infer what you are doing/who you are meeting, work patterns, when your desk is unattended, etc., which can be sensitive."* Another participant said: *"you could EASILY use it [sensor data] to follow someone around the building by government, uni, or other parties obtaining this information."* Another participant expressed their concern by saying: *"If an absence is recorded then the data would be used potentially to the detriment of a employee"*.

Combination of sensors: 9 participants chose multiple sensors, of whom 7 of them explicitly commented that they think a combination of these sensors would reveal personal information about them. For example one of the participants who chose CO_2, Sound Level, Brightness, and Occupancy expressed their concern stating that: *"I work in am open plan office environment, so inferences are not always possible, but a combination of sensors (e.g. sound and movement sensors) at several locations would, I imagine, allow triangulation to identify fairly precisely a specific desk. This would for example enable tracking of movement in the building, times at desk etc."*

Smart card data: One interesting concern shared by 5 participants was the personal data collected via their smart card around the smart building. Although this (e.g. contactless access points) was not listed as a sensor in the previous question, some of our participants expressed their concern about the privacy invasion which can be possible through such data collection and they mistakenly thought occupancy is determined though smart card data. For example one of the participants commented: *"I imagine occupancy is determined by number of university cards swiped to gain access to rooms and areas. These can probably be traced back to the individual user in order to determine where they were at a particular time. The other environmental variables I don't think can be used to identify people in this way"*.

Others: Other comments (5) included concerns around camera images and possible microphone recordings as well as confusion about data storage and the fact that this data collection approach is not voluntary in a smart building. For example, one of the participants commented: *"..., Cameras may be watching me walking around the building. Sound levels [collect personal data] because it may be possible for microphones to pick up on conversations"*.

User Concerns (Q24): In Q23, we asked our participants to choose any of the sensor data which they would deny access to if they could. In a follow-up question (Q24), we asked them to tell us what other concerns they have. The following concerns were extracted from the comments given by 24 participants.

Transparency: 8 participants expressed concern about a lack of clarity throughout the process of the data collection, processing, sharing, and its usage, especially when it is publicly available. For example one of our participants commented: *"Currently data collection is not transparent at all. I have no idea (or only from hearsay) what is collected, how, with which resolution/precision, by who, why, who has access and what is done with this data. I'm also not a big data expert, so I'd need explanations on what is possible e.g. what can be inferred about individuals from environmental sensors."*

Monitoring and tracking at work: Similar to Q17.a, some of our participants (7) showed concern about being monitored and tracked at work and its consequences. For example, one comment included: *"[I'm concerned about] Misuse of the data to cut services or to track productivity."*

Smart card, camera and microphone: The same concerns seen in Q17.a about collecting data from smart cards, cameras, and microphones in the building were expressed here too. 9 of our participants said they are worried about the data being collected about them by at least one of these means. For example, one participant said: *"I'm aware of various cameras in use, and not always sure their use is justified. Building users have no way to opt out of having their image captured, so putting up a sign warning people isn't sufficient, if the use isn't critical to the operation of the University."*

Others: Other concerns around user privacy included the combination of sensor data with other sensor data and/or other sources of information and the data collected from individual offices. For example, one participant said: *"I'm "lucky" to work in an open plan office where above aspects are of less concern but to academics and people with their own office it should be a concern."*

User Suggestions (Q25): In another follow-up question, the participants were asked to provide more comments about anything that would make them more comfortable about their concerns. 25 participants provided comments and we extracted the following:

Transparency: A large number of the comments (15) were asking for more clarification in all aspects of any data collection in their work space via smart building sensors and they even made a couple of suggestions. For example, one of the participants commented: *"[I would like to see] more transparency. I would be very interested in some form of dashboard (general/individual) that answers all the questions above and shows me in easily understandable form through for example graphs with textual explanations statistics, trends etc. ..."*

Consent: 8 comments explicitly asked for a form of consent and opt-out options (from data collection and to avoid monitored areas) for the residents of the smart building. For example, one comment included: *"When researchers want to collect data, they need to consult with the building occupants and be willing to show examples of the raw collected so that we can make an informed decision about finding a route around the monitored area. There should always be an alternative route to avoid the monitored space."*

Privacy enhancing solutions: 13 participants suggested ways to protect their privacy better, including: stop collecting certain data; collect data ethically; use security measurements for data storage and processing such as data anonymization and noise inclusion; limit use of data to certain people (e.g. researchers) and for certain purposes (e.g. building safety) through access control mechanisms. Example comments include: *"Usage of data limited to special cases: security and emergency situations"*, and *"Remove the occupancy data"*.

Physical comfort: A few participants asked for more physical comfort and expected that to be automatically provided by a smart building e.g., the optimal use of smart card for various purposes such as opening doors and booking rooms, and better air conditioning in terms of the quality of the air and its temperature.

Revisited Questions (Qs 33–34): These questions were repeat of Qs 24–25. We had 14 and 15 answers, respectively, where 8 of them included *"As before"* and *"The same"*. The concerns extracted from the remaining comments have been seen in the previous sections. There was one new concern raised by a few participants in relation to the public access to this smart building data which may enable all sorts of misuse e.g. *"crime"* or *"domestic terrorism"*.

4   Discussion

In this section, we further discuss some of our findings, provide recommendations for various stakeholders, and point to future research directions.

4.1   Further Analysis

Privacy concern: As discussed before, most of our participants were generally concerned about their data privacy (Fig. 1). They also had a basic knowledge about the types of sensors available in the smart building (Fig. 2). However, only around half of our participants expressed concern about data collection by these sensors. While this concern slightly shifted after knowing about sensors and their risks, the general trend stayed the same (Fig. 4). When analysing our results, we could not find any significant correlation between user general data privacy concern and the concern they expressed in relation to smart building data. In other words, although most of our participants were concerned about their general privacy, only half of them were bothered about smart building privacy and there was no significant correlation between these groups.

Demography breakdown: In addition, our demographic break down (Table 1) demonstrates that there is not any significant differences on user privacy concern about sensors across the age ranges. The participants from different age groups chose around the same number of sensors for Qs 17, 26 (personal data collection), Qs 18, 27 (usage), Q20 (who access), Q28 (access purpose), and Qs 23, 32 (deny access). The only exception was the age group of 30 to 40 who chose more sensors in comparison to other groups in response to most questions.

Table 1. Average number of sensors chosen by each age category for the related questions before and after being informed about smart building sensors and risks.

Age group	No. of participants	Qs 17, 26 (data collection)	Qs 18, 27 (usage)	Q20 (who access)	Q28 (access purpose)	Qs 23, 32 (deny access)
Under 20	9	1.1, 1.4	0.8, 1.1	1	0.8	1, 0.7
20–30	34	0.5, 0.3	0.8, 1	0.9	0.9	0.6, 0.7
30–40	19	1.3, 2.2	1.6, 1.7	2.5	1.7	0.6, 1.2
Above 40	19	0.9, 1.4	0.6, 0.9	0.8	0.8	0.6, 0.8

Benefits vs. risks: While analysing the participants' comments, we realised that some of our participants were not convinced about the benefits of data collection in a smart building. For example someone commented: *"I think there is a technological utopianism around smart buildings and smart cities; the notion that: if we just had more data, we could solve problems. This means that consciously or not, we are enabling the collection, aggregation, and storage of huge amounts of data about us. The more data is stored, the easier it is to triangulate with other data and identify individuals - and the more tempting it is as a target. From a privacy and security perspective alone, we should be building in more privacy-by-design. But the underlying premise of simply collecting more data to solve problems is false: actually, many of the issues people face are individual and social, and will not be solved through more data alone. For example if you have two people in an office, one of whom prefers it colder and the other warmer, the data about whether it is 'objective' warm or cold doesn't address the underlying issue. You can't split the difference without dissatisfying both of them, and you can't necessarily solve it without moving one or the other away."* Other similar comments highlighted how some of the participants were disappointed about some of the basic features that they expected from a smart building (e,g, physical comfort) and thought the data collection and processing should be refocused.

We also noticed that many of the participants say they don't understand the usage of this data collection and its benefits to them, and hence desired more transparency. Similar research in other contexts has shown that multiple factors influence user willingness to adopt a technology. For example for a Contact Tracing Covid-19 app, these factors include: the technology features, benefits to themselves and community, the technology provider, privacy and accuracy [11]. In this study, we did not evaluate the impact of various factors concerning user views and preferences in a smart building and leave it as future work.

4.2 Recommendations

Our studies demonstrate that the current practices for empowering users in smart buildings are not enough since most of our participants expressed serious privacy concerns about data collection in such buildings. Here we provide a set of recommendations for different stakeholders in order to improve user privacy:

– **Regulations:** We believe that there are many blind spots in the current regulations on user data privacy (e.g. the GDPR) in the context of smart buildings. Therefore, providing clarification in the law and potentially developing context-specific regulations by standardisation bodies will significantly impact the current practices.
– **Smart building owners/managers:** Through our research, as well as the comments provided by our participants, we have identified many areas where the smart building owners and managers can improve the user experience. A more transparent practice is on the top of this list, which can be enabled by induction sessions, online pages, visual dashboards, explicit consent, opt-out

options, etc. To ensure ethical and governance requirements are met when sharing smart building data, a socio-technical ethical process for owners and managers has already been proposed by our research team using the USB as a case study [14].

– **Occupants:** The current practices by smart buildings do not offer much to users to enhance their privacy. However, when occupants of such buildings are concerned about their privacy at work, they should be able to communicate their concern with their employer. We believe that such feedback will raise awareness around the issue and impact the existing practices.

4.3 Limitations

As mentioned before, it took 15 minutes on average for our participants to complete this questionnaire, with three outliers. When excluding those three, the average time decreased to 11 minutes. It is possible that the long number of the questions might have caused some levels of questionnaire fatigue e.g. not every one provided answers to the open answer questions.

In addition, the questionnaire was completed by our participants during the lock down (as a result of the Covid-19 pandemic) and while they were working from home. For the same reason, we could not arrange for in-person interviews and conducted all the experiments online. Working from home might have impacted the number of the attendees, the concerns and preferences in various ways. We plan to address the above by conducting more studies in the future and hopefully when people are back to their workplaces.

5 Conclusion

This paper presents the first user study on the privacy concerns and preferences of the occupants of smart buildings when used as their workplace. 81 participants who were residents of a real-world smart building took part in our study which was conducted through an online questionnaire.

Our results show that smart building users have serious privacy concerns about data collection in smart buildings. First, around half of our participants believed that at least one type of sensor in the building collects personal data about them, enabling monitoring and tracking at work. Second, although we did not ask the participants about the smart card and camera data directly, they expressed concerns about these types of data, especially when combined with other sensor data enabling surveillance at work. Third, most of our participants believed that more transparency is required throughout the whole cycle of data collection, storage, processing, usage and beyond. And finally, some of our participants believed that the current approaches for getting consent from them is not efficient and does not empower them.

Given that the privacy of the data generated by smart buildings via sensors is not directly covered in the law (e.g. the GDPR), this topic requires the immediate attention of the research community and industry, not only to prevent any misuse of such data, but also to empower the users and give them control over the data that is generated by and/or about them.

Acknowledgement. We thank those working in the USB (researchers, admins, building managers, industry contacts, etc.) and beyond who contributed to the ideas of this research and provided feedback on the structure of our questionnaire. We would like to thank Dr Ehsan Toreini, Durham University, UK, for his help with the thematic analysis of this paper. We thank our participants who took part in this user study and provided valuable comments.

A   Questionnaire

A.1   Background Information

1. How often are you in the USB (USB) normally?

Less than once a week	Once a week	2–3 days a week	4–5 days a week

2. What is your role in the university?

Undergrad/PGT	Professional support
RA/Lecturer/PhD	Visitor/Industry Partner/Other

2a) If you selected Undergrad/PGT: Have you covered security and/or privacy in lectures? -Yes -No) If you selected RA/Lecturer/PhD: Is your research focused on security and privacy? -Yes -No

3. Does your role involve aspects of computer science? -Yes -No

4. How old are you?

Under 20 y	20–30 y	30–40 y	40–50 y	50–60 y	60+ y

5. Where are you from?

UK	EU	Outside of the UK/EU

A.2   Views on Privacy

6. It usually bothers me when companies ask me for personal information.

Strongly disagree	Disagree	Neither agree nor disagree	Agree	Strongly Agree

7. Companies should not use personal information unless it has been authorised by the individuals who provided the information.

Strongly disagree	Disagree	Neither agree nor disagree	Agree	Strongly Agree

8. When companies ask me for personal information, I sometimes think twice before providing it.

Strongly disagree	Disagree	Neither agree nor disagree	Agree	Strongly Agree

9. It bothers me to give personal information to so many companies.

Strongly disagree	Disagree	Neither agree nor disagree	Agree	Strongly Agree

10. I am concerned that companies are collecting too much personal information about me.

Strongly disagree	Disagree	Neither agree nor disagree	Agree	Strongly Agree

11. I am concerned about my privacy in the workplace.

Strongly disagree	Disagree	Neither agree nor disagree	Agree	Strongly Agree

12. How would you rate your knowledge of data privacy regulations?

1(low)	2	3	4	5(high)

A.3   Awareness of USB Data Collection and Access

13. Are you aware of what data is collected, relating to the building environment, within the USB? -Yes -No -Partially.

14. Select all the environmental data types below you think are collected within the USB.

CO_2	Sound level	Temperature	Humidity	Air pressure	Occupancy	Brightness

15. How do you think this data is used? Select all that apply.

Building operation (e.g. temperature regulation, air conditioning)
Maintenance (e.g. errors and alarm notification)
Work related operations (e.g. room booking, room utilisation)
Security (e.g. access control)
Research (e.g. improved energy management)
Student/staff information (e.g. study space availability)
Public information (e.g. CO_2 output, energy use)

16. Select all the roles below you think can access the environmental data collected within the USB.

Building operations management	Estates support service	Security
Professional support	Academics	Students
External third parties (e.g. maintenance, energy suppliers)	Public	Other

A.4 USB Privacy Concerns

17. For each of the sensors below, do you think that the data they collect in your workspace is personal data? Select all that apply.

CO_2	Sound level	Temperature	Humidity	Air pressure	Occupancy	Brightness

17a) If you answered yes to any of the above, please say why. (Open Answer)

18. For each of the sensors below, are you concerned with how the collected data in your workspace will be used? Select all that apply.

CO_2	Sound level	Temperature	Humidity	Air pressure	Occupancy	Brightness

19. Allowing access to the data collected in my workspace will be beneficial to me

Strongly disagree	Disagree	Neither agree nor disagree	Agree	Strongly Agree

20. For each of the sensors below, are you concerned with who could access the data collected in your workspace? Select all that apply.

CO_2	Sound level	Temperature	Humidity	Air pressure	Occupancy	Brightness

21. Access to the data collected in my workspace should be disclosed more clearly.

Strongly disagree	Disagree	Neither agree nor disagree	Agree	Strongly Agree

22. Do you think that the data collected is secure?

Strongly disagree	Disagree	Neither agree nor disagree	Agree	Strongly Agree

23. If you had the choice, which of the following types of data collected from your workplace would you deny access to? Select all that apply.

CO_2	Sound level	Temperature	Humidity	Air pressure	Occupancy	Brightness

24. Are there any other concerns you have about access to data being collected in your workspace? (Open Answer)

25. If you are concerned, what would make you more comfortable in your workspace? (Open Answer)

A.5   Information Page

This page is here to inform you on current data collection and access within the USB. The USB has been designed for a variety of activities including teaching, laboratory research, events, and the testing of real-time smart technologies for urban sustainability (https://www.ncl.ac.uk/helix/urban/). On average, the building houses approximately 1,200 students, 55 academic staff and 120 post-doctoral researchers as well as regular visitors from across academia, industry and government. Large parts of the USB are also accessible to the general public. In excess of 4000 digital sensors are integrated into open spaces and the building structure itself making it one of the most densely monitored buildings in the world. Over 1 million data points are collected on average per day and used by the automated building management systems to control a large part of the USB's operation. As well as a teaching and research centre, the USB is also designed to be a Building-as-a-Lab providing a test bed and demonstrator for understanding the relationship between buildings and their internal and external environments. The building is home to groups focusing on research in data science, energy systems integration, water management, energy storage, IoT, and security. The thousands of sensors make it possible to collect and analyse data about how the building is used, its performance and efficiency against defined standards, and how it interfaces with the energy, water, internet, and other national and international networks. Access to large parts of this data is publicly available online (https://3d.usb.urbanobservatory.ac.uk/). Another access point is an Application Programming Interface (API) which enables users to download real-time and historical data down to specific room and sensor type (e.g. occupancy sensor, room temperature). Note, the data from single occupant workspaces is collected for building operational purposes but is not publicly accessible. The key types of workspace environmental data available are: CO_2, Temperature, Humidity, Brightness, and Occupancy (whether a room is occupied, not the number of occupants). Even without access to occupancy level data, existing research indicates it is possible to track and monitor the number of occupants in workspaces to a high degree of accuracy using climate data such as CO_2 and room temperature. As well as through environmental sensors, other sensor-based information may exist in a smart building. For example, in the USB, data is gathered regarding the use of smart cards being swiped (door entry, printing, student attendance, and using lifts). Other digital and physical information such as timetables, room bookings, calendars and office name plates also exist. Current research indicates aggregating these different types of data with environmental data could potentially be used to track and monitor individuals or small groups of individuals.

A.6   USB Privacy Concerns (Revisited)

26. Which of the sensors below, found in the USB, do you think collect personal data? Select all that apply.

CO_2	Temperature	Humidity	Occupancy	Brightness

27. Of the sensors below, are you concerned with how the collected data in your workspace will be used? Select all that apply.

CO_2	Temperature	Humidity	Occupancy	Brightness

28. Of the sensors below, are you concerned that this data is accessible for more than operational purposes? Select all that apply.

CO_2	Temperature	Humidity	Occupancy	Brightness

29. Allowing access to the data collected in my workspace will be beneficial to me.

Strongly disagree	Disagree	Neither agree nor disagree	Agree	Strongly Agree

30. Access to the data collected in my workspace should be disclosed more clearly.

Strongly disagree	Disagree	Neither agree nor disagree	Agree	Strongly Agree

31. Do you think that the data collected is secure?

Strongly Disagree	Disagree	Neither agree nor disagree	Agree	Strongly Agree

32. If you had the choice, which of the following data types collected from your workspace would you deny access to? Select all that apply.

CO_2	Temperature	Humidity	Occupancy	Brightness

33. Are there any other concerns you have about access to data being collected in your workspace? (Open Answer)

34. If you are concerned, what would make you more comfortable in your workspace? (Open Answer) 35. Which of these workspace controls would you like to have in the USB? Select all that apply.

Control over who can access my workspace data
Control over what data can be accessed about my workspace
Control over when my data can be accessed about my workspace
Control over what my workspace data is used for e.g. specific research
Control over what parts of my workspace data I think is sensitive

A.7   Consent

36. I understand what my data will be used for and I am okay with my data being used. -Agree

References

1. Abdi, N., Ramokapane, K.M., Such, J.M.: More than smart speakers: security and privacy perceptions of smart home personal assistants. In: SOUPS (2019)
2. Acumen: Smart Building Market - Global Industry Analysis, Market Size, Opportunities and Forecast, 2019–2026. https://www.acumenresearchandconsulting.com/smart-building-market
3. Bailey, M., Dittrich, D., Kenneally, E., Maughan, D.: The Menlo report. IEEE Secur. Privacy 10(2), 71–75 (2012)
4. Bugeja, J., Jacobsson, A., Davidsson, P.: On privacy and security challenges in smart connected homes. In: 2016 European Intelligence and Security Informatics Conference (EISIC), pp. 172–175. IEEE (2016)
5. Calì, D., Matthes, P., Huchtemann, K., Streblow, R., Müller, D.: CO_2 based occupancy detection algorithm: experimental analysis and validation for office and residential buildings. Build. Environ. 86, 39–49 (2015)
6. Corporation, B.B.: Barclays scraps 'big brother' staff tracking system. https://www.bbc.co.uk/news/business-51570401

7. Corporation, B.B.: British Airways faces record £183m fine for data breach. https://www.bbc.co.uk/news/business-48905907
8. Crager, K., Maiti, A.: Information leakage through mobile motion sensors: user awareness and concerns. In: EuroUSEC (2017)
9. Das, A., Acar, G., Borisov, N., Pradeep, A.: The web's sixth sense: astudy of scripts accessing smartphone sensors. In: 2018 ACM SIGSAC Conference on Computer and Communications Security, CCS 2018, pp. 1515–1532 (2018)
10. Díaz, J., Jiménez, M.: Experimental assessment of room occupancy patterns in an office building. Comparison of different approaches based on CO_2 concentrations and computer power consumption. Appl. Energy **199**, 121–141 (2017)
11. Kaptchuk, G., Hargittai, E., Redmiles, E.M.: How good is good enough for covid19 apps? The influence of benefits, accuracy, and privacy on willingness to adopt. arXiv preprint arXiv:2005.04343 (2020)
12. Kohnstamm, J., Madhub, D.: Mauritius Declaration on the Internet of Things. https://edps.europa.eu/sites/edp/files/publication/14-10-14_mauritius_declaratio n_en.pdf
13. Mace, J.C., Melo Czekster, R., Morisset, C., Maple, C.: Smart building risk assessment case study: challenges, deficiencies and recommendations. In: 16th European Dependable Computing Conference (EDCC), pp. 59–64 (2020)
14. Mace, J.C., Morisset, C., Smith, L.: A socio-technical ethical process for managing access to smart building data. In: Living in the Internet of Things (2019)
15. Mehrnezhad, M.: A cross-platform evaluation of privacy notices and tracking practices. In: EuroUSEC (2020)
16. Mehrnezhad, M., Toreini, E.: What is this sensor and does this app need access to it? Informatics **6**(1), 7 (2019)
17. Mehrnezhad, M., Toreini, E., Shahandashti, S.F., Hao, F.: Stealing pins via mobile sensors: actual risk versus user perception. Int. J. Inf. Secur. **17**(3), 291–313 (2018)
18. Mundt, T., Krüger, F., Wollenberg, T.: Who refuses to wash hands? Privacy issues in modern house installation networks. In: BWCCA, pp. 271–277 (2012)
19. Murphy, I.: Google fails to overturn €50 million fine. https://www.enterprisetimes. co.uk/2020/06/22/google-fails-to-overturn-e50-million-fine/
20. Naeini, P.E., et al.: Privacy expectations and preferences in an IoT world. In: SOUPS (2017)
21. Office for National Statistics: Construction output QMI. https://www.ons.gov. uk/businessindustryandtrade/constructionindustry/methodologies/constructionou tputqualityandmethodologyinformation
22. Pappachan, P., et al.: Towards privacy-aware smart buildings: capturing, communicating, and enforcing privacy policies and preferences. In: 2017 IEEE 37th International Conference on Distributed Computing Systems Workshops (ICDCSW), pp. 193–198. IEEE (2017)
23. Preibusch, S.: Guide to measuring privacy concern: review of survey and observational instruments. Int. J. Hum. Comput. Stud. **71**(12), 1133–1143 (2013)
24. Saputro, N., Yurekli, A., Akkaya, K., Uluagac, S.: Privacy preservation for IoT used in smart buildings. Security and Privacy in Internet of Things (IoTs): Models, Algorithms, and Implementations, pp. 129–160 (2016)
25. Smith, H.J., Milberg, S.J., Burke, S.J.: Information privacy: measuring individuals' concerns about organizational practices. MIS Q. **20**, 167–196 (1996)
26. Sookhak, M., Tang, H., He, Y., Yu, F.R.: Security and privacy of smart cities: a survey, research issues and challenges. IEEE Commun. Surv. Tutor. **21**(2), 1718–1743 (2019)

27. Szczurek, A., Maciejewska, M., Pietrucha, T.: Occupancy determination based on time series of CO_2 concentration, temperature and relative humidity. Energy Build. **147**, 142–154 (2017)
28. Tabassum, M., Kosinski, T., Lipford, H.R.: "I don't own the data": end user perceptions of smart home device data practices and risks. In: SOUPS (2019)
29. TEECOM: Smart Buildings & Data Responsibility: What to Know Now. https://teecom.com/smart-buildings-data-responsibility-what-to-know-now/
30. Van Zoonen, L.: Privacy concerns in smart cities. Gov. Inf. Q. **33**(3), 472–480 (2016)
31. Varmarken, J., Le, H., Shuba, A., Markopoulou, A., Shafiq, Z.: The TV is smart and full of trackers: measuring smart TV advertising and tracking. Proc. Priv. Enhanc. Technol. **2020**(2), 129–154 (2020)
32. Verma, U.: What building owners need to know about GDPR and occupant data privacy. https://inbuildingtech.com/smart-buildings/gdpr-smart-buildings-office/
33. Waterson, J.: Daily Telegraph installs workplace monitors on journalists' desks. https://www.buzzfeed.com/jimwaterson/telegraph-workplace-sensors
34. Zeng, E., Mare, S., Roesner, F.: End user security and privacy concerns with smart homes. In: SOUPS, pp. 65–80 (2017)
35. Zoethout, T.: GDPR: a fateful course for smart buildings? https://www.elektormagazine.com/news/gdpr-a-fateful-course-for-smart-buildings

Work in Progress: Towards Usable Updates for Smart Home Devices

Julie M. Haney$^{(\boxtimes)}$ and Susanne M. Furman

National Institute of Standards and Technology (NIST), Gaithersburg, MD, USA
{julie.haney,susanne.furman}@nist.gov

Abstract. *Background.* Smart home device updates are important tools for remediating security vulnerabilities.

Aim. We aim to understand smart home users' perceptions of and experiences with updates.

Method. We interviewed 40 smart home users and analyzed a subset of data related to updates. We are also planning a broader, follow-on survey.

Results. Users experienced inconsistency in update transparency and methods, were confused about how and if updates are applied, and seldom linked updates to security.

Conclusion. Our efforts will provide a new understanding of smart home updates from a usable security perspective and how those are similar/different to views on updates of conventional IT.

Keywords: Smart home · Updates · Cybersecurity · Usability

1 Introduction

Internet of things (IoT) smart home updates are a critical mechanism by which manufacturers can distribute patches to remediate security vulnerabilities. Updates may be one of the few tools users have to secure their devices since other configurable security options are limited or unavailable. Unfortunately, technologists have found that update mechanisms may be inconsistent across devices [8]. Even among security professionals, the number one threat to IoT was viewed as "difficulty patching Things, leaving them vulnerable" [16]. Despite technology experts identifying issues, the user perspective on smart home updates has not yet been fully explored.

To better understand experiences and challenges with smart home updates, we analyzed a subset of data from a broader, in-depth interview study of 40 smart home users aimed at investigating general experiences with, perceptions of, and opinions about smart home devices, including aspects of privacy and

---

Certain commercial companies/products are identified in this paper to foster understanding. This does not imply recommendation or endorsement by NIST.

© Springer Nature Switzerland AG 2021
T. Groß and L. Viganò (Eds.): STAST 2020, LNCS 12812, pp. 107–117, 2021.
https://doi.org/10.1007/978-3-030-79318-0_6

security. This paper[1] focuses on analysis of update-related data only. By exploring this subset of the interview data, we begin to gain insights into perceptions and usability of smart home updates, including what role, if any, users perceive updates as playing with the security of their devices. Preliminary analysis suggests that users experience inconsistency in update transparency and methods, as well as confusion about how and if updates are applied. More concerning, most study participants did not relate smart home device updates to security, so they might not have been as inclined to install updates immediately.

Since updates were not a major focus of the interview study, we wish to delve deeper into user update experiences and perceptions, especially on a per-device basis. To that end, we are planning a follow-up survey to gather responses from a broader population of smart home owners. When completed, we hope our research will have several contributions. We will provide novel insights into end user perceptions, experiences, and challenges with updates within the context of smart home devices from both a usability and security perspective. In addition to identifying similarities to prior research focused on updates of other types of computing devices, we hope to discover ways in which smart home device updates may be different or more challenging. Our results may also inform the design of smart home device update mechanisms and notifications to provide a more usable platform for deploying critical security patches when necessary.

2   Related Work

2.1   User Update Behaviors

While no prior studies have explored update behaviors for smart home technologies, researchers have investigated these behaviors for other information technology (IT). People delay software updates for a number of reasons, including a lack of awareness of the upgrade value; interruption of computing activities; and possible negative consequences of applying the update [6,18]. Users may also have a difficult time understanding the relationship between software updates and security [6]. Ultimately, users must balance the risk and costs of updating against potential benefits [19].

2.2   IoT Updates

A number of critical security vulnerabilities for smart home devices have been identified in recent years, highlighting the need for timely updates [2]. However, there are unique challenges to IoT updates [9]. IoT manufacturers may be inexperienced with security feature and update mechanism design. Economic incentives for providing updates and long-term support for inexpensive and disposable devices may not exist, leaving devices vulnerable to attack. NIST discovered that

---

[1] An extended version with appendices for participant demographics and interview questions can be found at https://www.nist.gov/publications/towards-usable-updates-smart-home-devices.

information on IoT updates is not always readily available to consumers and that updates are not always done in a secure manner [8]. From a technology perspective, IoT devices are often memory, processor, and battery constrained, making updates more challenging to deploy while managing integrity and confidentiality of the updates and potential software dependencies [1,11,12].

Several researchers focused on security labels for IoT products. Emami-Naeini et al. [4] showed consumer openness to IoT privacy and security labels, including update information. Morgner et al. [15] investigated consumer preferences for security update information on mandatory IoT product labels. They concluded that security update labels, especially those focused on the availability period (how long the manufacturer guarantees to provide updates) may have a significant impact on consumer product selection.

Although the technical limitations of IoT updates and potential of labels have been discussed, to the best of our knowledge, no prior literature addresses potential usability issues with *smart home* updates through the eyes of consumers, a gap our study hopes to address. Lin and Bergmann [14] suggested that smart home devices should implement updates with little or no user intervention. Emami-Naeini et al. [4] interviewed smart home users, noting that most desired automatic updates because of convenience. However, they made no further observations for recommendations with respect to updates. Other researchers explored user perceptions of smart home privacy and security but did not discuss updates (e.g., [17,20,21]).

3   Methodology

From February to June 2019, we interviewed 40 smart home users to understand their perceptions of and experiences with smart home devices. NIST's Research Protections Office approved the study. Prior to the interviews, we informed participants of the study purpose and how data would be protected with generic identifiers (e.g., P14_U) not linked to individuals.

3.1   Participant Recruitment and Demographics

We hired a consumer research company to recruit adult users of smart home devices from a database of individuals living in a large U.S. metropolitan area who had agreed to be contacted about research opportunities. To determine eligibility, prospective participants completed an online screening survey about their smart home devices, their role with the devices (e.g., administrator, user), and other demographic information. After reviewing the screening information, we selected participants if they were active users of at least two different types of smart home devices. In line with current interview compensation rates in our region, participants were given a $75 prepaid card.

Participants had diverse professional backgrounds with only eight in an engineering or IT field. Thirty-two of the 40 participants had installed and administered their devices (indicated with an A after the participant ID), and eight were non-administrative users of the devices (indicated with a U). Fifty-five percent were male and 45% were female. Seventy percent were between the ages of 30 and 49. Participants were highly educated with 45% having a master's degree or above and another 50% with a BS/BA. All but one participant had three or more individual smart home devices, with 38 having three or more different categories of devices.

3.2   Data Collection and Analysis

We developed a semi-structured interview protocol covering several topics: purchase and general use; installation and maintenance (including updates); privacy; security; and safety. In this paper, we focus only on data related to updates. An IoT content expert who had professionally worked on IoT security in addition to having an extensive, custom smart home, reviewed the interview questions to ensure the use of correct terminology and the consideration of appropriate aspects of smart home ownership. We piloted the interview with four smart home owners from our institution (two device administrators and two non-administrators/users) to determine face validity of questions and language. Based on feedback from the content expert, we added questions for potential "do-it-yourself" users who customize smart home software and hardware to their own specifications (e.g., via writing custom code). After the pilots, minor adjustments were made to simplify the wording of several questions. Because modifications were minor, the pilot interviews were included in our analyzed data set. After the protocol was finalized, we collected data via 36 additional semi-structured interviews (40 interviews total including pilots) lasting on average 41 min. Interviews were audio recorded and transcribed.

We analyzed the interview data using both deductive and inductive coding practices. Initially, each member of the research team individually coded a subset of four interview transcripts using an *a priori* code list based on research questions and open coded for additional concepts as needed. We then met to discuss codes and develop a codebook. Coding then continued until all transcripts were coded by two researchers, who then met to examine and resolve differences in code application and identify relationships and central themes.

4   Preliminary Results

4.1   Update Modes and Notifications

The interviews revealed that update modes may vary from smart home device to device, with some updating automatically and others requiring users to manually initiate updates. In addition, participants discovered available updates in different ways depending on the device. A participant who owned multiple devices said: *"Some of them notify me, others update automatically, and others I'll find out about either through an email or just because I'm kind of monitoring technology news in general"* (P15_A). Another commented:

"Some devices will send me a text message. . . saying that we're going to be updating a device at this time, and it will apply the updates automatically. Other devices, I need to go into their own specialty apps and check what firmware is running and then check for an update. Some devices, I actually have to go to a website and download something, and then my phone, for instance, will update the device" (P11_A).

Smart home devices that notify users of available updates do so in a variety of ways. Notifications "pushed" to the device's user interface or via the companion app before or after update installation are most common. For example, an owner of a smart doorbell explained how she finds out about updates: *"I see an alert. It says, 'Your Ring doorbell has a new update. Do you want to allow it? Do you want to accept it?' "* (P36_A). Several participants received emails alerting them of available or just-installed updates. Some devices with screen interfaces, such as smart thermostats and televisions, displayed the update notification directly on the device itself. Other smart home owners did not receive push notifications to tell them updates were available. Rather, they had to manually open the companion app and check.

4.2 Update Purpose and Urgency

Participants most often viewed updates as fixing or adding non-security functionality. For example, one participant stated, *"I accept all updates because I believe they'll make things more functional, add new features that I didn't have before"* (P36_A). Interestingly, this perception led to mixed feelings regarding the urgency of applying updates. Several participants who had experienced issues with their devices believed updates were a high priority. A participant who owns a smart video doorbell and security cameras noted that smart home devices *"would have the highest priorities than any of the other apps on my phone. . . because that's the security of my home"* (P31_A). Another participant talked about experiencing frequent glitches with his devices. Therefore, he viewed regular updates to his devices as being critical:

"To me it's not a choice for, at least, internet of things. Sometimes for my computer, I don't update as soon as they tell me I should. I wait for a while to see if anybody reports bad bugs with the new update. I feel that I have to [for a smart home device] in order for it to work at its best" (P13_A).

However, others thought updates to functionality were lower priority or unnecessary as long as the device appeared to be working properly. A participant described her indifference with respect to updates, *"I don't think that the end user actually really cares. As long as the thing works, it works"* (P40_U). Other participants did not feel they could properly assess the criticality of the update because the manufacturer did not reveal the purpose of the update: *"The information on what the update achieves is unclear"* (P31_A).

4.3 Uncertainty About Update Status

Participants reflected that they may not observe update notifications, do not recall setting an option to automatically install updates, or are not sure if there are configurable options for setting update parameters. These inconsistencies may lead to a sense of uncertainty about whether their devices are being updated or even can be updated. One user remarked about his virtual assistant, *"I don't know when it's [virtual assistant] doing its updates. Like ever. They never ask me. They never prompt me"* (P7_A).

Some participants assumed that the lack of notifications meant that updates must be happening automatically. While possibly true with some devices, this assumption might be flawed for other products. A participant lamented, *"They don't notify me when there's an update. I guess I just kind of assume that they happen as they go. You would think that I'd get an email, but I guess I don't. That might be nice" (P23_A).*

Even though users may have an assumption of automatic updates, the uncertainty due to lack of notification leaves some with a sense of discomfort. For example, one participant stated: *"I'm assuming that updates are being done silently in the background. I don't really know, and it sort of gives the impression that you bought this thing and it's not evolving... that it's not expanding and getting new updates"* (P24_A).

4.4 Updates to Apps vs. Updates to Devices

In addition to uncertainty about update status, the interviews revealed that participants often conflated updates to smart home device companion app software (typically installed on a smartphone) with updates to device firmware. They did not realize that updates to apps were not necessarily accompanied by device updates and vice-versa. This was evidenced by participants referencing typical smartphone app update indicators when asked how they know smart home device updates are available. For example, a user of an Android-based phone explained, *"I get a notification. It doesn't say specifically which apps need to be updated. It just says 48 apps need to be updated. Then I go into Google Play, and see my apps, and individually determine which ones I want to update"* (P31_A).

4.5 Update Concerns

Even when update availability was visible, participants voiced concerns about updates causing issues or breaking functionality on their smart home devices. For example, one participant voiced frustration with updates to his smart televisions: *"I've had to reset my TVs many times because the software update didn't work or kind of messed things up"* (P10_A). Updates also have the potential to invalidate previous user configuration settings or necessitate new ones: *"as they come out with updates, particularly significant updates that change the interface, for example, that might be cause for me to go back in and redo some of the settings"* (P15_A).

Two participants expressed concerns about a lack of updates should a manufacturer stop supporting a product. One of these commented,

> *"I would hope that over time the companies that support these devices would continue to update their firmware and basically make them more reliable. I think in some cases that's happened, but I think in other cases the devices just get abandoned"* (P11_A).

4.6   Relationship to Security

Although some updates can be a conduit to fix security vulnerabilities in smart home devices, study participants rarely linked updates to security, with only five mentioning updates in the context of security. Most discussed updates in terms of fixing functionality or adding features. When asked what mitigation actions they take to address any security concerns they might have, only three mentioned applying updates or upgrading products.

Interestingly, two participants recognized the importance of applying updates, but were also concerned about potential security-related consequences. One participant liked that updates to his devices could be done via the internet, but at the same time was concerned because *"it means that someone's reaching in... There's some kind of access from the outside"* (P26_A). Another saw potential for updates to weaken security:

> *"I guess one area where I would be worried about would be adding features that may threaten my privacy and security... I would want to know that the update also gave me the capability of disabling or turning off that feature I might be concerned about"* (P15_A).

5   Discussion

5.1   Comparison to Traditional Updates

We note similarities between our results and those from previous research studies in Related Work. Similarities included: a lack of awareness of the importance of applying updates; a lack of information about the update purpose hindering users' ability to weigh risk and cost against potential update benefits; concern about possible negative consequences of applying updates; and concern about surprise new features being added.

Although similarities exist, we identified several differences in user experiences with smart home updates as compared to updates explored in prior studies. We did not find evidence of concerns about interruption, likely because users do not have the same kind of interactive sessions with smart devices as they would on a tablet, phone, or computer. Our findings additionally suggest that, because devices are often controlled with a mobile companion app, some updates may be overlooked since several participants did not understand the difference between a phone update, an app update, and a device update. We also discovered that participants were concerned about manufacturers discontinuing product support (and therefore, no longer issuing updates) due to the dynamic smart home market. As opposed to updates for more-familiar and widely-used operating systems, applications, and hardware (e.g., those from Apple and Microsoft), our participants were often unaware if updates were available, how to configure automatic updates, or how to check update status. Confusion about update mechanisms may be amplified by the number of smart home devices users own, especially if the products are from various manufacturers with different update models and different modes of notification.

We also acknowledge that the update experience for smart home devices may necessarily have to be different than traditional IT updates because of processing/memory constraints and limited interactive interfaces. Therefore, more research is warranted to investigate a suitable, usable update interface that can accommodate device limitations.

5.2 Informing Usable Updates

Study results may inform more usable update interfaces and mechanisms. Although our focus was on home users, improved update usability can also be especially valuable for IoT administrators in organizations who have to maintain large numbers of devices.

Insufficient information about the purpose and benefit of updates may result in users lacking a sense of urgency about applying updates, especially if devices appear to be working fine. Users may also be uncertain about update status and availability. To help users make informed decisions, manufacturers could provide greater transparency of update purpose and importance of applying an update (perhaps via a criticality rating), which is in concert with Vaniea and Rashidi's recommendation for easy-to-find information on updates [19]. As also recommended by other standards and government organizations [3,5,7,9], manufacturers could be more forthcoming about their update model and support so that users are aware of how update availability will be made known, what actions users should take to install updates, what update configuration and notification options (if any) are available, and how manufacturers will handle discontinuation of product support. Some of these update attributes were addressed in prior work on product labels [4,15] and showed promise in impacting consumer purchase decisions and providing transparency. However, more research needs to be done to determine whether consumers would even read the labels.

In addition to lack of transparency, many of our participants expressed discomfort or frustration with updates and their ability to control them. Providing additional information on updates can help users feel more confident in their update decisions. In addition, manufacturers could provide options for users to configure automated updates (as recommended in [14]) with configurable notifications of success afterwards. Users could be given options to schedule if and when they receive notifications. To mitigate concerns that updates might break the device or result in unwanted features or settings, devices could support a rollback mechanism, as recommended by others [8,13,19]. Users may then be more likely to install an update if they have a way out should there be a problem.

Although we identified issues related to lack of transparency, it must be noted that it is currently unclear as to whether or not consumers would actually read any additional information or in what format they would wish to receive the information. In addition, too much information could be overwhelming and result in user frustration or users just ignoring the information. Therefore, future research should be done to account for consumer preferences.

6   Limitations and Planned Future Work

In addition to typical limitations of interview studies (e.g., self-report and social desirability biases), our study results may have limited generalizability. Our sampling frame of mostly well-educated individuals living in a high-income region in the U.S. may not be fully representative of the global smart home user population. However, our participant population does appear to typify early adopters of smart home devices as identified in industry surveys (for example, [10]).

Our interview study was meant to be exploratory with a goal of identifying areas warranting additional investigation. As such, the interview protocol was broad in covering multiple aspects of smart home ownership and did not focus solely on updates. We also did not ask about updates on a per-device basis (just generally), so are not able to determine if there are different perceptions or experiences depending on the type of device and manufacturer and if some devices are doing a better job at updates than others.

In recognition that more research should be done to delve deeper into users' smart home update experiences, we are in the initial planning phase for an online, quantitative survey of a larger, more diverse sample of smart home users. In addition to asking more questions about perceptions of updates (e.g., importance, purpose), we will obtain per-device experiences and explore what kind of options, if any, users would like in order to gain greater insight and control of update mechanisms. We will also investigate users preferences for update-related information, e.g., what kind of information they would like to receive (if any at all) and desired formats and communication mechanisms.

References

1. Bauwens, J., Ruckebusch, P., Giannoulis, S., Moerman, I., Poorter, E.D.: Over-the-air software updates in the internet of things: an overview of key principles. IEEE Commun. Mag. **58**(2), 35–41 (2020)
2. Consumer Product Safety Commission: Status report on the Internet of Things (IoT) and consumer product safety. https://www.cpsc.gov/s3fs-public/Status-Report-to-the-Commission-on-the-Internet-of-Things-and-Consumer-Product-Safety.pdf (2019)
3. Department for Digital, Culture, Media and Sport: Code of practice for consumer IoT security. https://www.gov.uk/government/publications/code-of-practice-for-consumer-iot-security (2018)

4. Emami-Naeini, P., Dixon, H., Agarwal, Y., Cranor, L.F.: Exploring how privacy and security factor into IoT device purchase behavior. In: Proceedings of the 2019 CHI Conference on Human Factors in Computing Systems, pp. 1–12. ACM, Glasgow, United Kingdom (May 2019)
5. ETSI: TS 103 645 Cyber security for consumer internet of things. https://www.etsi.org/newsroom/press-releases/1549-2019-02-etsi-releases-first-globally-applicable-standard-for-consumer-iot-security (2019)
6. Fagan, M., Khan, M.M.H., Buck, R.: A study of users' experiences and beliefs about software update messages. Comput Hum. Behav. **51**, 504–519 (2015)
7. Fagan, M., Megas, K.N., Scarfone, K., Smith, M.: NISTIR 8259 Foundational cybersecurity activities for IoT device manufacturers. https://nvlpubs.nist.gov/nistpubs/ir/2020/NIST.IR.8259.pdf (2020)
8. Fagan, M., Yang, M., Tan, A., Randolph, L., Scarfone, K.: Draft NISTIR 8267 Security review of consumer home Internet of Things (IoT) products. https://nvlpubs.nist.gov/nistpubs/ir/2019/NIST.IR.8267-draft.pdf (2019)
9. Federal Trade Commission: Internet of things privacy and security in a connected world (2015). https://www.ftc.gov/system/files/documents/reports/federal-trade-commission-staff-report-november-2013-workshop-entitled-internet-things-privacy/150127iotrpt.pdf
10. GfK: Future of smart home study global report (2016). https://www.gfk.com
11. Gupta, H., Oorschot, P.C.V.: Onboarding and software update architecture for IoT devices. In: 17th International Conference on Privacy, Security and Trust (PST), pp. 1–11. IEEE, Fredericton, Canada (August 2019)
12. Hernández-Ramos, J.L., Baldini, G., Matheu, S.N., Skarmeta, A.: Updating IoT devices: challenges and potential approaches. In: 2020 Global Internet of Things Summit (GIoTS), pp. 1–5. IEEE, Virtual (June 2020)
13. IoT Security Foundation: Secure design best practice guides (2019). https://www.iotsecurityfoundation.org/wp-content/uploads/2019/11/Best-Practice-Guides-Release-2.pdf
14. Lin, H., Bergmann, N.: IoT privacy and security challenges for smart home environments. Information **7**(3), 44 (2016)
15. Morgner, P., Mai, C., Koschate-Fischer, N., Freiling, F., Benenson, Z.: Security update labels: establishing economic incentives for security patching of IoT consumer products. In: Proceedings of the 2020 IEEE Symposium on Security and Privacy, pp. 429–446. IEEE, Oakland, CA, USA (May 2020)
16. SANS Institute: Securing the Internet of Things Survey (2014). https://www.sans.org/reading-room/whitepapers/covert/paper/34785
17. Tabassum, M., Kosinski, T., Lipford, H.R.: "I don't own the data": end user perceptions of smart home device data practices and risks. In: Proceedings of the Fifteenth Symposium on Usable Privacy and Security, pp. 435–450. USENIX, Santa Clara, CA, USA (August 2019)
18. Vaniea, K., Rader, E., Wash, R.: Betrayed by updates: How negative experiences affect future security. In: Proceedings of the 2014 SIGCHI Conference on Human Factors in Computing Systems (CHI 2014), pp. 2671–2674. ACM, Toronto, Canada (April 2014)
19. Vaniea, K., Rashidi, Y.: Tales of software updates: The process of updating software. In: Proceedings of the 2016 SIGCHI Conference on Human Factors in Computing Systems (CHI 2016), pp. 3215–3226. ACM, San Jose, CA, USA (May 2016)

20. Zeng, E., Mare, S., Roesner, F.: End user security and privacy concerns with smart homes. In: Proceedings of the Thirteenth Symposium on Usable Privacy and Security, pp. 65–80. USENIX, Santa Clara, CA, USA (July 2017)
21. Zheng, S., Apthorpe, N., Chetty, M., Feamster, N.: User perceptions of smart home IoT privacy. In: Proceedings of the ACM on Human-Computer Interaction (CSCW 2018), vol. 2, pp. 1–20. ACM, Jersey City, NJ, USA (November 2018)

Decentralized Systems and Digital Ledgers

WARChain: Blockchain-Based Validation of Web Archives

Imre Lendák[1,3]✉ ⓘ, Balázs Indig[2] ⓘ, and Gábor Palkó[2] ⓘ

[1] Faculty of Informatics, Eötvös Loránd University, Budapest, Hungary
lendak@inf.elte.hu
[2] Centre of Digital Humanities, Faculty of Humanities, Eötvös Loránd University,
Budapest, Hungary
[3] Faculty of Technical Sciences, University of Novi Sad, Novi Sad, Serbia
http://t-labs.elte.hu

Abstract. Background. Web archives store born-digital documents, which are usually collected from the Internet by crawlers and stored in the Web Archive (WARC) format. The trustworthiness and integrity of web archives is still an open challenge, especially in the news portal domain, which face additional challenges of censorship even in democratic societies.

Aim. The aim of this paper is to present a light-weight, blockchain-based solution for web archive validation, which would ensure that the crawled documents are authentic for many years to come.

Method. We developed our archive validation solution as an extension and continuation of our work in web crawler development, mainly targeting news portals. The system is designed as an overlay over a blockchain with a proof-of-stake (PoS) distributed consensus algorithm. PoS was chosen due to its lower ecological footprint compared to proof-of-work solutions (e.g. Bitcoin) and lower expected investment in computing infrastructure.

Results. We implemented a prototype of the proposed solution in Python and C#. The prototype was tested on web archive content crawled from Hungarian news portals at two different timestamps which consisted of 1 million articles in total.

Conclusions. We concluded that the proposed solution is accessible, usable by different stakeholders to validate crawled content, deployable on cheap commodity hardware, tackles the archive integrity challenge and is capable to efficiently manage duplicate documents.

Keywords: Web archive · Validation · Blockchain · Proof-of-stake · Web crawling · Censorship

1 Introduction

Web archives are snapshots of web content collected by processes called crawlers. The contents of such web archives are trusted only as much as the institutions or

ⓒ Springer Nature Switzerland AG 2021
T. Groß and L. Viganò (Eds.): STAST 2020, LNCS 12812, pp. 121–134, 2021.
https://doi.org/10.1007/978-3-030-79318-0_7

individuals who created them, e.g. we can (mostly) trust the archive stored by national archives in democratic countries are unaltered and stored as they were crawled in the past. This is an open societal challenge, as there is broad consensus about the significance of being able to research and access web content which was available five, ten or even more years ago. Unfortunately, there are various reports about attempts to alter web archives. That is an additional reason warranting the development of solutions which distribute trust and allow different stakeholders (e.g. archive holders and researchers) to participate in the validation of archived content. Considering the fact that web archival efforts are usually understaffed, underfunded and lack computer scientists and system administrators to develop and maintain their systems, any solution in this domain should be easy to deploy, maintain and run on cheap hardware attainable in limited budgets.

Our goal is therefore to propose a blockchain-based web archive validation solution which tackles trust, is simple and cheap to implement. It should be accessible to different web archive stakeholders, e.g. national archives, research institutions and groups, as well as the general public. Essentially it can be one piece of a puzzle allowing future generations to enjoy and research the Internet as it was in the past.

2   Related Works

Digital (cultural) heritage can be regarded as an unwanted orphan: most undertakings in the domain face the lack of financial resources (i.e. formal funding) and entirely rely on the competence and enthusiasm of the human element involved [16]. Web archives are used for long-term storage of (usually static) born-digital documents harvested from the web[1] [6,7,10,20]. They allow content to be replayed in the future in close resemblance to their original versions at the time of capture [2]. The Internet Archive's (IA) Wayback Machine [11] is the largest web archive[2]. Standardized data access via uniform application programming interfaces to the IA and other archives is usually supported by the Memento framework[3] [3]. A memento is a timestamp-archived version of a resource retrieved from the web in the past. Content retrieved from a web archive (i.e. a memento) is often marked with an archival replay banner consisting of data about the memento (i.e. archived resource) and the corresponding original resource [1].

In legal environments it is imperative to know that a memento was not forged or altered beyond the necessary changes for replay, e.g. rewriting links inside documents. The Signed Exchanges is a step towards achieving those goals, yet its reliance on short-lived digital signatures limits its applicability in long-term web archival projects. When combined with Certificate Transparency, it might become a viable temporally-aware digital signature validation model[4].

---

[1] http://www.digitalpreservation.gov/formats/fdd/fdd000236.shtml, last accessed, 2020/05/15.

[2] Internet Archive, https://archive.org/.

[3] https://tools.ietf.org/html/rfc7089, last accessed, 2020/05/15.

[4] https://tools.ietf.org/html/rfc6962, last accessed, 2020/05/15.

Web Packaging is a novel standard for bundling and optionally signing resources for authenticity preservation and non-repudiation[5]. The Text Encoding Initiative (TEI) recommendation allows versioning and annotation of enriched articles, allows to store metadata and the body of the document structurally in one file, as well as the verification of the authenticity of the source text [18].

The above initiatives aim to address real-life threats of censorship and tampering in web archives, which is a justified research and development effort, as there were reports about manipulated web archives, e.g. blog posts in the Wayback Machine[6]. Lernet et al. [14] go one step ahead and present proof-of-concept attacks for showing deliberately modified resources to users without tampering with the archive content itself.

Additional important challenges in web archives are duplicates, as well as unwanted metadata and boilerplate text [8,15,17,19]. Countering the above listed challenges in the web archival domain is a task which is yet to be fully solved. Currently trust is reputation-based, which means that we either trust an institution or individual maintaining a web archive, or we do not. There are proposals to rely on blockchain technology [13] and apply a distributed ledger[7] on the Ethereum infrastructure to ensure the long-term integrity of public web archives [5] thereby ensuring public trust in the archived resources. Essentially, they are advocating a shift from institutional trust to technological trust, i.e. instead of institutions, they propose to trust technology (i.e. the blockchain), which is guaranteed to be impartial. When considering blockchain-based solutions, the use of proof-of-stake[8] solutions significantly reduces the computing power necessary to reach distributed consensus and thereby becomes a viable alternative to platforms based on proof-of-work[9]. The Ethereum Casper PoS blockchain was scheduled to be introduced in January 2020, but it was delayed[10].

Based on the above we concluded that data acquisition, storage, retrieval, analysis, indexing/searching and visualization are the key topics and challenges for both practitioners and researchers active in the web archival domain. Conservation and preservation are on the radar but defined as concepts of lesser relevance. Security in general with topics such as trust, integrity (i.e. protection against alteration), censorship and other forms of unwanted filtering and modification are seldom addressed issues in digital heritage in general and web archives specifically [16] [Figure 14].

---

[5] https://github.com/WICG/webpackage, last accessed 2020/07/08.

[6] http://blog.archive.org/2018/04/24/addressing-recent-claimsof-manipulated-blog-posts-in-the-wayback-machine, last accessed 2020/07/08.

[7] https://www.w3.org/TR/prov-overview, last accessed 2020/07/08.

[8] https://medium.com/coinmonks/implementing-proof-of-stake-part-2-748156d5c85e, last accessed 2020/07/08.

[9] https://www.gov.uk/government/news/distributed-ledger-technology-beyond-block-chain, last accessed 2020/07/08.

[10] https://medium.com/chainsafe-systems/ethereum-2-0-a-complete-guide-casper-and-the-beacon-chain-be95129fc6c1, last accessed, 2020/07/08.

3   Solution

We propose to introduce a system architecture shown in Fig. 1, which consists of different participants, namely crawlers, validators, archived content storage and consumers. Crawlers, storage and consumers are components in existence. Crawlers harvest document from the web [12], stored in archives (depicted by the WARC Store processes) and subsequently used by consumers. The novel elements of this system are WARChain validator processes. The task of these proposed nodes is to participate in a distributed consensus algorithm with the goal to validate each new web archive entry generated by the crawlers, as well as to certify the validity of each entry when requested by peer nodes or archive consumers depicted by the laptops in the bottom right of Fig. 1. This solution is intended to replace similar, informal validation systems based on documents hashes and private document repositories (e.g. in Zenodo communities[11]). It is important to note that we propose to introduce a distributed system of multiple such nodes implemented at different stakeholders worldwide.

We propose that the validators reach distributed consensus by relying on a proof-of-stake (PoS) blockchain. We advocate for the use of PoS as opposed to proof-of-work (PoW) solutions, which consume significant amounts of computing power and electricity, thereby increasing their ecological footprint, i.e. they are dirty solutions. The 'stake' in such a system would not be measured by the size of financial deposits, but instead by the trust placed in the institutions participating in the system which host validator nodes. The trusted systems are depicted in Fig. 1 by the icons of academic and government institutions, which can be national archives, universities or other trusted institutions. One such participating institution could host different node types, e.g. a university or other research outfit might host a crawler, a storage node, one or more validators and customers, who in this context would be the researchers accessing the trusted web archives.

In our proposed architecture not all node types participate in the PoS block-chain. We propose that only the WARChain validator nodes participate in the blockchain. The general idea is that while crawler and storage nodes could be set up by anybody with an Internet connection, validators might be hosted only by trusted institutions, which stake the public trust put in them while partici-pating. Ideally, only national archives and highly respected higher education and research institutions would be allowed to delegate validator nodes to the system, thereby making it a semi-private blockchain used for a specific a purpose. This is different from the general-purpose blockchains usually utilized by cryptocur-rencies and other common usage scenarios. The authors of the ARCHANGEL solution [5] present a somewhat similar solution, but with the notable difference of relying on a public proof-of-work blockchain, which wastes significant amounts of energy and not formally introducing the different node types shown in Fig. 1.

Essentially, we propose a system in which web archives (i.e. the collections of documents crawled from the web) are crawled and stored similarly to the

---

[11] Zenodo, https://zenodo.org/.

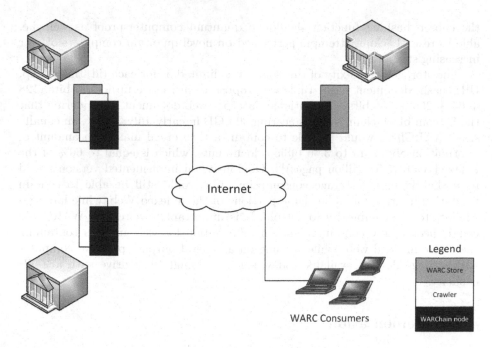

Fig. 1. WARChain system architecture

current state of the art, in storage nodes utilizing on-premise or cloud-based glacier storage which can be rented even on a limited budget. The novel processes participating in the WARChain are used only for storing the limited information necessary for web archive validation. We propose a system in which crawlers harvest documents from the web, persist them into the storage nodes as well as generate tuples of additional validation information consisting of the following pieces of information:

- Crawler process or institution identifier. Storage complexity: up to 128 bits for a globally unique identifier.
- Crawl date. The timestamp of document crawl. Storage complexity: up to 64 bits for a Unix timestamps.
- URL hash. A hash of the URL of the crawled document. Storage complexity (i.e. length): 256 bits.
- Document hash. A hash of the document harvested from the URL specified. Storage complexity (i.e. length): 256 bits.

The above tuple ensures that each raw document stored in the storage archive has a unique and irrefutable link to its corresponding block and/or transaction within the blockchain, i.e. the crawler identifier, crawl date and URL hash uniquely identify a web document crawled by a specific crawler at a specific time.

We propose to use strong one-way hashing functions (e.g. SHA256) which are expected to be available and secure for many years to come. Additionally, the chosen hashing function should be quantum computer-proof as well, i.e. able to resist hacking attempts performed on novel quantum computers of ever increasing strength.

The storage complexity of this solution is limited as for each (id, timestamp, URL hash, document hash) tuple we propose to introduce up to 704 bits (128 + 64 + 256 + 256 bits) of additional data per web document. Considering that the Bitcoin block-chain's size is nearing 300 GB in early July 2020[12], an equally sized WARChain would be able to contain a theoretical maximum amount of information about up to 3.66 billion documents, which is equal to 66% of the indexed Web (5.57 billion pages)[13]. Obviously, an implemented version would have slightly higher storage consumption, but would still be able to contain validation information about large portions of the indexed Web, while having a similar storage complexity to Bitcoin. It is important to note that WARChain could theoretically contain validation information for web archives containing the entire indexed web, while running on a general-purpose personal computer with storage devices available today, e.g. on a single disk drive with a 2 TB capacity.

4   Implementation

In Fig. 1 we visualized crawlers, storage, validators and consumers. Our team implemented and experimented with all of the listed components. We discussed crawlers and storage in [8] and [9]. As a proof-of-concept for the solution introduced in the previous section, we implemented the EduPoS lightweight proof-of-stake (PoS) blockchain for educational purposes. We also implemented the WARChain as an overlay over that system and published our prototype on Github[14]. In this section we discuss the implementation of both elements. We present EduPoS in short and the WARChain in more detail.

4.1   The EduPoS Blockchain

The Unified Modeling Language (UML) class diagram of the EduPoS blockchain developed for experimentation and education purposes is shown in Fig. 2. The general purpose solution consists of nodes which form a decentralized distributed system. The nodes connect to a random subset of other validator nodes and thereby create a sparsely connected distributed system in which the Gossip protocol[15] can be successfully executed. We did not implement likelihood-based connectivity which would be influenced by a higher probability of connecting new nodes to existing nodes with higher numbers of connections (edges) [4].

---

[12] https://www.blockchain.com/charts/blocks-size.

[13] https://www.worldwidewebsize.com.

[14] https://github.com/lendak/warchain.git.

[15] https://medium.com/chainsafe-systems/ethereum-2-0-a-complete-guide-casper-and-the-beacon-chain-be95129fc6c1, last accessed, 2020/07/08.

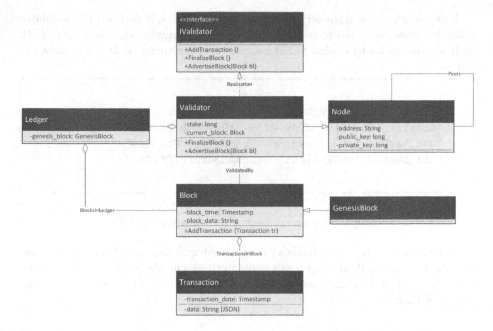

Fig. 2. EduPos proof-of-stake blockchain class diagram

Nodes group transactions into blocks of configurable numbers of transactions and propagate them through the network of nodes. When a node fills a new block with transactions, a distributed consensus algorithm is started. It reaches consensus (i.e. makes a decision to append the new block to the blockchain, if the majority contacted validator nodes approves the change.

The very first block inside the chain is modeled as a genesis block. The chain itself is contained inside the distributed ledger, whose copies are maintained by each validator node. The methods used for maintaining the aggregations and associations between the class instances are not shown in Fig. 2.

The EduPoS blockchain was implemented in the C# programming language for simplicity and ease of use on the Windows platform. Due to its simplicity it can be easily ported to Python or other programming languages and therefore made cross-platform.

4.2 Validators

Our implementation of the WARChain validator nodes extended the general purpose EduPoS with the following domain-specific functionality:

1. A searchable dictionary of (URL hash, document hash) pairs.
2. A counter and reporting capabilities for duplicate entries.
3. Detection and reporting of potentially tampered-with documents which are reachable via a shared URL, but differ between crawls.

Instead of generic data serialized into binary or JSON format, the validator nodes implemented custom code for handling the (crawler id, crawl time, URL hash, document hash) tuples. One example tuple serialized to JSON is shown in Listing 1.

```
{
  "crawl_time":  "2020-07-07 23:17",
  "crawler_id": "6520d949-4168-419e-bb4b-3de6a64f1ad3",
  "doc_hash": "ef2c97cedc8ea42b36d170a879bd3dce",
  "url_hash": "8637941c6610942c90834f6fe79ff482"
}
```

Listing 1. Document hash representation in JSON

The document and URL hashes were created with the SHA256 cryptographic one-way function with an empty salt value in this example. SHA256 is considered a strong one-way function, which will most probably remain secure for a long period of time.

4.3   Crawler Simulator

As we intended to work with large WARC files and switch between different versions of our prototypes, we needed an efficient way to experiment with real-life WARC files. Therefore, we decided to implement a two-state crawler simulator as a combination of Python and C# code. The Python element works with WARC files by relying on the WARCIO streaming library[16]. It extracts URL and article data and saves them to easily accessible Excel and comma separated formats. We decided to extract the newspaper articles from archives we worked with, i.e. we focused only on article text and removed the HTML markup and media files by relying on existing functionality in the BeautifulSoup library[17] and our own custom WARC content filtering.

The part of the crawler simulator written in C# loads the cleaned URL and article data, creates transactions and pushes them into the WARChain. The C# element was wrapped as a Windows console application.

5   Experiments

We started our experiments with the assumption that the implementation of the underlying proof-of-stake blockchain (i.e. the WARChain) was correct and that it inherently supports distributed consensus and immutability of blocks. Further, that meant that we assumed that the data stored inside the chain is unchangeable even in the presence of one or more malicious participants in the

---

[16] https://github.com/webrecorder/warcio.

[17] https://www.crummy.com/software/BeautifulSoup/.

system depicted in Fig. 1. Instead of checking the functionality of the underlying blockchain, our intention was to show that the proposed solution can run effortlessly on commodity computer hardware and that it manages duplicate entries and integrity checking in the web archival context. Along this line of thought, our first experiment focuses on the efficiency and ease of use of the system, followed by the verification of the system's strong integrity validation and duplicate management capabilities.

Table 1. Overview of the experimental setup

Test hardware	Intel i7-9750 CPU, 16 GB RAM, SSD
Web archive #1 [documents]	467,115
Web archive #2 [documents]	592,896
Crawlers	1 or 2
WARChain validator nodes	1 or 12

We conducted our experiments in a setup which consisted of the following elements (see Table 1 for a summary):

1. One or more crawler simulators implemented as a mix of components developed in the Python and C# programming languages. The simulators extracted articles from WARC files populated from the same newspaper portal [9]. The WARC content was crawled at two different dates and the two archives contained 467115 and 592896 article entries.
2. The WARChain consisted of a varying number of nodes.

As we needed an efficient way to compare both article text and URL values between the two archives, we used the SHA256 cryptographic one-way function to hash both the URLs and the article texts and compared those hash values when looking for exact URL/article matches.

The experiments were run on a high-end personal computer with an Intel i7-9750 CPU, 16 GB RAM and a pair of non-raid SSD drives.

5.1   Experiment #1: Proof of Concept

The specific goal of our first experiment was to show that the proposed solution is not just easy to deploy, but also able to run on commodity personal computers, thereby allowing any stakeholder with limited funds to install it on any computer with an appropriate network connection.

The starting point of the experiment was a WARChain system consisting of a single validator node for simplicity. This setup was similar to a situation in which a single institution implemented a single WARChain node. We populated the validator node by running one crawler simulator, taking the smaller WARC file (467k entries) as input and finalizing blocks after a configurable number of received transactions (default 10,000). For simplicity, our experimental setup did not include any storage nodes. It is important to note that we started this experiment with a completely empty ledger (i.e. blockchain).

We measured the memory consumption and time necessary to populate the single node. Our measurements are shown in Table 2 below.

Table 2. Memory consumption and average transaction time

Memory consumption	101.3 MB
Average transaction time	0,0193 ms
Transactions per block	10,000

The memory consumption was measured as the memory used by the single validator node when it was wrapped as a Windows console application and run on the high-end personal computer we used during our tests. Memory use was higher than expected due to the implementation overhead in our blockchain. This can be optimized as part of future research.

The average transaction time was measured by dividing the time needed to add all transactions created for the documents in the input archive (9 s in total on average) by the number of documents (467,115 documents). As in this experiment we had only a single validator node, our time complexity measurements did not include the overhead caused by the communication infrastructure and the distributed consensus algorithm. Considering that we propose to rely on a novel proof-of-stake blockchain implemented by a controlled amount of nodes, the time to validate transactions can and should be significantly lower than the currently measured 5–10 min available in Bitcoin[18] or Ethereum[19].

5.2 Experiment #2: Validation

The specific goal of our second experiment was to test the system's capability to efficiently detect and report alterations in web documents collected by crawlers at different timestamps and potentially different WARChain stakeholders. We started by repeating experiment #1 and followed that up by running the crawler simulator on the second, extended dataset collected from the same news portal at a different timestamp. This second web archive consisted of 592,896 entries as mentioned above. We sent one transaction for each of these entries. We expected the system to be capable to discern the following types of document entries:

1. New entries which were included only in the second archive.
2. Modified entries which existed in both archives, but were different.
3. Removed entries which were inside the first, smaller dataset, but not included in the second, larger WARC file.

---

[18] https://www.blockchain.com/charts/median-confirmation-time.
[19] https://ethgasstation.info/blog/ethereum-transaction-how-long.

We focused on the documents which were included in both crawls, but were different. This kind of discrepancy between two crawls of the same news portal might be caused by tampering or censoring (Table 3).

Table 3. Document validation across multiple web archives

Web archive overlap [documents]	173,784
Web archive overlap [%]	37%
Integrity check failures [documents]	0

We found that the overlap between the two archives was only partial as 173,784 URLs were shared between the two archives (about 37% overlap). We did not find document discrepancies between the two datasets which would point to possible integrity issues, namely all shared documents between the two archives were exact copies. More specifically, this meant that we found 173,784 shared URL hashes between the two datasets and the corresponding articles were equal. Thereby we concluded that there were no alterations made to documents between the collection times of the two web archives we used in our experiments.

We were surprised to see a smaller than expected overlap between the two archives, which we intend to investigate in the future, i.e. we will find out why only 37% of the articles were shared between the archives collected at different times from the same news portal. It was either caused by a change in the crawler implementation, or there might be more sinister reasons behind this finding.

We decided to not measure the average time it took to perform a single integrity check, as we reckoned that it is near zero compared to the length of other tasks performed in the system, first of all the crawling process and reaching the distributed consensus.

5.3 Experiment #3: Duplicate Detection

In our third experiment we wanted to assess the merits of the proposed solution in duplicate document detection. We initialized a slightly different experimental environment with a blockchain consisting of 12 validator nodes (could not add more on a single computer) and ran two crawler simulators which were inserting validation information at two different WARChain nodes. When looking at Fig. 1, this can be understood as if there were 12 black processes (validators) and 2 white processes (crawlers) (Table 4).

With this experiment we tested the way the system would behave in a more realistic setting in which multiple web crawlers collect documents from potentially overlapping parts of the web. As the blockchain is not designed to perform update and delete operations, we allowed each crawler to create new transactions for each crawled document. This way the blockchain contained numerous (see Table 1 for a quantitative measure) transactions essentially describing the

Table 4. Duplicate detection environment

WARChain nodes	12
Crawler simulators	2
Storage nodes	0

same archived content by different crawlers, i.e. there were duplicate transaction entries in the blockchain which differed only in the crawler identifier and/or crawl timestamp of the JSON representation shown in Listing 1. If the system were implemented on a global scale with participation of many validators and crawlers, then the above described duplicate data entry feature of the system would be quite useful in detecting duplicate crawling efforts carried out by different organizations and teams worldwide, as well as allowing cross-validation between the duplicate content crawled.

6   Conclusion and Future Work

We stated that the long-term authenticity of web archives is an open scientific challenge. We proposed to solve this challenge with WARChain, a light-weight, blockchain-based solution for web archive validation. The WARChain relies on a proof-of-stake blockchain, thereby requiring less computing power compared to proof-of-work solution, like Bitcoin. Due to the high cost of storing data in any blockchain, we separated archive storage from the blockchain-based archive validation. The nodes participating in the WARChain stored only tuples consisting of crawler identifier, archive date, URL hash and document hash. We thereby relied on two layers of cryptography, one to hash the URLs and documents, and the other to hash the blocks in the blockchain.

We implemented the EduPoS prototype blockchain and the WARChain as an overlay over that system. The EduPoS was necessary as the Ethereum Casper PoS blockchain was not yet publicly available during our work. Our implementation consisted of a mix of Python and C# code. We validated the solution by testing it on two medium-sized web archives crawled from a news portal and consisting of approximately 500,000 entries each. We extracted the article texts from the archived documents and worked with hashed URL and article values. The experiments conducted showed that the system can run on cheap commodity hardware, it is capable to validate vast amounts of archived web content and is able to manage duplicate entries resulting from multiple crawls. If a similar system were deployed at multiple digital archives worldwide, we could distribute technological trust between those participants, who would ideally be national archives and research institutions. That kind of distributed trust and non-repudiation would ensure that the web archives created by crawlers are not tampered with and available for validation even many years in the future.

As future work, we intend to experiment with additional web archives, port the system to work on mainstream proof-of-stake blockchains as they become available (e.g. Ethereum Casper) and to implement a more fine-grained duplicate detection solution based on minhashing, i.e. to split the article texts into sentences or bags of words and store multiple hash values for each text document. Additionally, any PoS-based solution needs to somehow penalize misbehavior of nodes, which we still need to explore and experiment with in the future.

Acknowledgement. This research was supported by the Institutional Excellence Program for Higher Education (FIKP) of the Republic of Hungary.

References

1. Alam, S., Kelly, M., Weigle, M.C., Nelson, M.L.: Unobtrusive and extensible archival replay banners using custom elements. In: Proceedings of the 18th ACM/IEEE on Joint Conference on Digital Libraries. JCDL 2018, New York, NY, USA, pp. 319–320. Association for Computing Machinery (2018). https://doi.org/10.1145/3197026.3203881
2. Alam, S., Weigle, M.C., Nelson, M.L., Klein, M., de Sompel, H.V.: Supporting web archiving via web packaging (2019)
3. Alam, S., Weigle, M.C., Nelson, M.L., Melo, F., Bicho, D., Gomes, D.: Mementomap framework for flexible and adaptive web archive profiling. In: Proceedings of the 18th Joint Conference on Digital Libraries. JCDL 2019, pp. 172–181. IEEE Press (2019). https://doi.org/10.1109/JCDL.2019.00033
4. Barabasi, A.L., Albert, R.: Emergence of scaling in random networks. Science **286**(5439), 509–512 (1999). https://doi.org/10.1126/science.286.5439.509, http://www.sciencemag.org/cgi/content/abstract/286/5439/509
5. Collomosse, J., et al.: Archangel: trusted archives of digital public documents. In: Proceedings of the ACM Symposium on Document Engineering, DocEng 2018, New York, NY, USA. Association for Computing Machinery (2018). https://doi.org/10.1145/3209280.3229120
6. Gomes, D., Miranda, J., Costa, M.: A survey on web archiving initiatives. In: Gradmann, S., Borri, F., Meghini, C., Schuldt, H. (eds.) TPDL 2011. LNCS, vol. 6966, pp. 408–420. Springer, Heidelberg (2011). https://doi.org/10.1007/978-3-642-24469-8_41
7. Holzmann, H., Goel, V., Anand, A.: Archivespark: efficient web archive access, extraction and derivation. In: Proceedings of the 16th ACM/IEEE-CS on Joint Conference on Digital Libraries. JCDL 2016, New York, NY, USA, pp. 83–92. Association for Computing Machinery (2016). https://doi.org/10.1145/2910896.2910902
8. Indig, B., Kákonyi, T., Novák, A.: Crawling in reverse - lightweight targeted crawling of news portals. In: Kubis, M. (ed.) Proceedings of the 9th Language and Technology Conference: Human Language Technologies as a Challenge for Computer Science and Linguistics (LTC 2019), pp. 81–86. Wydawnictwo Nauka I Innowacje (2019)
9. Indig, B., Knap, Á., Sárközi-Lindner, Z., Timári, M., Palkó, G.: The ELTE.DH pilot corpus - creating a handcrafted Gigaword web corpus with metadata. In: Proceedings of the 12th Web as Corpus Workshop, Marseille, France, pp. 33–41. European Language Resources Association (2020). https://www.aclweb.org/anthology/2020.wac-1.5

10. Johnson, V., Thomas, D.: Interfaces with the past... present and future? scale and scope: the implications of size and structure for the digital archive of tomorrow. In: Proceedings Digital Heritage Conference, vol. 1 (2013)
11. Kelly, M., Alam, S., Nelson, M.L., Weigle, M.C.: InterPlanetary wayback: peer-to-peer permanence of web archives. In: Fuhr, N., Kovács, L., Risse, T., Nejdl, W. (eds.) TPDL 2016. LNCS, vol. 9819, pp. 411–416. Springer, Cham (2016). https://doi.org/10.1007/978-3-319-43997-6_35
12. Kelly, M., Weigle, M.C.: Warcreate: Create wayback-consumable warc files from any webpage. In: Proceedings of the 12th ACM/IEEE-CS Joint Conference on Digital Libraries. JCDL 2012, New York, NY, USA, pp. 437–438. Association for Computing Machinery (2012). https://doi.org/10.1145/2232817.2232930
13. Lemieux, V.L.: Blockchain technology for record keeping: help or hype? In: Technical Report. University of British Columbia (2016)
14. Lerner, A., Kohno, T., Roesner, F.: Rewriting history: changing the archived web from the present. In: Proceedings of the 2017 ACM SIGSAC Conference on Computer and Communications Security. CCS 2017, New York, NY, USA, pp. 1741–1755. Association for Computing Machinery (2017). https://doi.org/10.1145/3133956.3134042
15. Milligan, I.: Lost in the infinite archive: the promise and pitfalls of web archives. Int. J. Humanit. Arts Comput. **10**(1), 78–94 (2016)
16. Münster, S.: Digital heritage as a scholarly field-topics, researchers, and perspectives from a bibliometric point of view. J. Comput. Cult. Herit. **12**(3), 1–27 (2019). https://doi.org/10.1145/3310012
17. Pomikálek, J.: Removing boilerplate and duplicate content from web corpora. Ph.D. thesis, Masaryk university, Faculty of informatics, Brno (2011)
18. Schreibman, S., Siemens, R., Unsworth, J.: A Companion to Digital Humanities. John Wiley & Sons, Hoboken (2008)
19. Sigurðsson, K.: Managing duplicates across sequential crawls. IWAW 2006, p. 99 (2006)
20. You, L.L., Pollack, K.T., Long, D.D.E.: Deep store: an archival storage system architecture. In: 21st International Conference on Data Engineering (ICDE 2005), pp. 804–815 (2005). https://doi.org/10.1109/ICDE.2005.47

Cyber 9/11 Will Not Take Place: A User Perspective of Bitcoin and Cryptocurrencies from Underground and Dark Net Forums

Simon Butler[✉] [iD]

Information Security Group, Royal Holloway, University of London, Egham, UK
Simon.Butler.2015@live.rhul.ac.uk

Abstract. Background. There is a historical narrative of fear surrounding cyber-crime. This has extended to cryptocurrencies (CCs), which are often viewed as a criminal tool. **Aim.** To carry out the first user study of CCs for illicit activity, from the perspective of underground and dark net forums. **Method.** We conducted a qualitative study, using a content analysis method, of 16,405 underground and dark net forum posts selected from *CrimeBB*, a dataset of 100 million posts curated by the Cambridge Cybercrime Centre. **Results.** Firstly, finality of payments emerged as a major motivator for the use of CCs. Second, we propose an Operational Security Taxonomy for Illicit Internet Activity to show that CCs are only one part of several considerations that combine to form security in illicit internet transactions. Third, the dark net is hard to use and requires significant study, specialist equipment and advanced knowledge to achieve relative security. **Conclusion.** We argue that finality is the main advantage of CCs for this user group, not anonymity as widely thought. The taxonomy shows that banning CCs is unlikely to be effective. Finally, we contend that the dark net is a niche for criminal activity and fears over cybercrime cause the threat to be exaggerated.

Keywords: Bitcoin · Cryptocurrencies · Underground and dark net forums · User studies · Cybercrime · Security

1 Introduction

On the 25 February 2015, the Superintendent of New York State's Department of Financial Services (DFS) delivered a speech at Columbia Law School about the role of regulators after the Great Financial Crisis. In a section on cyber security in the financial sector, the Superintendent made clear the extent of his department's fears:

> We are concerned that within the next decade (or perhaps sooner) we will experience an Armageddon-type cyber event that causes a significant disruption in the financial system for a period of time – what some have termed a "cyber 9/11" [1].

Simon Butler was supported as part of the EPSRC Centre for Doctoral Training in Cyber Security at Royal Holloway, University of London (EP/K035584/1).

T. Groß and L. Viganò (Eds.): STAST 2020, LNCS 12812, pp. 135–153, 2021.
https://doi.org/10.1007/978-3-030-79318-0_8

On the very same day, DFS released its revised proposed rules for businesses with CC services; the so-called 'Bitlicense' regulation, which came into force a few months later. This highlights the rhetoric of extreme fear that often surrounds matters of cybercrime. Indeed, for several decades there were predictions that 'Cyberwar is Coming!', to which Thomas Rid responded that 'Cyber War Will Not Take Place' [2].

The narrative surrounding CCs has also often been security led, providing ample material for the media. Stories have run of the FBI's fears of Bitcoin's popularity with criminals [3], of the Chairman of the Federal Reserve commenting that CCs are 'great if you are trying to hide or launder money' [4] or even more recently, in 2019, when CCs made headlines when described as a national security threat by the US Treasury Secretary [5]. There is a War on Terror, a War on Drugs, and also a long-standing struggle between the state and those that desire privacy through strong encryption. If you add to this concern over control of one of mankind's most important constructs – money – then CCs find themselves amongst several of the world's most hotly contested debates; in no small part, due to their connection with illicit activity on the dark net.

Yet, some 11 years after Bitcoin was invented, CCs have not played a critical role in a Cyber War, a Cyber 9/11, or been responsible for an explosion in dark net crime that threatens society. The DFS Superintendent said of virtual currencies in a 2013 interview that 'it feels as if the major advantage they're providing is anonymity' [6]. And in evidence given in 2014, DFS was told that illicit activity using virtual currencies 'reduces or even eliminates practical barriers to entry' thereby enabling the purchase of drugs globally with 'essentially the push of a button' [7]. There is little dispute that CCs are used for criminal activity, but how useful are they really? Is anonymity their major advantage? And is purchasing on the dark net as simple as clicking a button? We take a social constructivist approach to these questions. What do the users *themselves* say of their attitudes and motivations towards the usage of CCs for illicit purposes?

We follow this introduction with a background section to highlight the importance of this topic. We examine some existing user studies of CCs and also some wider work on the dark net. This exposes the gap in the literature that we aim to address through three research questions. Methodology and ethical considerations were key to researching a sensitive subject and so we consider these aspects in detail. We then discuss our results, which are achieved through analysis of underground and dark net forum posts. Our study presents several implications for policy, before closing with the conclusion.

2 Background

2.1 User Studies

CCs are an important topic of research. The world is moving increasingly towards a digital future and the methods with which we transact have undergone more evolution in the last 100 years than the previous two millennia [8]. The very form of money is changing; from new initiatives like Facebook's Libra to the prospect of Central Bank Digital Currencies. Bitcoin emerged amongst this change, at some level in response to the Great Financial Crisis but also 'as a symptom of monetary plurality in the twenty-first century' [9]. The control of money, the form and properties of money, the relationship of money to society; all have emerged as important topics in recent years.

Early academic interest in Bitcoin was largely technical, as the original CC seemingly delivered on a long past of cryptographic endeavour and previous attempts to build digital cash [8]. The examination of CCs focussed on issues such as their ability to scale and their security – prompting calls from several researchers for more to be done from a social perspective [10–14]. A number of studies of user experiences of CCs have now been conducted. One of the first surveys of Bitcoin users was a web-survey of 7500 students. Amongst that group, politics and Libertarianism were an influence for using Bitcoin, whilst novelty was more of a draw than anonymity. The study concludes that Bitcoin means different things to different people [11]. Whilst this seems a simple observation, it is telling as there is a tendency in the debate about CCs to make sweeping statements, such as that CCs are a tool for criminals. The reality is, of course, more nuanced and varied. It is only by researching different groups that we can learn of the different attitudes and motivations that invariably exist between them.

In another earlier study of 1000 users, almost half identified as Libertarian [15]. This political dimension was also identified in a 2013 investigation of Bitcoin from a semiotics perspective, which analysed archived conversations of those involved in Bitcoin. The researchers showed that Bitcoin 'provides an alternative to currencies and payment systems that are seen to threaten users' privacy, limit personal liberty, and undermine the value of money through state and corporate oversight' [16]. Many other studies have now taken place to understand user experiences and motivations for using CCs, usually employing interview or web-survey methods [12, 17–21]. In 2015, researchers used the Technology Acceptance Model (TAM) to organise their results; interviewees expressed concerns over ease of use, and one merchant worried about price volatility. In terms of usefulness, low cost was a major driver, with anonymity not viewed as an issue [22]. Several other studies draw similar conclusions but analysed from different perspectives, such as human-computer interaction [19, 23–25].

As well as being limited to specific groups, such as students or a country by geography, the other main similarity in all these user studies is the focus on legitimate usage. There is a gap in the literature concerning the attitudes and motivations of users of CCs for illicit purposes. This is particularly important given the security-led concerns that are expressed about CCs. This paper addresses this crucial gap by conducting the first user study of CCs from an illicit perspective, in order to contribute to the debates about their existence. Furthermore, several of the studies discussed took place prior to 2017 when CCs gathered mainstream attention. This study contributes to recent knowledge of views up to late 2019.

2.2 Dark Net Studies

Usage of CCs on the dark net is an oft-cited concern yet none of the user research discussed so far addresses this issue. The dark net is a rich area of study but, again, the use of CCs on them is a largely neglected subject. Although there is a suggestion that 'cryptomarkets' will increase the volume of illegal substances for sale, researchers challenge the assumption that this will only increase harm [26]. Drug quality can be higher and physical violence lower on dark net markets [27]. Policy makers must give careful thought to the dark net, as the effects of it are not universally negative.

Another interesting study reveals that the risk of arrest is also reduced on the dark net; there were only 391 arrests worldwide up to December 2016 [26]. This is a modest figure and should be borne in mind in relation to the findings of Kethineni, Cao and Dodge [28], who conclude, in their work applying space transition theory to Bitcoin usage on the dark net, that a lack of deterrence is one attraction of the internet to criminal behaviour. Indeed, research suggests that trade on markets increased after media coverage of successful law enforcement action on the Silk Road [29]. The research community notes that there is a lack of work assessing the effectiveness of strategies towards illicit markets [30]. Is it that CC properties enable dark net activity or is the problem more due to a lack of deterrence? Interestingly Bancroft and Reid [31] note, with regard to dark net anonymity, that this property is not a precondition for internet drug selling as drug trading exists on the internet without attempts to hide identity.

The dark net has proven to be a popular area of research for social scientists. A significant part of the literature focusses on the drugs dimension, in reflection of the status of this topic in wider society. This study adds to this knowledge with a focus on the payment mechanism, which is seldom discussed. It is important for policy makers to understand the role that CCs play on the dark net, as they consider the risks they pose.

3   Research Questions

This research seeks to explore attitudes and motivations towards the use of cryptocurrencies. To do this, we aimed to carry out the first user study of cryptocurrencies (CCs) for illicit activity, from the perspective of underground and dark net forum users. We do not seek to make any moral or legal judgement on the actions of any individuals but use the term 'illicit activity' as other researchers have done [32], as a collective term to aid discussion of a variety of actions on the internet, such as buying illegal drugs on a dark net market. The following three sub-questions were chosen in support of our aim:

Q1. What properties of cryptocurrencies are important to users for illicit activity?
Q2. What are users' attitudes and experiences of using CCs for illicit activity?
Q3. To what extent are CCs an enabler of illicit underground and dark net activity?

4   Research Method

4.1   Data Collection Method

In Gehl's field guide for studying the dark net [33] the author implores for more 'humanistic inquiry' and provides advice based on many years of studying this location of research. Gehl notes that ethnographic work on the dark net has mainly focussed on marketplaces and not on other sites, such as 'forums and social networking sites' [33]. These forums are places where discussion about the dark net takes place, including how to use the system [33]. This includes discussion of cryptocurrencies, as the main payment method of the dark net. This study explores the attitudes and motivations towards the usage of cryptocurrencies and so forums and social networking sites were chosen as the most suitable research targets. Of particular relevance here, in terms of illicit activity, are underground forums on the internet (such as hacker sites) and forums on the dark net which require specialist software (such as the Tor browser) to access.

There are two broad strategies used by researchers to gather information on forums. The first is active engagement with users; however, this comes with significant ethical and practical implications but also with greater potential risk to participants and even researcher safety [34]. The second broad strategy is without active engagement. This can involve a bespoke scraping (downloading data) of target websites but there are also repositories of these scrapes available for research use. Considering researcher reflectivity and positionality, we selected using a repository of scraped data as the most appropriate strategy, as there were no advantages to the other methods for this study.

4.2 Sample Selection

There are a number of scraped datasets available for research. Gehl describes one 50GB source covering dates between 2011–2015 [33]. Another extensive dataset called CrimeBB has been assembled by Cambridge University's Cybercrime Centre (CCC). This dataset has been professionally curated and covers a more extensive period. For these reasons, it was chosen as the sample for research. CrimeBB was created in recognition of the fact that prior research had relied on insufficient and out of date datasets [35]. Furthermore, underground forums provide a place for criminals to discuss and exchange information, products and services – as such, they help researchers better understand 'behaviours of offenders and pathways into crime' [36].

CCC makes CrimeBB available to other researchers 'under a legal agreement, designed to prevent misuse and provide safeguards for ethical research' [35]. The dataset continues to grow as more forums are included. In 2019, CrimeBB had data from fifteen underground forums, such as Hackforums which is the largest of its kind in the English language [37]. CrimeBB also includes dark net forum data. As such, the dataset is one of the largest available to researchers, covering a wide timespan and a variety of different internet and dark net forums. Several research papers are connected to the CrimeBB dataset [33–40].

4.3 Data Analysis

The first task was to download a SQL dump for each forum available from CCC. These were then restored in a Postgres database. In total, data from 18 underground and dark net forums were added, amounting to some 100 million posts. Search terms were then employed as SQL statements to focus the relevancy of the data. Using 'Bitcoin' as an initial search term produced a selection that was still more than 200,000 posts. As a test, we coded a selection of 100 posts and found that took one hour. To code all the 'Bitcoin' posts would take in the region of one year of full-time work. Another factor that influenced selection strategy was the disparity in the size of the forum dumps. The largest forum accounted for approximately 80 per cent of the 100 million posts, whilst the smallest produced less than 100 posts containing 'Bitcoin'.

Based on the coding test and the results for each forum using the 'Bitcoin' search term, we adopted the following method to obtain our selection for coding and analysis. For any forum with more than 2000 'Bitcoin' results, 'Bitcoin' was combined with other search terms to reduce the results. For small forums with less than 2000 'Bitcoin' results, these other terms were searched for in addition to 'Bitcoin'. The effect being to widen search terms for small forums and combine search terms for larger forums.

'Bitcoin' was chosen as the 'master' search term as it is the overwhelmingly dominant CC. As the first of its type, there would also have been many years of posts where it was the only CC. To select other search terms, the 200,000 'Bitcoin' posts were then analysed using IBM SPSS Modeler's text analytics capabilities. This offers an auto-categorisation of content. By reviewing the categorisations by order of content volume, we identified new search terms of interest. We also then added a further three related terms based on experience. The following table shows the final search terms, which resulted in a total selection of 23,223 posts (Table 1):

Table 1. Final search term selection

Master term	Top 500 SPSS categories	Other SPSS categories	Related terms
Bitcoin	Money	Zcash	Dash
	BTC	Police	Feds
	Cryptocurrency	Criminal	Jail
	Monero	Privacy coin	

The posts were then exported to Microsoft Excel. Here, 180 posts were removed as they no longer had discernible forum identifiers. Duplicates were also then removed resulting in a final 16,405 posts, equating to 164 h of estimated coding time. Coding is central to most qualitative data analysis and software tools are often used to assist [42]. We attempted to use Nvivo but found that it took too long to process codes. After considering other options, QDA Miner Lite was selected for coding and analysis.

5 Ethics

Ethical considerations were central to the design of this study, as sites of illicit activity need extra consideration for participants and researchers. There is a risk of personal harm and also the potential to stray into illegal activity [34]. Using CrimeBB minimised many risks. The ethical principles of the Association of Internet Researchers (AoIR) were also used to assess the implications of the research conducted in the study [43]. A key point raised by AoIR is about expectations of privacy. This is a contested issue but a widely held position is that 'informed consent is not legally required to access data from publicly available forums, as they are in the public domain' [44]. There has been extensive research on internet forums, and of CrimeBB, so we did not seek informed consent. Other significant considerations highlighted by AoIR were minimised in this study. There was no interaction with any individuals from the dataset, which alone eliminated a great deal of risk and negates the need for a communications strategy.

The guidance of the British Society of Criminology (BSC) [45] also informed the methodology. Even though forums are public, information gained from the internet 'should always be critically examined and the identity of individuals protected unless it is a salient aspect of the research' [45]. This research aims to explore group behaviour and usage of cryptocurrencies, it is not necessary, therefore, to identify users by their usernames. Furthermore, the British Sociological Association [44] advises that data from online forums should not be copied verbatim. This research abides by the guidance of both organisations and does not present usernames or verbatim quotations.

BSC provides further ethical guidance concerning the law and obligations for researchers. In the UK, individuals (including researchers) are not legally obliged to report crimes they witness to the police unless an act relates to terrorism, child abuse or money laundering [45]. The nature of the data analysed here was unlikely to relate to the first two categories. One advantage of using a professionally curated dataset is that images are often removed as part of the scraping process. This reduces the chance of viewing certain types of data. The obligation with regards to money laundering relates to the Proceeds of Crime Act 2002 and relates primarily to the regulatory sector [45]. An ethics note by the University of Sheffield also comments that most information collected by researchers is likely to amount to intelligence or hearsay – it is not 'hard proof of criminality' [46]. There was, therefore, a negligible chance that this research revealed anything that would cause concern with respect to the obligations mentioned. However, if that likelihood had occurred then the protocol would have been to discuss any material with University staff before taking further action. A full ethics review of this study was approved by the University's Research Ethics Committee.

6 Results and Analysis

Neither usernames nor verbatim quotations are used in this paper. In this section, where a specific post from CrimeBB is discussed, we use the term 'author' generically in lieu of any username connected to a post.

6.1 It's About Finality, Not Anonymity

Cryptocurrencies present a user with an alternative financial system with differentiated properties. Among the key properties are anonymity (or pseudonymity), speed, low-cost (usually), decentralisation (no third-parties), self-sovereignty, immutability of the blockchain and finality [8]. We define finality here as a payment transaction that, once made, cannot practically be undone. For the university students surveyed by Bashir, Strickland and Bohr [11], there was a political motivation towards usage and novelty was a greater draw than anonymity. But how does this view change amongst different user groups with different needs and wants? Specifically, which properties were most important for adoption of cryptocurrencies by underground and dark net forum users?

Whilst anonymity *generally* is important to those conducting illicit activities, it was the property of finality that emerged strongly from the coding. Many authors spoke of difficulties with using traditional finance and discussion about PayPal, in particular, was of note. It is difficult in a predominantly qualitative work such as this to quantitatively support what, at a certain level, is something of a subjective judgement that arose from analysing the posts. However, some key search terms were submitted into QDA using the text retrieval function in order to give the reader a sense of the frequency that certain terms appeared in the 16,405 posts, as shown in Table 2.

Table 2. Total number of posts containing the selected search term

Search term	Number of posts with hits
Anonymity	396
Anonymous	776
Pseudonymous	23
PayPal	3325
Chargeback/Charge back	333 (123/210)
Privacy coin	109
Monero/XMR	1337 (993/344)
Dash	238
Zcash	130
Verge	53
Decentralised/Decentralized	360 (54/306)
Speed	1233
Cost	855
Immutable	11
Libertarian	27
Cypherpunk	3

The meaning derived from this table is crude, but it is useful in discussion of the properties that were important to the users of this study. Of note, there was very little discussion observed of the Libertarian or Cypherpunk ideals that are often mentioned in connection to CCs. The other figures from Table 2 need to be handled cautiously. Some terms, like 'speed' and 'cost', appear relatively frequently but may have been used in many different contexts among the posts. Others, such as 'decentralis(z)ed', were present in many 'generic' posts that served as introductions to CCs. In contrast, the difficulty that many users had with traditional finance stood large as a theme in its own right. The term 'chargeback' is singular in its meaning compared to 'cost' for example, which caused it to emerge, along with 'PayPal', as significant codes of interest. Notably, neither of these terms were used in the initial filtering of posts from CrimeBB.

In 2014, PayPal extended the time to raise a dispute from 45 to 180 days. The feeling among many authors on CrimeBB was that this was great for scammers and terrible for sellers - the issue being that a trade could be made, only for a buyer to complain later causing accounts and funds to be frozen. Furthermore, the view was that third parties tended to side with the buyer rather than the seller. The result was that many people looked for alternatives without chargebacks – Bitcoin was one of several useful solutions. In 2014 when Bitcoin was relatively unknown, there were sellers considering accepting only Bitcoin despite the fear of losing most of their customers by rejecting more accepted payment methods. It is also important to note that this issue was not limited to illicit activity - a lot of this discussion took place on the underground forums, even as far back as 2012 where authors had problems using Liberty Reserve. Discussion also highlighted some of the other reasons why people were frustrated with traditional finance and sought alternatives: PayPal, for example, is not supported in every country, under 18s are restricted from many financial services and others talked of their problems using existing services after having had previous financial difficulty. All these experiences led to the adoption of Bitcoin (primarily) as a tool open to all.

One limitation of CrimeBB is the periods covered. Underground forum posts are from as early as 2010, whilst the dark net forums date from 2014 onwards[1]. We are not, therefore, able to see dark net posts from the very early days of Bitcoin or indeed of the Silk Road era. However, there is a crossover from the underground forums where these matters are discussed. Much is also known of the dark net and the Silk Road from these times from existing research, where Bitcoin was long established as a payment mechanism for trade. And it was and is the finality of transactions that has been at the heart of Bitcoin's acceptance for illicit activity as it overcomes one of the difficulties of the internet – that of trust. As one author puts it, there is little trust on the internet. Another urges others to trust in cryptography over anything a human might say. Finality, with an immutable public ledger, enabled trust to increase, above that of the alternatives that existed at the time. Authors note that they could verify funds had been sent and be secure knowing they would not suffer chargebacks or other problems - a situation enhanced further with escrow and eventually multi-signature transactions.

The volume of posts, and their strength and tone, caused finality to emerge as the most useful property of CCs. This finding aligns with Anderson's paper pre-dating Bitcoin that 'reveals that revocability is more important' than traceability for online fraudsters using 'nonbank payment services' [47]. Speed was not a top concern in our sample when, in the case of purchasing drugs on the dark net as an example, packages were to arrive by post. Reduced cost of transactions was an attractive feature, but lower down the order than the benefits of finality. The other structural characteristics of Bitcoin contribute to achieving this benefit but were not the overt reason why it was adopted – finality solved real problems of existing alternatives. But what of anonymity? Was this not the main advantage of Bitcoin and cryptocurrencies as many believe?

6.2 Anonymity Isn't Everything

Table 2 shows that anonymity is a frequent term in posts. The dark net forums, in particular, are dense with discussions about operational security, or how not to get caught. A first important point authors note is that complete anonymity is impossible to achieve – the best that can be hoped for is sufficient security to be practically safe. Secondly, anonymity is achieved through a raft of measures, not solely through one method such as the payment mechanism. A layering of protection is needed to create obscurity. (There will be more on this in the following sub-sections). These are important distinctions, as anonymity is not, therefore, the 'main advantage' offered by CCs. They can aid in the endeavour but do not solve the issue in its entirety.

---

[1] One of the foreign language dark net forums has posts as far back as 2012.

Analysis of CrimeBB is also interesting from a longitudinal perspective, as we observe the changes in attitude and behaviour towards CCs. It also reveals the spectrum of user knowledge about the properties of CCs and how to use them for illicit activity. There is strong evidence from 2011/12 that many users believed that Bitcoin was fully anonymous. They were likely using the Silk Road thinking that tracking or any form of identification was not possible. Despite this, there were other users, as early as 2012, who were aware of the pseudonymous nature of Bitcoin. In one such post, an author expresses his exasperation that others keep claiming that Bitcoin is completely anonymous. There is a clear difference in understanding between those that are technically savvy and well-read, and those who are not. To those that are not, there was a belief that Bitcoin was as anonymous as cash and served that purpose as 'cash on the internet'. Posts show that users felt it was anonymous as they did not have to provide a genuine name when creating a wallet.

By 2014, the underground forums evidence a widespread recommendation to use third party 'tumbler or mixer' services with Bitcoin as the prevailing method to increase the obscurity of any trail. Ultimately though, as one author explains, Bitcoin is only as anonymous as the individual behind it. Despite this, claims of Bitcoin's complete anonymity continue through all years, as well as posts of disbelief at this lack of knowledge. Remarkably, in 2019 there is even evidence that users were buying CCs on regulated exchanges with real-world details and then sending funds directly to illicit sites. There is a noticeable difference between the underground and dark net forums in these matters. In general, the dark net forums are heavily dominated by operational security discussion and so are much more aware of the issues and take them more seriously. This makes sense and Tor appears to filter some of the banality that the easier access of underground forums enables.

Using tumblers continued to be a widespread practice from 2014 to 2016. After this time, however, users moved away from this method, citing trust (some services have control of your funds and can disappear with them) and also efficacy – you may be mixing your 'dirty' coin and receiving another 'dirty' coin in return. In 2017, one of the main tumblers closed their services as they changed their philosophy, realising that Bitcoin was intended as a transparent system. This change also aligns with the other significant development of this time, which was the emergence of privacy coins, designed with enhanced anonymity in mind in comparison to Bitcoin.

Table 2 is again a useful reference at this point. Dash, or Darkcoin as it was previously known, had some prominence in the 2014–15 period but posts show that users moved from it, questioning if its technology enabled any more security than Bitcoin. Instead, it was Monero that emerged as the most talked-about privacy coin of choice. By 2018, there was a marked clamour about the use of Monero, with some proclaiming it the rescuer and future of dark net markets. This is supported by Monero's daily transaction chart, which has been on an upward trend since early 2019 and now regularly records more daily transactions than the peak of the 2017 bubble [48]. Despite the increased security on offer from Monero, Bitcoin retains its prominence even on dark net markets. Why is this the case? That is exactly the question that many authors pose. In 2018, one author commented that Monero was not an option on many markets. A 2019 post notes that Bitcoin is awful for anonymity or privacy. It also becomes noticeable at this time that there is anger towards Bitcoin as users cannot understand why anyone would use it for illicit activity when it has a traceable, public ledger. There are even outright calls and advice to stop using it on the dark net. Others thought it obsolete in terms of the privacy it offers and even described it as terrible for illicit activity.

Several explanations arise. Firstly, there are the network effects that Bitcoin has achieved. It is *the* CC that is universally available and accepted. People have also learnt how to use it over 11 years of operation. One seller questions the ability of buyers to use a new currency (Monero), suggesting it would be easier to accept Bitcoin and take responsibility for anonymity as part of their own operational security. Another user explains that there is no cyber law enforcement in their country, meaning there is nothing to worry about if using Bitcoin. This question of deterrence also emerges in many other posts. The widespread opinion is that law enforcement only cares about large dark net participants – if you are a buyer of small quantities then again Bitcoin will probably do. Similarly, another author states that major criminals do not need Bitcoin and that it is a poor tool for money laundering. Some other users fall into the categories of careless, misinformed, stupid, entrenched and even lazy, as author explanations for the continued use of Bitcoin. Additionally, Monero is viewed as harder to get and to use than Bitcoin. Users also worry that a connection to Monero looks suspicious. In a 2019 post, another author asks why anyone would use Monero, as none of the markets had multi-signature transactions – leaving participants to run the risk of market exit scams. One final post gets to the crux of the issue – the main advantage of Bitcoin is not anonymity.

That Bitcoin is still widely used even though it is common knowledge that it does not offer strong anonymity is prima facie evidence that this is not the main advantage on offer. To return to a point made earlier, anonymity is not and should not be sought from one element of activity. It takes many aspects of operational security to achieve sufficient anonymity – that is, a transparent currency can be used for an illicit payment as long as other countermeasures are used. For example, a user could acquire a currency with fraudulent details; in this case, it does not matter that the transaction is not anonymous. And so it is with Bitcoin and CCs. The payment mechanism is only one part of a whole set of other considerations that work to achieve the desired anonymity. It is not singularly important for Bitcoin to be anonymous – if it was, it would not be used. In this way, we can say that dark net markets are not dependent on CCs or a perceived advantage of anonymity. They can survive without this necessity.

How, though, is this possible? The following sub-sections will explore this in more detail. For now, we can summarise that illicit activity requires an overall level of anonymity, but this is not achieved through Bitcoin or a privacy coin. In this way, Bitcoin can be pseudonymous and still be used, as long as other methods are employed. Privacy coins enhance anonymity, but they are still not a singular solution. Countless posts (amongst those that care) take place on underground and dark net forums discussing how to best transact. This will now be examined.

6.3   The Payment Mechanism

The payment mechanism used to conduct illicit activity is just one of a suite of considerations that a conscientious user must scrutinise if they hope to achieve a sufficient level of operational security. To aid discussion of this, we propose an Operational Security Taxonomy for Illicit Internet Activity, shown in Fig. 1. As the reader can see, there is a great deal to consider if you seek to conduct illicit activity as securely as possible. The seven areas of security are not exhaustive but capture the main elements that contribute towards relative anonymity. The dashed boxes are also not exhaustive but illustrate some of the considerations in each area. At the top, there is a cross-cutting theme of 'procedures', which applies to all seven security areas. For example, a procedure may be implemented to erase all hard disks weekly, or in relation to shipping to ensure that a home address is free of illicit material prior to an expected delivery.

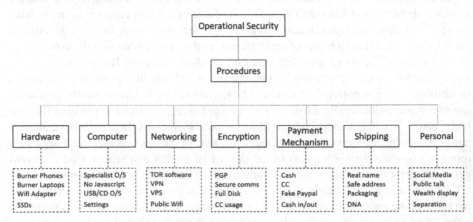

Fig. 1. Operational security taxonomy for illicit internet activity

Our focus here is on the payment mechanism. We begin with the following claim – banning CCs would not materially reduce illicit internet activity. In many areas of the taxonomy, we can think of there being 'tools for the job'. The history seen through CrimeBB shows that when one payment mechanism falls, another is quickly found. When Liberty Reserve ceased, other options were soon adopted. As difficulties with traditional finance grew, demand for Bitcoin increased. And now, as Bitcoin is scrutinised, many want to move to Monero. There are always alternative payment mechanisms. Table 3 highlights some of those used in CrimeBB.

The table shows that a ban on CCs would only restrict one potential mechanism, leaving several other options. If we consider just the bearer type, we see that it is an ultimate recourse should every other type become unavailable. Bearer assets are owned by the holder and so offer a finality of transaction, like CCs. Cash is the most common example and finality explains why 'cash is still king' for criminal transactions [8]. Indeed, as several authors point out, cash is the main mechanism for purchasing drugs more widely. Another author describes successfully sending cash through the mail system – established techniques such as this would be extremely difficult to counter and exist as proven payment mechanisms should other methods disappear. Gift cards are another readily available bearer mechanism discussed and used in a multitude of posts.

Several authors question the logic of a ban on CCs. They view cash as being a greater enabler of criminal activity than CCs and believe there is a hypocrisy in targeting CCs

Table 3. Selection of payment mechanisms in CrimeBB

Payment type	Example mechanisms
Cryptocurrencies	Bitcoin/Litecoin/Monero/Dash/Zcash
Payment Processors	PayPal, Western Union, MoneyGram, Skrill (Moneybookers), Payza, Webmoney, Moneypak
Bearer Assets	Cash, Gift Cards
Fintech	Perfectmoney, Cashapp, Venmo, Greendot, Dwolla, Perfectmoney, UKash, Virwox, Paysafecard
Gaming Currency	Runescape Gold, Second Life Linden Dollars
Traditional Finance	Bank Account, Credit/Debit Cards, Prepaid Debit Cards, Polish Bank Cards

over cash or the traditional financial system. Authors acknowledge that CCs are used in crime but ask if that is different from any other payment mechanism. It is worth noting at this point the central role that cash also plays in illicit internet activity. Not only is it used as a payment mechanism, it also acts as a fundamental tool for achieving anonymity. One of the most discussed topics, particularly on the dark net forums, is the subject of 'cashing in or out' of CCs. As CCs are still a relatively small market and not accepted widely in the world, authors describe the need to transfer any CCs into and out of cash for use in the real world. In this way, cash can often be thought of as the anonymity wrapper applied around a pseudonymous Bitcoin transaction. This again explains why anonymity is not the main property needed from CCs as an illicit payment mechanism - as long as anonymity can be achieved elsewhere as part of the process.

In fact, the increasing difficulties of cashing in/out, arguably brought on by improving regulation of legitimate CC services, has deterred some illicit activity. One author describes being put off from selling on the dark net due to this difficulty of cashing out. There is a further interesting paradox to consider about the efficacy of bans. Currently, most illicit transactions have a connection to legitimate services. This brings opportunity for enforcement. However, a ban would likely push users to illicit mechanisms and reduce some of these opportunities. Cash can be sent in the mail or deposited into a bank account. Or legitimate mechanisms would be used fraudulently, such as registering for services using fake identification. These methods are harder to stop and arguably leave less opportunity for enforcement. In this way, a ban would reduce opportunity for legitimate users and merely push illicit activity towards other established mechanisms that are harder to control. Dark net market activity would be temporarily affected but users would likely soon find alternatives, as they have done after Liberty Reserve ceased or the repeated closure of markets themselves. Legitimate services drain liquidity away from illicit methods, making them rarer and harder to use.

Finally, policy makers must consider whether they could even achieve a ban. The nature of CCs means that they cannot be shut down as easily as a centralised service like Liberty Reserve. And as long as a decentralised CC system persists, there is little that can be done about individuals meeting in the real-world to trade CCs for cash, for example. As one author puts it, criminals could still use Bitcoin if it was banned and only ordinary users would be affected. Another writes that Bitcoin is simple for legitimate activity but hard for illicit. Regulated exchanges combined with a transparent record of transactions make illicit payments harder. On this point, an author writes that analysis of the Bitcoin blockchain has been central to all dark net market prosecution and that, if you use Bitcoin, you must ensure that every aspect of your operational security is infallible. In another post, the author decries the hype around CCs or that they are revolutionary to simply say that they are just a useful tool to transact with, like other monies. CCs are, then, useful for illicit activity as they are a useful payment mechanism. But it is too simple to say they are 'great' for criminals - there is far more to consider in terms of their usage. They are a tool among many, as the taxonomy shows, but as an individual mechanism, they come with significant disadvantages to the illicit actor.

6.4   Dark Nets Are Hard

A recent research paper that also analysed CrimeBB came to the conclusion that 'cybercrime is (often) boring' [41]. To this, we add that cybercrime, particularly on the dark net, is hard. The dark net is fraught with risk – scammers abound, and law enforcement action has been successful to an extent. The taxonomy shows that there is a significant educational and technical barrier in order to illicitly transact relatively securely on the internet. Even for a careless user, the minimum required to use the dark net is a computer with Tor set up, a delivery address and a working knowledge and possession of CCs. We contend, therefore, that dark net markets are a niche and are unlikely to grow significantly in comparison to traditional counterparts. The dark net may reduce risk in acquiring narcotics, for example, but it is arguably much easier, as some of the authors claim, to get cash and buy drugs in the real-world. Dark net markets only cater for a small volume of overall crime [8] – the threat should not be overexaggerated.

There are countless guides and posts on the underground and dark net forums discussing how to conduct illicit transactions. Even just the payment mechanism part of the taxonomy requires substantial knowledge. Users must also keep up with changing methodologies as services come and go, regulation tightens, and behaviours evolve. One author describes studying for many months before being able to start selling on a market. Another author tells of mental exhaustion from researching how to buy. The author thought it would be simple, perhaps as easy as 'pushing a button' - the reality was the opposite. There is no better example of this than the Dark Net Market's Buyer Bible [49]. This is a guide written for users wanting to purchase on dark net markets – it is 133 pages long. We cannot discuss the Bible or the taxonomy in full detail from a buyer's or seller's perspective as it would be too long but here follows a few items that highlight some of the complexity involved: use a non-windows, Linux based machine for a specialist operating system such as Tails or Whonix on a portable media (USB/CD), acquire a VPN service anonymously, learn to use PGP for encryption, use pre-installed IP tables as needed, disable JavaScript in the browser, get onion addresses from a reputable website, use a self-destructing messaging service, acquire BTC using cash from an ATM using a disguise and burner phone, convert Bitcoin to Monero using a non-exchange wallet… Advice for sellers is even more exhausting.

This also shows why privacy coins are not a panacea for anonymity. The user must acquire the Monero, for example, most probably with Bitcoin. Websites exist to highlight services such as VPN providers and decentralised exchanges that aid in anonymity [50]. For example, a popular service on CrimeBB is xmr.to, which will send Bitcoin to a recipient in exchange for Monero. Or morphtoken.com which exchanges cryptocurrencies e.g. Monero for Bitcoin. However, even with these tools a user still needs to cash in/out, plus do every other part of the taxonomy securely. It is a difficult task.

We must also consider the environment of the dark net itself. One user from the early days commented on how much more difficult it had become. Whilst there was early disdain about law enforcement capability, authors now acknowledge much improvement since the Silk Road market. There is evidence of some fear of law enforcement activity. However, an author notes in 2014 that arrest is more likely in the real-world. As such, the view remains that buyers of small amounts have little to worry about. The extent of deterrence on the dark net is therefore limited. Operation has become more difficult, but buyers do not think there is much chance of law enforcement interest in their activities. The role that Bitcoin analysis has played in prosecution is known but sellers continue, believing that they can operate if they take sufficient precaution. Recent views from 2019, though, show that marketplaces are hard to trust and often disappear after short periods. This all leads to a sense of containment if nothing else, as authors hope for improved days based on innovation using new technologies. The desire for a truly decentralised marketplace using Monero is there to see. There is a paradox here, that every law enforcement success leads to a Darwinian hardening of the system, which one day could leave little in way of enforcement opportunity.

To finish this section, we consider the words from three final posts. One author reminds readers that even if you do everything right (according to the taxonomy), using the dark net still requires trust and 'hope'. Hope that someone else has not done something to compromise your security, such as a seller that is caught who has not deleted customer addresses. Another reminds that people make errors and security cannot be applied retrospectively. You must get everything right from the beginning, which is difficult and can lead to silly mistakes getting you caught (as in the case of Ross Ulbricht). This leads us to the final comment, that the dark net appears to be easy and safe to use – but it isn't. It is a risky domain and it requires a lot of research and capability to use it relatively securely. And for these reasons, it is not for everyone.

7 Discussion

7.1 Implications for Policy

This paper challenges the notion that the main advantage of using CCs for illicit activity is anonymity. Users adopted CCs because they were a useful tool that solved real-world problems. Finality was the property most sought. Policy makers should recognise the issues people had that led to this adoption. It is important that traditional systems are inclusive and fair to all; they should not drive users to alternative choices.

Banning CCs is unlikely to do more than disrupt illicit internet activity. If anything, this reduces opportunity for legitimate use, pushes liquidity to illicit methods and reduces law enforcement opportunity by reducing contact with regulated systems. There are many other payment mechanisms that could be used for illicit activity; some, such as cash, are even harder to monitor than CCs. A ban would also likely be ineffective due to the decentralised nature of CC systems.

Law enforcement action has contained dark net activity and created a degree of deterrence, but little at the small buyer level. For these buyers, research shows that the dark net may reduce harm. Policy makers must also consider the evolutionary nature of markets and the impact that future technology could have on law enforcement impact.

Illicit internet activity is hard to achieve relatively securely, as the taxonomy shows. Dark net markets are therefore a niche and are unlikely to explode in size. The creators of Silk Road and AlphaBay markets were not from traditional crime groups. Policy should consider the threat that the dark net measurably poses and react accordingly. There is a danger that headlines make it seem more of a threat than it is. It is unlikely that dark net markets will capture significant shares of real-world counterparts.

7.2 Limitations

CrimeBB covers limited periods for each forum, meaning there is a wide range in the amount of material available. It is, though, a fantastic resource and our thanks go to CCC for their efforts in making this dataset available. It reduces many problems associated with research in this domain.

Particular care was taken in choosing search terms and using a content analysis method enabled themes to emerge naturally. As a qualitative study, we do not claim to 'prove' our findings but justify them based on the reading that emerged. We would have liked to have used quotations from posts to show the discussions that led to our results, but our ethical guidance advised against this. CrimeBB is, of course, available to other researchers should they wish to know more or to reproduce the results.

8 Conclusion and Future Work

This research addresses a gap in the literature by conducting the first user study of CCs for illicit activity. It also adds to the research on the dark net by focussing on payment mechanisms, rather than well-researched aspects such as harm or drug availability.

We present several significant findings that have implications for policy. Anonymity is not the main advantage of CCs for this user group, finality is. This challenges established assumptions and shows the value of qualitative research in this subject. Bitcoin is not as anonymous as cash but, in many respects, has proven to be the next best thing on the internet for illicit transactions. Is it great for criminals? The answer is a predictable yes and no. Yes, in that it proved to be a useful payment mechanism, offering finality and open access to those cut off from traditional finance; in the lexicon of TAM, it had a utility that led to adoption. No, in that using CCs for illicit activity is difficult, they are traceable and the dark net itself can be an inhospitable place. Even privacy coins do not solve the anonymity problem; users must still cash in and out and must also overcome significant barriers to use CCs relatively safely, as shown by the taxonomy. Finally, banning CCs is unlikely to be effective; determined users will switch to another payment mechanism, some of which are already established and proven. Or they will find a way to continue using CCs. The dark net is a niche; it is not an existential threat, and neither are CCs.

Society continues to wrestle with questions of liberty and security. 9/11 shifted us towards security and Snowden moved the dial back towards liberty. Debates about these issues and the question of balance between them endure - but we need to take care in our response to perceived threats [51]. Or, at the very least, continue to look for ways 'out of the impasse of security' [52]. We hope this study contributes to this aim.

References

1. mondovisione.com: New York State Department of Financial Services Superintendent Remarks at Columbia Law School (2015). https://m.mondovisione.com/. 30 June 2020
2. Rid, T.: Cyber war will not take place. J. Strateg. Stud. **35**(1), 5–32 (2012). https://doi.org/10.1080/01402390.2011.608939
3. Zetter, K.: FBI Fears Bitcoin's Popularity with Criminals. Wired (2012). https://www.wired.com/2012/05/fbi-fears-bitcoin/. Accessed 09 Jan 2019
4. Shi, M.M.: Fed Chair: Cryptocurrencies Are 'Great' For Money Laundering. Coindesk (2018). https://www.coindesk.com/fed-chair-cryptocurrencies-are-great-for-money-laundering. Accessed 09 Jan 2019
5. Rappeport, A., Popper, N.: Cryptocurrencies Pose National Security Threat, Mnuchin Says. The New York Times (2019). https://www.nytimes.com/2019/07/15/us/politics/mnuchin-facebook-libra-risk.html. Accessed 31 July 2019
6. Farrell, G., Larson, E.: Lawsky Says 'So Be It' If Transparency Harms Bitcoin. bloomberg.com (2013).
7. US Department of Justice: Department of Financial Services Hearing on Law Enforcement and Virtual Currencies (2014). https://www.justice.gov. Accessed 30 June 2020
8. Butler, S.: Criminal use of cryptocurrencies: a great new threat or is cash still king? J. Cyber Policy **4**(3), 326–345 (2019). https://doi.org/10.1080/23738871.2019.1680720
9. Dodd, N.: The social life of Bitcoin. Theory Cult. Soc. **35**(3), 35–56 (2017). https://doi.org/10.1177/0263276417746464
10. Karlstrøm, H.: Do libertarians dream of electric coins? The material embeddedness of Bitcoin. Distinktion J. Soc. Theory **15**(1), 23–36 (2014). https://doi.org/10.1080/1600910X.2013.870083
11. Bashir, M., Strickland, B., Bohr, J.: What motivates people to use Bitcoin? In: Spiro, E., Ahn, Y.-Y. (eds.) SocInfo 2016. LNCS, vol. 10047, pp. 347–367. Springer, Cham (2016). https://doi.org/10.1007/978-3-319-47874-6_25
12. Abramova, S., Böhme, R.: Perceived benefit and risk as multidimensional determinants of bitcoin use: a quantitative exploratory study. In: Proceedings of Thirty-Seventh International Conference on Information Systems (ICIS 2016), pp. 1–20, December 2016
13. Alshamsi, A., Andras, P.P.: User perception of Bitcoin usability and security across novice users. Int. J. Hum. Comput. Stud. **126**, 94–110 (2019). https://doi.org/10.1016/J.IJHCS.2019.02.004
14. Hayes, A.: The socio-technological lives of Bitcoin. Theory Cult. Soc. **36**(4), 49–72 (2019). https://doi.org/10.1177/0263276419826218
15. Bohr, J., Bashir, M.: Who uses Bitcoin? An exploration of the Bitcoin community. In: 2014 Twelfth Annual International Conference on Privacy, Security and Trust, pp. 94–101 (2014). https://doi.org/10.1109/PST.2014.6890928

16. Maurer, B., Nelms, T.C., Swartz, L.: "When perhaps the real problem is money itself!" The practical materiality of Bitcoin Soc. Semiot. **23**(2), 261–277 (2013). https://doi.org/10.1080/10350330.2013.777594
17. Roussou, I., Stiakakis, E.: Adoption of digital currencies by companies in the European Union: a research model combining DOI and TAM. In: 4th International Conference on Contemporary Marketing Issues (2016)
18. Shahzad, F., Xiu, G., Wang, J., Shahbaz, M.: An empirical investigation on the adoption of cryptocurrencies among the people of mainland China. Technol. Soc. **55**, 33–40 (2018). https://doi.org/10.1016/J.TECHSOC.2018.05.006
19. Mendoza-Tello, J.C., Mora, H., Pujol-López, F.A., Lytras, M.D.: Social commerce as a driver to enhance trust and intention to use cryptocurrencies for electronic payments. IEEE Access **6**, 50737–50751 (2018). https://doi.org/10.1109/ACCESS.2018.2869359
20. Gao, X., Clark, G.D., Lindqvist, J.: Of two minds, multiple addresses, and one ledger: characterizing opinions, knowledge, and perceptions of Bitcoin across users and non-users. In: Proceedings of the 2016 CHI Conference on Human Factors in Computing Systems (2016). https://doi.org/10.1145/2858036.2858049
21. Krombholz, K., Judmayer, A., Gusenbauer, M., Weippl, E.: The other side of the coin: user experiences with Bitcoin security and privacy. In: Grossklags, J., Preneel, B. (eds.) FC 2016. LNCS, vol. 9603, pp. 555–580. Springer, Heidelberg (2017). https://doi.org/10.1007/978-3-662-54970-4_33
22. Baur, A.W., Bühler, J., Bick, M., Bonorden, C.S.: Cryptocurrencies as a disruption? Empirical findings on user adoption and future potential of bitcoin and co. In: Janssen, M., et al. (eds.) I3E 2015. LNCS, vol. 9373, pp. 63–80. Springer, Cham (2015). https://doi.org/10.1007/978-3-319-25013-7_6
23. Presthus, W., O'Malley, N.O.: Motivations and barriers for end-user adoption of bitcoin as digital currency. Procedia Comput. Sci. **121**, 89–97 (2017). https://doi.org/10.1016/j.procs.2017.11.013
24. Sas, C., Khairuddin, I.E.: Exploring trust in bitcoin technology: a framework for HCI research. In: Proceedings of the Annual Meeting of the Australian Special Interest Group for Computer Human Interaction, pp. 338–342 (2015). https://doi.org/10.1145/2838739.2838821
25. Tsanidis, C., Nerantzaki, D.M., Karavasilis, G., Vrana, V., Paschaloudis, D.: Greek consumers and the use of Bitcoin. Bus. Manag. Rev. **6**, 30–31 (2015)
26. Aldridge, J., Stevens, A., Barratt, M.J.: Will growth in cryptomarket drug buying increase the harms of illicit drugs? Addiction **113**(5), 789–796 (2018). https://doi.org/10.1111/add.13899
27. Barratt, M.J., Ferris, J.A., Winstock, A.R.: Safer scoring? Cryptomarkets, social supply and drug market violence. Int. J. Drug Policy **35**, 24–31 (2016). https://doi.org/10.1016/j.drugpo.2016.04.019
28. Kethineni, S., Cao, Y., Dodge, C.: Use of bitcoin in darknet markets: examining facilitative factors on bitcoin-related crimes. Am. J. Crim. Justice **43**(2), 141–157 (2017). https://doi.org/10.1007/s12103-017-9394-6
29. Ladegaard, I.: We know where you are, what you are doing and we will catch you: Testing deterrence theory in digital drug markets. Br. J. Criminol. **58**(2), 414–433 (2018). https://doi.org/10.1093/bjc/azx021
30. Holt, T.J.: Identifying gaps in the research literature on illicit markets on-line. Glob. Crime **18**(1), 1–10 (2017)
31. Bancroft, A., Scott Reid, P.: Challenging the techno-politics of anonymity: the case of cryptomarket users. Info. Commun. Soc. **20**(4), 497–512 (2016). https://doi.org/10.1080/1369118X.2016.1187643
32. Paquet-Clouston, M., Haslhofer, B., Dupont, B.: Ransomware payments in the bitcoin ecosystem. Papers Presented to 17th Annual Workshop on the Economics of Information Security, Innsbruck, Austria, 18–19 June 2018 (2018). https://doi.org/10.1016/j.specom.2007.01.008

33. Gehl, R.W.: Archives for the dark web: a field guide for study. In: levenberg, l., Neilson, T., Rheams, D. (eds.) Research Methods for the Digital Humanities, pp. 31–51. Springer International Publishing, Cham (2018). https://doi.org/10.1007/978-3-319-96713-4_3

34. Barratt, M.J., Maddox, A.: Active engagement with stigmatised communities through digital ethnography. Qual. Res. **16**(6), 701–719 (2016). https://doi.org/10.1177/1468794116648766

35. Pastrana, S., Thomas, D.R., Hutchings, A., Clayton, R.: CrimeBB: enabling cybercrime research on underground forums at scale. In: Proceedings of the 2018 World Wide Web Conference (WWW 2018). Republic and Canton of Geneva, Switzerland, pp. 1845–1854 (2018). https://doi.org/10.1145/3178876.3186178

36. Caines, A., Pastrana, S., Hutchings, A., Buttery, P.J.: Automatically identifying the function and intent of posts in underground forums. Crime Sci. **7** (2018). Article number: 19. https://doi.org/10.1186/s40163-018-0094-4

37. Pastrana, S., Hutchings, A., Thomas, D., Tapiador, J.: Measuring eWhoring. In: Proceedings of the Internet Measurement Conference (IMC 2019), pp. 463–477. ACM, New York (2019). https://doi.org/10.1145/3355369.3355597

38. Thomas, D.R., Pastrana, S., Hutchings, A., Clayton, R., Beresford, A.R.: Ethical issues in research using datasets of illicit origin. In: IMC 2017: Proceedings of the Internet Measurement Conference, pp. 445–462. Association for Computing Machinery (ACM), New York (2017)

39. Pastrana, S., Hutchings, A., Caines, A., Buttery, P.: Characterizing eve: analysing cybercrime actors in a large underground forum. In: Bailey, M., Holz, T., Stamatogiannakis, M., Ioannidis, S. (eds.) RAID 2018. LNCS, vol. 11050, pp. 207–227. Springer, Cham (2018). https://doi.org/10.1007/978-3-030-00470-5_10

40. Hutchings, A., Pastrana, S.: Understanding eWhoring. In: Proceedings of 4th IEEE European Symposium on Security and Privacy, EURO S and P 2019, pp. 201–214 (2019). https://doi.org/10.1109/EuroSP.2019.00024

41. Collier, B., Clayton, R., Hutchings, A., Thomas, D.R.: Cybercrime is (often) boring: maintaining the infrastructure of cybercrime economies. In: Workshop on the Economics of Information Security (2020). https://doi.org/10.17863/CAM.53769

42. Bryman, A.: Social Research Methods, 4th edn. Oxford University Press, Oxford (2012)

43. Markham, A., Buchanan, E.: Ethical decision-making and internet research: recommendations from the AoIR ethics working committee (Version 2.0) (2012)

44. Sugiura, L.: Researching Online Forums (2017)

45. BSC: British Society of Criminology Statement of Ethics 2015 (2015)

46. The University of Sheffield: Research Involving Illegal Activities (2018)

47. Anderson, R.: Closing the Phishing Hole-Fraud, Risk and Nonbanks (2007)

48. bitinfocharts.com: Monero Transactions Chart (2020). https://bitinfocharts.com/comparison/monero-transactions.html. Accessed 03 July 2020

49. Anon: Dark Net Market's Buyer Bible (2018)

50. KYCNOT.ME: Exchanges (2020). https://kycnot.me/. Accessed 29 June 2020

51. Amoore, L., De. Goede, M.: Governance, risk and dataveillance in the war on terror. Law Soc. Change **43**, 149–173 (2005). https://doi.org/10.1007/s10611-005-1717-8

52. Neocleous, M.: Critique of Security. Edinburgh University Press, Edinburgh (2008)

Self-Governing Public Decentralised Systems
Work in Progress

Moritz Platt[(✉)] and Peter McBurney

Department of Informatics, King's College London, London, UK
{moritz.platt,peter.mcburney}@kcl.ac.uk

Abstract. The selection of members responsible for data replication is a challenge in decentralised record-keeping systems. In 'permissioned' systems, this crucial task is performed by a central authority or consortium. In 'permissionless' systems, however, the selection process is not trivial and comes with risks. Malicious actors, in a privileged position, can tamper with data, threatening the integrity of the system as a whole. Permissionless membership selection protocols, popularised with the dissemination of distributed ledger technology, have the objective of limiting the influence of a single entity on the wider network. They do so by approximating a participant's legitimacy to participate in record maintenance. These approximations come with downsides, in terms of attackability, system performance, supported use-cases and resource requirements. In this paper, we propose a prototypical membership selection protocol that uses the measure of personhood as an approximation of legitimacy. Interpreting a decentralised system as a political system, we frame the membership selection problem as one of political representation. We propose a protocol that democratically attributes a personhood score to members, thus creating a self-governing public decentralised system. This work in progress lays out a roadmap for the formal evaluation of self-governing public decentralised systems and describes the anticipated challenges in their implementation. Our proposals provide a means to evolve the membership selection protocol when a closed, permissioned system evolves to an open, permissionless system, as several commercial platforms intend to do.

Keywords: Socio-technical systems · Self-governance · Distributed ledger technology · Blockchain · Decentralisation · Consensus · Permissionless networks · Membership selection

1 Introduction

A challenge that any decentralised record-keeping system, that operates in a potentially-distrusting environment, faces is how to select members to perform

We are grateful for financial support from the UK EPSRC VOLT Project, grant number EP/P031811/1. We thank the anonymous reviewers whose comments helped to improve this manuscript.

© Springer Nature Switzerland AG 2021
T. Groß and L. Viganò (Eds.): STAST 2020, LNCS 12812, pp. 154–167, 2021.
https://doi.org/10.1007/978-3-030-79318-0_9

validation of records and record evolvement. Building on earlier work in distributed system design, the peer-to-peer electronic cash system 'Bitcoin' [37] solved this membership selection problem, bringing with it a new paradigm of decentralised record-keeping based on 'proof-of-work' (cf. Sect. 2.1). It is distinguished from earlier approaches by being truly permissionless, in the sense that 'any network participant has the ability to create a candidate record' [44, p. 61]. This paradigm laid the foundation for a variety of similar protocols. Addressing the challenge of preventing illegitimate updates to shared data, by nefarious actors, is the main contribution underlying Nakamoto's work. Proof-of-work based protocols have been widely criticised for their environmental impact [13,35] and for poor throughput characteristics when compared to centralised systems [11].

Recognising these shortcomings, alternative approaches for selecting participants in public decentralised systems have been proposed. These are commonly differentiated by their trust assumption, i.e. whether the protocol gives certain entities, on a network, extended permissions in the membership selection process [38, p. 7]. Given that these selection processes often resemble votes, parallels to the political realm are obvious. Following this line of thought, it can be speculated that membership selection in decentralised systems follows mechanisms similar to those present in archetypes of self-governance. This paper evaluates whether self-governance could provide inspiration for a novel membership selection protocol, that combines the advantages of different degrees of openness in the membership selection process of a decentralised system.

2 State of the Art

Fault-tolerance of distributed systems has been part of the research agenda in computer science for a long time. Among the early findings, most relevant to self-governing public decentralised systems[1], is the work of Lamport et al. [28]. They show how a decentralised system behaves when actors spread incorrect or conflicting information, or withhold information. They describe how a system tolerates a limited fraction of these actors, often referred to as 'byzantine' actors. Douceur [15] makes another instrumental finding, showing how a 'single faulty entity', often referred to as a 'sybil' actor, can gain control of a redundant network by 'presenting multiple identities'.

In the absence of an overseeing authority with special privileges, public decentralised systems must be able to rely on the adherence of the majority of their members to the system's protocol. While redundancy allows systems to tolerate a proportion of 'byzantine' actors, 'sybil' actors can never be tolerated. Unsurprisingly, most of the research in distributed ledger technology revolves around these two concepts.

Hellwig et al. [22] define the terms 'anonymity' and 'pseudonymity' in the context of cryptocurrencies, describing anonymous transactions as those that

---

[1] This section only discusses approaches that are relevant to self-governing systems. Bach et al. [1] and Natoli et al. [38] provide comprehensive surveys of beyond this.

'do not require a name' and pseudonymous transactions as transactions in which 'a false name is used'. This is reflected by the use of 'addresses', self-created pseudonymous identifiers, that are easy to generate within a very large address space. Pseudonymity on cryptocurrency networks is infamously heavily abused [25].

2.1 Proof-of-Work

In his work on the Bitcoin protocol, Nakamoto [37] formalised the need for consensus on two dimensions; the validity of blocks (i.e. the comprehensive validity of all transactions in a block) and the ordering of blocks. The predominant goal of the consensus algorithm, in this protocol, is to counteract the 'double-spend problem', a well-known problem in the realm of electronic payments, that allows dishonest actors (in the absence of a control mechanism) to over-spend their funds. Solutions to this problem were proposed much earlier but encompassed a pre-defined actor (or set of actors) to assume the role of trusted third party [9], or required tamper-proof hardware [50]. Thus, pre-proof-of-work payment systems relied on a permissioned approach, in which certain participants (e.g. banks or payment system operators) had special privileges.

Nakamoto's contribution was to introduce a permissionless approach to membership selection. The goal of membership selection in Bitcoin is to select a 'miner' to validate the transactional data and act as an ordering authority, immutably linking the current set of transactions with all previous sets. This problem can't be solved by selecting actors randomly, since they are not uniquely identifiable on a network, in fact, they can generate arbitrary numbers of pseudonyms, making a random selection highly susceptible to 'Sybil Attacks'. These are attacks in which a single malicious entity presents multiple identities [15], thus improving their chances of being selected. The main purpose of proof-of-work in membership selection is to create an environment in which a participant ('miner') is incentivised to act honestly. The Bitcoin protocol, similar to other proof-of-work protocols, is designed to be incentive-compatible, i.e. it should accomplish its goal of evolving the decentralised data correctly, if all participants follow the rules and are capable of handling the informational requirements [16]. This is based on the assumption that those who expended computing resources, by participating in proof-of-work, have an incentive not to introduce incorrect data because they would otherwise threaten the value of their reward.

Along with Bitcoin, numerous other decentralised record-keeping systems, specifically cryptocurrencies, utilise proof-of-work protocols [36]. Proof-of-work systems have been found to be 'dreaded with various attacks' with 'robust and practical security solutions' to those being absent [10]. Attacks can roughly be divided into two classes; 'Goldfinger' attacks [27], where adversaries seek to disrupt the validation of records and record evolement on a public distributed system (e.g. double-spending [24] or brute-force attacks [23]), and attacks that do not threaten the system as a whole but lead to financial gain or loss for individual participants in the protocol (e.g. refund attacks [34], transaction malleability [51] or denial-of-service attacks against participants [49]).

2.2   Proof-of-Stake

Deuber *et al.* [13] names avoiding 'computational waste' as the main motivation for the blockchain community to research alternatives to proof-of-work. King and Nadal [26] proposed 'ppcoin', a peer-to-peer cryptocurrency, with proof-of-stake, taking inspiration from earlier discussions of the concept among Bitcoin circles [43]. In their design, being able to prove ownership of currency, along with proving how long it has been held, will determine the difficulty of creating a new block, thus making those participants who have held larger quantities of currency for longer more influential in record evolvement. Compared to proof-of-work, this shifts the responsibility of maintaining and evolving decentralised data from those who invest computing resources to those who hold the most currency.

This fundamentally changes the incentives for behaving dishonestly. Gui *et al.* [20] show that proof-of-stake is less vulnerable to both double-spending attacks and sabotage attacks than proof-of-work. Li *et al.* [30] discuss how this new paradigm has brought with it new forms of attacks; specifically, 'nothing at stake' attacks, where malicious validators generate conflicting blocks to slow down consensus time and 'long range' attacks in which malicious actors create forks from historic blocks, allowing them to form longer chains, based on an out-dated view of stake. A notable proof-of-stake protocol is 'Algorand', which 'assigns weights to users proportionally to the monetary value they have in the system' [18]. Thin *et al.* [47] verified that 'Tendermint', an exemplary proof-of-stake protocol, can reach consensus when at least $\frac{2}{3}$ of a proof-of-stake network are in agreement. The 'Ethereum' blockchain, utilising a proof-of-work approach from inception, is planned to migrate to a 'proof of stake-based finality system which overlays an existing proof of work blockchain' [6] with the next version of the platform.

2.3   Delegated Proof-of-Stake

Larimer [29] proposed a variation to proof-of-stake, introducing a delegation scheme, in which 'shareholders may delegate their voting power to a representative'. This delegation is implemented via proxy signatures [4]. Delegating the right to validate and evolve records to other participants is useful in an environment where there is a majority of participants that are not interested in, or capable of, providing validation. Delegated proof-of-stake has been considered a suitable building block for election-based protocols, such as 'Snow White' [12], a protocol that supports committee reconfiguration and remains robust in the presence of sporadic participation.

2.4   Proof-of-Personhood

Borge *et al.* [5] show how, by conducting 'pseudonym parties', 'sybil attacks' (cf. Sect. 2) can be prevented. They use this as the foundation of the 'PoPCoin' protocol in which proving 'personhood', i.e. the existence as a human individual, grants membership on a network.

2.5   Proof-of-Authority

Permissionless membership selection (cf. Sects. 2.1–2.4) is not appropriate in all contexts. An environment in which anyone can create a candidate record is undesirable in scenarios where there is a need for limiting the audience or participation. Drivers for rejection of an open approach can be privacy concerns (i.e. who can access the data to be validated), or regulatory concerns (e.g. where regulatory requirements exist that govern who can partake in a certain activity). In such contexts, membership selection can be achieved by policy, i.e. through a pre-defined list of privileged members. The practice of employing a central party, or consortium, to decide who is allowed to perform record validation activities is known as 'proof-of-authority'. An example of an implementation of this approach is the 'Ripple Protocol Consensus Algorithm' [8], that employs a pre-defined 'Unique Node List' of trusted servers, with no facility for altering this list via the standard protocol. The transaction ordering and timestamping services described in the 'Corda' protocol operate similarly. Here, it is the responsibility of the network governing body to establish and maintain a list of notaries [21]. Facebook's 'Libra' payment system plans to adopt a similar approach, with a set of pre-approved validators [31].

2.6   Voting 'On-Ledger'

In addition to concerns of membership selection, voting can be conducted on-ledger, i.e. on top of an already-established system. It is important to note that e-voting can be conducted on-ledger, irrespective of the membership selection paradigm. That means that entities that engage in on-ledger voting do not necessarily have to be 'members', in the sense of the outlined membership selection paradigms.

Dhillon et al. [14] point out that large-scale decentralised online voting poses challenges around the governance of voting networks and delegations of votes. On a smaller scale, McCorry et al. [33] show how a 'self-tallying internet voting protocol with maximum voter privacy' can be implemented on top of the Ethereum blockchain. The voting functionality here is implemented 'top-of-Stack', i.e. the voters do not have to participate in proof-of-work (cf. Sect. 2.1) but can cast their votes via Ethereum transactions.

3   Problem Motivation

Some parallels can be drawn between membership selection methodologies, in decentralised systems, and processes of political representation that can be observed in the analogue world. The virtual constituency of those who can create candidate records, in a decentralised system (cf. Fig. 1), can be compared to a constituency in the political sense, albeit not a well-defined, stable state-level constituency, but a transnational fast-evolving one. This group can rely on the legal framework of the governing system to gain a high degree of certainty that the codified rules of the system will be enforced by the executive branch.

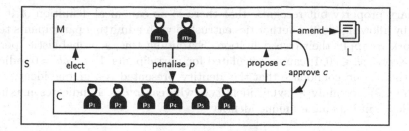

Fig. 1. A decentralised system S, comprised of regular participants $(p_{1..n})$ and participants with additional duties ('miners' $m_{1..n}$) who are appointed or elected to fulfil these duties. Participants propose candidate records, c, to be included in the entirety of public records. Miners decide, based on a legislative framework, L, whether a candidate record is permissible and, based on this evaluation, either approve it or, penalise the responsible participant for proposing an impermissible record.

The group of participants who validate candidate records, approve and evolve them, can be compared to a government, particularly the legislative and executive branches of government. Depending on the underlying membership protocol, miners are appointed (cf. Sect. 2.5) or elected (cf. Sects. 2.1–2.4) via probabilistic methods that roughly resemble a majority vote (e.g. the majority computing power in the case of proof-of-work, or the majority of funds in the case of proof-of-stake). Participants who create candidate records make these available to miners, who in turn validate that these are compliant with the legal framework. Should a candidate record be found to be compliant, miners will endorse it publicly. Should the candidate record found to be in breach of the framework, participants may be penalised. It can be assumed that the legislative framework is deterministic, meaning all honest miners will come to an identical conclusion on compliancy when evaluating a record[2].

4 Solution

The previous section shows how democratic political representation can be considered an archetype for member selection in decentralised systems. While numerous approaches have been developed to approximate democratic member selection (cf. Sect. 2), no scalable protocol to implement the democratic ideal of 'One Person/One Vote' in membership selection currently exists. This section shows how the reason for this is the difficulty of determining who should be considered eligible to vote, rather than the implementation of the voting protocol itself. It will employ the concept of 'personhood' as an approximation of eligibility, building on the definition of Borge *et al.* [5], who specify 'personhood' as the property of having a unique identity in the real world. We define personhood as

---

[2] Deterministic, automatically evaluable, 'smart contracts' [46] are a concept at the intersection of law and computer science. While natural language contracts require interpretation, computer language contracts are designed not to [7].

a binary property but recognise that there is no canonical definition of it [17], thereby allowing elected authorities entrusted with admitting participants to the network to apply their own definition. Extending this, a probabilistic 'personhood score' $ph \in [0, 1]$ can be calculated for participants. Here, $ph = 0$ indicates that there is no confidence that the identity presented is a unique identity (i.e. it is almost certainly a 'sybil' identity), whereas $ph = 1$ indicates maximum confidence in it being a unique identity.

4.1 'One Person/One Vote' in Delegated Proof-of-Stake

In a delegated proof-of-stake system S (cf. Sect. 2.3) members $p_{1..n}$ form a constituency C. They can delegate participation in the consensus protocol to other parties on the network, miners ($m_{1..n}$), thus approximating a vote. Since delegation privileges in this protocol are aligned with the currency holdings of the delegating party, this pattern corresponds to the 'One Share/One Vote' paradigm, well-known in the realm of corporate securities [19]. Given that delegated proof-of-stake effectively already implements a 'One *Share*/One Vote' paradigm, it can be easily restructured to support a 'One *Person*/One Vote' paradigm by introducing additional constraints to limit the number of shares and how they can circulate. These constraints could be introduced into 'system contracts'[3].

  i. Delegated proof-of-stake is performed using personhood tokens as stake.
 ii. Every person with voting rights on the network receives a fixed number of personhood tokens once they enter the network.
iii. There is no other source of personhood tokens.
 iv. Personhood tokens cannot be traded and are not given out as a reward.

4.2 Establishing Personhood

The requirements *i*, *iii* and *iv* of the previous section can easily be satisfied through minor modifications of existing protocols. An implementation could be forking existing delegated proof-of-stake protocol implementations (cf. Sect. 2.3) and changing validation code so that token movement becomes impermissible. The second requirement, however, raises a more significant problem. Here, it needs to be considered who should be admitted to the decentralised system, by whom and on what basis.

Gatekeeping Authority. A trivial solution to this problem is the introduction of a central 'gatekeeping authority' A. They could assign stake in the form of personhood tokens. Conceivably they would assign all participants $ph = 1$, having confidence in their onboarding process. A hypothetical protocol that implements this paradigm could require prospective participants to generate an address (cf.

---

[3] The term has been popularised by the 'EOS.IO' blockchain [3], where it is used to describe fundamental functionality of the core protocol that is not modifiable by individual users, as compared to user defined smart contracts.

Sect. 2) and to subsequently submit it to the authority along with proof of their identity. Should the identity information provided satisfy the requirements of the central authority, they would allocate voting right tokens and fund the address of the applicant.

This approach would effectively recreate a proof-of-authority protocol (cf. Sect. 2.5) with one centralised admitting entity. The shortcomings of this approach coincide with the shortcomings of a proof-of-authority protocol, namely, the fact that the governance structure needs to be determined at the inception of the network and can only be amended by the initiative of the admitting entity itself. This approach requires a permanently high degree of trust in the admitting entity.

Self-governed Evolving Constituencies. While a central gatekeeping approach is well-suited for cases in which few changes to the constituency of a system are to be anticipated, and in which the central authority is irrefutably trusted, it is inappropriate in a scenario in which the constituency is evolving. An evolving constituency is conceivable in self-governance scenarios, e.g. when a group of constituents choose to administer common resources through a joint governance process [40, 48], or when a group decides they require self-governance, for resolving grievances or making political decisions outside of a wider context governed by an external authority [41].

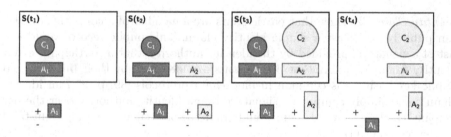

Fig. 2. A decentralised system S with a constituency that evolves over periods $t_{1..4}$. Initially, the first constituency C_1 is the only one to participate in delegated consensus on the network. They record their endorsement for identity authority A_1. In t_2 they also endorse authority A_2. Following this, in t_3, members endorsed by A_2 are on-boarded to the system. They endorse A_2. In the final period (t_4), a large number of participants discourage A_1, following which the value of the personhood tokens issued by them drops below the reputational threshold and C_1 loses their membership.

To replicate a self-governing structure in a decentralised system, the previously described 'gatekeeping' approach is a suitable point of departure. Conceptually, this means allowing multiple authorities $A_{1..n}$ in parallel. Delegated proof-of-stake protocols already bring all necessary technological primitives for voting, since delegation is a voting process in itself. Building on that, a second voting layer can be proposed. This voting layer would be responsible for the election of gatekeeping authorities into and out of the decentralised system.

As shown in Fig. 2, a decentralised system making use of evolving constituencies would be initialised with a 'genesis gatekeeping authority'[4]. This authority would act in the same way as described above, i.e. they would assign voting right tokens to members of the genesis constituency, following their principles of identity validation. The self-governing aspect would manifest itself by introducing new capabilities to the system:

1. Members of a constituency can endorse a gatekeeping authority on the network;
2. Members of a constituency can discourage a gatekeeping authority on the network.

The personhood score is relevant as it will determine the stake of a participant, i.e. how much voting power they can delegate to a miner of their choice. It also constitutes a weighting factor on an endorsement/discouragement. In a system utilising personhood scoring, participants would likely delegate their continuous participation in voting processes to agents acting on their behalf. Therefore, these systems would effectively constitute open agent societies that are likely to implement deliberative democracies, in which participants are both consumers of political information (i.e. the personhood scores of others) and producers of political information (by endorsing or discouraging authorities) [32].

Identity Claim. To show that participants are a member of a constituency, they can publicly broadcast a simple identity claim. This public record would consist of a signature, provided by the identity authority, that a participant claims identity from. Assuming that participants are identified by their public key, or public key hash, as is common in blockchain protocols [39, p. 25], an identity claim could simply comprise a signature by an identity authority over the participant's address. A valid claim would grant the participant a voting right token by the relevant authority.

Endorsement/Discouragement. As shown in the previous section, members can endorse or discourage gatekeeping authorities via a broadcast message. These actions directly impact the reputation of the authority and thus the personhood score the authority can grant. Per authority $A_{1..n}$ a vector of endorsement scores $e_{A_{1..n}}$ and a vector of discouragement scores $d_{A_{1..n}}$ are kept publicly. Participants add to either of the vectors via a message they broadcast. They can add at most one message to each vector. The value they add to the vector represents their personhood score as determined by the reputation of their gatekeeping authority. This means that the influence a participant can exert on the reputation of another authority is proportional to their reputation. This allows for basic arithmetic on the personhood score values of participants, depending on which

---

[4] The naming is inspired by the term 'genesis block', the genesis of the Bitcoin Blockchain.

constituency they belong to. A dampened personhood score (dph) depends on the reputation of the issuing authority: $dph = ||e||_1 / (||e||_1 + ||d||_1)$ if $||e||_1 + ||d||_1 > 0$, otherwise $dph = 0$. Here $||\cdot||_1$ denotes the L^1-norm. Consider an example of a network, with three identity authorities, $A_{1..3}$ with reputation of $A_1 = 0.8$ and $A_2 = 0.3$. Assuming that a member of A_1 has endorsed A_3 and a member of has A_2 discouraged A_3, the reputation value of A_3 would be $\frac{0.8}{0.8+0.3} \approx 0.7$. The reputational value of A_3 would be updated in the next iteration of the protocol.

Temporal Normalisation. A single malevolent authority can flood the network with sybil actors[5], who can disrupt any record-keeping and record-evolving activity on the network, permanently. Temporal normalisation can mitigate sybil attacks that go along with a sudden influx of bogus identities. Such attacks are likely to be preceded by an event in which a previously trustworthy private key is used to generate bogus identities on a network. This allows for participant's scores to increase over time. A time-normalised personhood score can be calculated using any normalisation function $f : [0,1] \times \mathbb{N} \mapsto [0,1]$, for example $f(dph, t) = dph \cdot (1 - \frac{1}{1+t})$, where dph is the personhood score of the participant at the current time and t is a measure of elapsed time, such as 'block height' added, since admission of the participant.

Constituency Size Ceilings. Assuming that attackers have perfect knowledge of the protocol and can therefore conduct attacks that take the maturing of personhood scores into account, the temporal normalisation approach alone cannot be effective. Under a reasonable temporal normalisation function, a large number of bogus identities can achieve a large cumulative time-normalised personhood score, even for small t. This makes the effectiveness of temporal normalisation dependent only on the rate at which attackers can create bogus identities. To counteract this phenomenon, an overall constituency size ceiling that limits the total number of identities, created by one authority, can be introduced. This can be a fixed value of maximum permissible identities issued per authority or a function that limits the permissible growth of the number of identities.

Diversity Dimension. In case of such a well-planned attack, the temporal and reputational safeguards would have limited effect. For these scenarios, a quantitative safeguard enforcing diversity should be introduced. This should give reputational signals from diverse sources more weight, thus potentially alleviating scenarios in which a large constituency of malicious actors is built up. Attackers can simulate diversity by creating multiple malicious sybil authorities. These newly established authorities would, however, be subject to the measures previously discussed, thereby limiting their influence.

Ousting. The result of removing an authority from a network has a notable side-effect: Any previous endorsements that any of the constituents of the ousted

---

[5] This is common in real-life, for example in the 2020 branch-stacking scandal in the Victorian branch of the Australian Labor Party, which led to resignations of senior ministers in the Victorian state government [42].

authority have made, become void once the authority is removed. Consequently, in a scenario where a malicious authority has constructed a tree-like endorsement structure to circumvent any of the safeguards discussed previously, child authorities will instantaneously lose the endorsement of the ousted parent's constituents.

Reputational Threshold. Once authorities are disproportionally discouraged on the network, they are likely to pose a threat to the integrity of the system. For this reason, deteriorating identity authorities should eventually lose all influence on the network, even if, in arithmetical terms, personhood tokens issued by them still hold value. To implement this, a lower bound for personhood scores can be introduced. Once an authority falls under that threshold, the personhood tokens issued by them would be devalued.

5   Conclusion and Future Work

In this paper, we have shown how a delegated proof-of-stake protocol can be evolved into a protocol supporting a self-governing public decentralised system. This supports the strategy of transitioning systems operated by a single entity to permissionless systems over time, which can be observed in major commercial blockchain initiatives [2, 45]. While, as a work in progress, the protocol proposed lacks formalisation, intuition suggests that the concept of evolving constituencies, backed by identity authorities, that can be added to and removed from a network dynamically, has merit. We have described how such an evolving system is more flexible than a proof-of-authority system, when constituencies change. We also outline how the protocol proposed might come closer to the ideal of 'one person/one vote' than other common approximations. We introduce a numeric 'personhood score', that allows for probabilistic calculations, taking into account the likelihood of a presented public key being the only identity of a given natural person. We anticipate attacks on such networks and show how damping of 'personhood scores' can mitigate those. Future work must focus on formalising the protocol to evaluate its robustness. A formal approach will ultimately prove or disprove its advantages over existing membership selection protocols, in the context of attacks.

References

1. Bach, L.M., Mihaljevic, B., Zagar, M.: Comparative analysis of blockchain consensus algorithms. In: Proceedings of the 41st International Convention on Information and Communication Technology, Electronics and Microelectronics, MIPRO 2018, Opatija, Croatia, pp. 1545–1550. IEEE (2018)
2. Baird, L., Harmon, M., Madsen, P.: Hedera: a public hashgraph network & Governing Council, September 2019. https://www.hedera.com/hh-whitepaper-v2.0-17Sep19.pdf. Accessed 22 Nov 2020
3. block.one: EOS.IO technical white paper (2018). https://github.com/EOSIO/Documentation/blob/master/TechnicalWhitePaper.md. Accessed 24 Aug 2020

4. Boldyreva, A., Palacio, A., Warinschi, B.: Secure proxy signature schemes for delegation of signing rights. J. Cryptol. **25**(1), 57–115 (2010). https://doi.org/10.1007/s00145-010-9082-x
5. Borge, M., Kokoris-Kogias, E., Jovanovic, P., Gasser, L., Gailly, N., Ford, B.: Proof-of-personhood: redemocratizing permissionless cryptocurrencies. In: Proceedings of the 2nd European Symposium on Security and Privacy Workshops, EuroS&P 2017, Paris, France, pp. 23–26. IEEE (2017)
6. Buterin, V., Griffith, V.: Casper the friendly finality gadget. arXiv e-prints arXiv:1710.09437, October 2017
7. Cannarsa, M.: Interpretation of contracts and smart contracts: smart interpretation or interpretation of smart contracts? Eur. Rev. Priv. Law **26**, 773–785 (2018)
8. Chase, B., MacBrough, E.: Analysis of the XRP ledger consensus protocol. arXiv e-prints arXiv:1802.07242, February 2018
9. Chaum, D., Fiat, A., Naor, M.: Untraceable electronic cash. In: Goldwasser, S. (ed.) CRYPTO 1988. LNCS, vol. 403, pp. 319–327. Springer, New York (1990). https://doi.org/10.1007/0-387-34799-2_25
10. Conti, M., Sandeep Kumar, E., Lal, C., Ruj, S.: A survey on security and privacy issues of Bitcoin. IEEE Commun. Surv. Tutor. **20**(4), 3416–3452 (2018)
11. Croman, K., et al.: On scaling decentralized blockchains. In: Clark, J., Meiklejohn, S., Ryan, P.Y.A., Wallach, D., Brenner, M., Rohloff, K. (eds.) FC 2016. LNCS, vol. 9604, pp. 106–125. Springer, Heidelberg (2016). https://doi.org/10.1007/978-3-662-53357-4_8
12. Daian, P., Pass, R., Shi, E.: Snow White: robustly reconfigurable consensus and applications to provably secure proof of stake. In: Goldberg, I., Moore, T. (eds.) FC 2019. LNCS, vol. 11598, pp. 23–41. Springer, Cham (2019). https://doi.org/10.1007/978-3-030-32101-7_2
13. Deuber, D., Döttling, N., Magri, B., Malavolta, G., Thyagarajan, S.A.K.: Minting mechanism for proof of stake blockchains. In: Conti, M., Zhou, J., Casalicchio, E., Spognardi, A. (eds.) ACNS 2020. LNCS, vol. 12146, pp. 315–334. Springer, Cham (2020). https://doi.org/10.1007/978-3-030-57808-4_16
14. Dhillon, A., Kotsialou, G., McBurney, P., Riley, L.: Voting over a distributed ledger: An interdisciplinary perspective, August 2020. https://doi.org/10.31235/osf.io/34df5
15. Douceur, J.R.: The Sybil attack. In: Druschel, P., Kaashoek, F., Rowstron, A. (eds.) IPTPS 2002. LNCS, vol. 2429, pp. 251–260. Springer, Heidelberg (2002). https://doi.org/10.1007/3-540-45748-8_24
16. Durlauf, S.N., Blume, L.E.: Incentive compatibility. In: Durlauf, S.N., Blume, L.E. (eds.) Game Theory, pp. 158–168. Palgrave Macmillan, London (2010)
17. Foster, C., Herring, J.: Theories of personhood. Identity, Personhood and the Law. SL, pp. 21–34. Springer, Cham (2017). https://doi.org/10.1007/978-3-319-53459-6_2
18. Gilad, Y., Hemo, R., Micali, S., Vlachos, G., Zeldovich, N.: Algorand. In: Proceedings of the 26th Symposium on Operating Systems Principles, SOSP 2017, Shanghai, China. ACM, October 2017
19. Grossman, S.J., Hart, O.D.: One share-one vote and the market for corporate control. J. Financ. Econ. **20**, 175–202 (1988)
20. Gui, G., Hortacsu, A., Tudon, J.: A memo on the proof-of-stake mechanism. arXiv e-prints arXiv:1807.09626, June 2018
21. Hearn, M., Brown, R.G.: Corda: A distributed ledger, August 2019. https://www.r3.com/wp-content/uploads/2019/08/corda-technical-whitepaper-August-29-2019.pdf. Accessed 24 Aug 2020

22. Hellwig, D., Karlic, G., Huchzermeier, A.: Privacy and anonymity. Build Your Own Blockchain. MP, pp. 99–121. Springer, Cham (2020). https://doi.org/10.1007/978-3-030-40142-9_5
23. Heusser, J.: SAT solving-an alternative to brute force bitcoin mining, February 2013. https://jheusser.github.io/2013/02/03/satcoin.html. Accessed 23 May 2020
24. Karame, G.O., Androulaki, E., Capkun, S.: Double-spending fast payments in Bitcoin. In: Proceedings of Conference on Computer and Communications Security, CCS 2012, Raleigh, NC, USA, pp. 906–917. ACM, New York (2012)
25. Kethineni, S., Cao, Y.: The rise in popularity of cryptocurrency and associated criminal activity. Int. Crim. Justice Rev. **30**, 325–344 (2019)
26. King, S., Nadal, S.: PPCoin: peer-to-peer crypto-currency with proof-of-stake, August 2012. https://decred.org/research/king2012.pdf. Accessed 19 Jan 2020
27. Kroll, J.A., Davey, I.C., Felten, E.W.: The economics of Bitcoin mining, or Bitcoin in the presence of adversaries. In: Proceedings of the 12th Workshop on the Economics of Information Security, WEIS 2013, Washington, D.C., USA, vol. 2013, p. 11 (2013)
28. Lamport, L., Shostak, R., Pease, M.: The Byzantine generals problem. ACM Trans. Program. Lang. Syst. **4**(3), 382–401 (1982)
29. Larimer, D.: Delegated proof-of-stake (DPOS) (2014). http://107.170.30.182/security/delegated-proof-of-stake.php. Accessed 3 May 2018
30. Li, W., Andreina, S., Bohli, J.-M., Karame, G.: Securing proof-of-stake blockchain protocols. In: Garcia-Alfaro, J., Navarro-Arribas, G., Hartenstein, H., Herrera-Joancomartí, J. (eds.) ESORICS/DPM/CBT-2017. LNCS, vol. 10436, pp. 297–315. Springer, Cham (2017). https://doi.org/10.1007/978-3-319-67816-0_17
31. Libra Association Members: The Libra payment system, April 2020. https://libra.org/en-US/wp-content/uploads/sites/23/2020/04/Libra_WhitePaperV2_April2020.pdf. Accessed 8 July 2020
32. McBurney, P., Parsons, S.: Engineering democracy in open agent systems. In: Omicini, A., Petta, P., Pitt, J. (eds.) ESAW 2003. LNCS (LNAI), vol. 3071, pp. 66–80. Springer, Heidelberg (2004). https://doi.org/10.1007/978-3-540-25946-6_4
33. McCorry, P., Shahandashti, S.F., Hao, F.: A smart contract for boardroom voting with maximum voter privacy. In: Kiayias, A. (ed.) FC 2017. LNCS, vol. 10322, pp. 357–375. Springer, Cham (2017). https://doi.org/10.1007/978-3-319-70972-7_20
34. Miller, A.: Feather-forks: enforcing a blacklist with sub-50% hash power (2013). https://bitcointalk.org/index.php?topic=312668.0. Accessed 29 Sept 2020
35. Mora, C., et al.: Bitcoin emissions alone could push global warming above 2°c. Nat. Clim. Change **8**(11), 931–933 (2018)
36. Mukhopadhyay, U., Skjellum, A., Hambolu, O., Oakley, J., Yu, L., Brooks, R.: A brief survey of cryptocurrency systems. In: Proceedings of the 14th Annual Conference on Privacy, Security and Trust, PST, Auckland, New Zealand, pp. 745–752 (2016). https://doi.org/10.1109/PST.2016.7906988
37. Nakamoto, S.: Bitcoin: a peer-to-peer electronic cash system (2008). https://bitcoin.org/bitcoin.pdf. Accessed 22 Nov 2020
38. Natoli, C., Yu, J., Gramoli, V., Esteves-Verissimo, P.: Deconstructing blockchains: a comprehensive survey on consensus, membership and structure. arXiv e-prints arXiv:1908.08316, August 2019
39. Orman, H.: Blockchain: the emperors new PKI? IEEE Internet Comput. **22**(2), 23–28 (2018)
40. Ostrom, E.: Self-governance and forest resources. Occasional Paper 20, Center for International Forestry Research (CIFOR), February 1999. https://www.cifor.org/publications/pdf_files/OccPapers/OP-20.pdf. Accessed 22 Nov 2020

41. Ostrom, E., Walker, J., Gardner, R.: Covenants with and without a sword: self-governance is possible. Am. Polit. Sci. Rev. **86**(2), 404–417 (1992)
42. Patrick, A., Marin-Guzman, D.: Everyone knew what was going on. The Australian Financial Review, June 2020
43. QuantumMechanic: Proof of stake instead of proof of work, July 2011. https://bitcointalk.org/index.php?topic=27787.0. Accessed 22 May 2020
44. Rauchs, M., et al.: Distributed ledger technology systems. A conceptual framework, August 2018. https://www.jbs.cam.ac.uk/wp-content/uploads/2020/08/2018-10-26-conceptualising-dlt-systems.pdf. Accessed 19 Jan 2020
45. Shehar, B., et al.: Moving toward permissionless consensus, June 2019. https://libra.org/wp-content/uploads/2019/06/MovingTowardPermissionlessConsensus_en_US.pdf. Accessed 22 Nov 2020
46. Szabo, N.: Formalizing and securing relationships on public networks. First Monday **2**(9) (1997). https://doi.org/10.5210/fm.v2i9.548
47. Thin, W.Y.M.M., Dong, N., Bai, G., Dong, J.S.: Formal analysis of a proof-of-stake blockchain. In: Proceedings of the 23rd International Conference on Engineering of Complex Computer Systems, ICECCS 2018, Melbourne, Australia. IEEE, December 2018
48. Townsend, R.E.: Fisheries self-governance: corporate or cooperative structures? Mar. Policy **19**(1), 39–45 (1995)
49. Vasek, M., Thornton, M., Moore, T.: Empirical analysis of denial-of-service attacks in the Bitcoin ecosystem. In: Böhme, R., Brenner, M., Moore, T., Smith, M. (eds.) FC 2014. LNCS, vol. 8438, pp. 57–71. Springer, Heidelberg (2014). https://doi.org/10.1007/978-3-662-44774-1_5
50. Waidner, M., Pfitzmann, B.: Loss-tolerance for electronic wallets. In: Proceedings of the 20th International Symposium Fault-Tolerant Computing, Newcastle Upon Tyne, UK, pp. 140–147. IEEE (1990)
51. Wuille, P.: Dealing with malleability (2014). https://github.com/bitcoin/bips/blob/master/bip-0062.mediawiki. Accessed 29 Sept 2020

Reflections on Socio-Technical Aspects of Security

Statistical Reliability of 10 Years of Cyber Security User Studies

Thomas Groß[✉]

School of Computing, Newcastle University, Newcastle upon Tyne, UK
thomas.gross@newcastle.ac.uk

Abstract. Background. In recent years, cyber security user studies have been appraised in meta-research, mostly focusing on the completeness of their statistical inferences and the fidelity of their statistical reporting. However, estimates of the field's distribution of statistical power and its publication bias have not received much attention.

Aim. In this study, we aim to estimate the effect sizes and their standard errors present as well as the implications on statistical power and publication bias.

Method. We built upon a published systematic literature review of 146 user studies in cyber security (2006–2016). We took into account 431 statistical inferences including t-, χ^2-, r-, one-way F-tests, and Z-tests. In addition, we coded the corresponding total sample sizes, group sizes and test families. Given these data, we established the observed effect sizes and evaluated the overall publication bias. We further computed the statistical power vis-à-vis of parametrized population thresholds to gain unbiased estimates of the power distribution.

Results. We obtained a distribution of effect sizes and their conversion into comparable log odds ratios together with their standard errors. We, further, gained funnel-plot estimates of the publication bias present in the sample as well as insights into the power distribution and its consequences.

Conclusions. Through the lenses of power and publication bias, we shed light on the statistical reliability of the studies in the field. The upshot of this introspection is practical recommendations on conducting and evaluating studies to advance the field.

Keywords: User studies · SLR · Cyber security · Effect estimation · Statistical power · Publication bias · Winner's curse

1 Introduction

Cyber security user studies and quantitative studies in socio-technical aspects of security in general often rely on statistical inferences to make their case that

Open Science Framework: osf.io/bcyte. An extended version of this work is available on arXiv: https://arxiv.org/abs/2010.02117.

T. Groß and L. Viganò (Eds.): STAST 2020, LNCS 12812, pp. 171–190, 2021.
https://doi.org/10.1007/978-3-030-79318-0_10

observed effects are not down to chance. They are to separate the wheat from the chaff. Indeed, null hypothesis significance testing and p-values indicating statistical significance hold great sway in the community. While the studies in the field have been appraised in recent years on the completeness and fidelity of their statistical reporting, we may still ask how reliable the underlying statistical inferences really are.

"*To what extent can we rely on reported effects?*" This question can take multiple shapes. First, we may consider the magnitude of observed effects. While a statement of statistical significance is dependent on the sample size at which the inference was obtained, the magnitude of an effect, its *effect size*, informs us whether an effect is practically relevant—or not. While small effects might not make much difference in practice and might not be economical to pursue, large effects estimated with confidence can guide us to the interventions that are likely carrying considerable weight in socio-technical systems.

Indeed, a second dimension of reliability pertains to the confidence we have in observed effects, typically measured with 95% confidence intervals. Here, we are interested how tightly the confidence interval envelops the effect point estimate. The rationale behind such a confidence interval is that if an experiment were repeated many times, we would expect 95% of the observed effect estimates to be within the stated confidence intervals. Wide intervals, thereby, give us little confidence in the accuracy of an estimation procedure.

This consideration is exacerbated if a study conducted many tests in the same test family. Given the risk of multiple comparisons to amplify false-positive rates, we would need to adjust the confidence intervals accounting for the multiplicity and, hence, be prepared to gain even less confidence in the findings.

Third, we may consider statistical power, the likelihood of finding an effect that is present in reality. To put it in precise terms, it is the likelihood of rejecting a null hypothesis when it is, in fact, false—the complement of the false negative rate. At the same time, statistical power also impacts the likelihood that a positive report is actually true, hence further impacts the reliability of a finding. The power distribution, further, offers a first assessment on the statistical reliability of the field.

Finally, we expand on the reliability of the field in terms of evaluating research biases that could undermine results. Two predominant biases of interest are (i) the publication bias [24], and (ii) the related winner's curse [3].

The publication bias, on the one hand, refers to the phenomenon that the outcome of a study determines the decision to publish. Hence, statistically significant positive results are more likely to be published, than null results—even if null results live up to the same scientific rigor and possibly carry more information for falsification. Furthermore, researchers might be incentivized to engage in research practices that ensure reporting of statistically significant results, introducing biases towards questionable research practices.

The winner's curse , on the other hand, refers to the phenomenon that underpowered studies tend to report more extreme effects with statistical significance, hence tend to introducing a bias in the mean effect estimates in the field.

To the best of our knowledge, these questions on reliability of statistical inferences in cyber security user studies have not been systematically answered, to date. Coopamootoo and Groß [6] offered a manual coding of syntactic completeness indicators on studies sampled in a systematic literature review (SLR) of 10 years of cyber security user studies, while also commenting on *post-hoc* power estimates for a small sub-sample. Groß [14] investigated the fidelity of statistical test reporting along with an overview of multiple-comparison corrections and the identification of computation and decision errors. While we chose to base our analysis on the same published SLR sample, we close the research gap by creating a sound empirical foundation to estimate effect sizes, their standard errors and confidence intervals, by establishing power simulations vs. typical effect size thresholds, by investigating publication bias and winner's curse.

Our Contributions. We are the first to estimate a large number ($n = 431$) of heterogenous effect sizes from cyber security user studies with their confidence intervals. Based on this estimation, we are able to show that a considerable number of tests executed in the field are underpowered, leaving results in question. This holds especially for small studies which computed a large number of tests at vanishingly low power. Furthermore, we are able to show that the reported effects of underpowered studies are especially susceptible to falter under Multiple-Comparison Corrections (MCC), while adequately powered studies are robust to MCC.

We are the first to quantify empirically that a publication bias is present in the field of cyber security user studies. We can further evidence that the field suffers from the over-estimated effect sizes at low power, the winner's curse. We conclude our study with practical and empirically grounded recommendations for researchers, reviewers and funders.

2   Background

2.1   Statistical Inferences and Null Hypothesis Significance Testing

Based on a—necessarily *a priori*—specified null hypothesis (and alternative hypothesis) and a given significance level α, statistical inference with *null hypothesis significance testing* [18, pp. 163] sets out to establish how surprising an obtained observation D is, assuming the null hypothesis being true. This is facilitated by means of a *test statistic* that relates observations to appropriate probability distributions. It is inherent to the method that the statistical hypothesis *must* be fixed, before the sample is examined.

The *p-value*, then, is the likelihood of obtaining an observation as extreme as or more extreme than D, contingent on the null hypothesis being true, all assumption of the test statistic being fulfilled, the sample being drawn randomly, etc. Indeed, not heeding the assumptions of the test statistic is one of the more subtle ways how the process can fail.

Statistical inferences carry the likelihood of a false positive or *Type I* error [18, pp. 168]. They are impacted, hence, by *multiplicity*, that is, the phenomenon that computing multiple statistical tests on a test family inflates the family-wise error rate. To mitigate this effect, it is prudent practice to employ *multiple-comparison corrections* (MCC) [18, pp. 415]. The Bonferroni correction we use here is the most conservative one, adjusting the significance level α by dividing it by the number of tests computed in the test family.

2.2   Effect Sizes and Confidence Intervals

We briefly introduce estimation theory [10] as a complement to significance testing and as a key tool for this study. An observed *effect size* (ES) is a *point estimate* of the magnitude of an observed effect. Its *confidence interval* (CI) is the corresponding interval estimate [18, pp. 313]. For instance, if we consider the popular 95% confidence interval on an effect size, it indicates that if an experiment were repeated infinitely many times, we would expect that the point estimate on the population effect were within the respective confidence interval 95% of the cases. The *standard error* of an ES is equally a measure of the effects uncertainty and monotonously related to the width of the corresponding confidence interval.

Notably, confidence intervals are often misused or misinterpreted [17,22]. For instance, they do *not* assert that the population effect is within a point estimate's CI with 95% likelihood.

However, used correctly, effect sizes and their confidence intervals are useful in establishing the practical relevance of and confidence in an effect [13]. They are, thereby, recommended as minimum requirement for standard reporting, such as by the APA guidelines [1] Whereas a statement of statistical significance or p-value largely gives a binary answer, an effect size quantifies the effect observed and, thereby, indicates what its impact in practice might be.

2.3   Statistical Power

In simple terms, *statistical power* $(1-\beta)$ [4] is the probability that a test correctly rejects the null hypothesis, if the null hypothesis is false in reality. Hence, power is the likelihood not to commit a false negative or *Type II* error.

It should not go unnoticed that power also has an impact on the probability whether a positively reported result is actually true in reality, often referred to as *Positive Predictive Value (PPV)* [19]. The lower the statistical power, the less likely a positive report is true in reality. Hence, a field affected by predominately low power is said to suffer from a *power failure* [3].

Statistical power is largely determined by significance level, sample size, and the population effect size θ. *A priori* statistical power of a test statistic is estimated by a power analysis [18, pp. 372] on the sample size employed vis-à-vis of the anticipated effect size, given a significance level α and target power $1 - \beta$.

Post-hoc statistical power [18, p. 391], that is, computed on observed effect sizes after the face, is not only considered redundant to the p-value and confidence intervals on the effect sizes, but also cautioned against as treacherously misleading: It tends to overestimate the statistical power because it discounts the power lost in the study execution and because it is vulnerable to being inflated by over-estimated observed effect sizes. Hence, especially small under-powered studies with erratic effect size estimates tend to yield a biased post-hoc power. Hence, post-hoc power statements are best disregarded.

We offer a less biased alternative approach in *power simulation*. In that, we specify standard effect size thresholds, that is, we parametrize the analysis on assumed average effect sizes found in a field. We then compute the statistical power of the studies given on their reported sample size against those thresholds. As the true average effect sizes of our field are unknown, we offer power simulations for a range of typical effect size thresholds.

2.4 Research Biases

Naturally, even well-executed studies can be impacted by a range of biases on per-study level. In this study, we consider biases of a field, instead. We zero in on two biases, specifically: (i) the publication bias and (ii) the winner's curse.

The *publication bias* [11, 20, 24, 27] refers to the phenomenon that the publication of studies may be contingent on their positive results, hence condemning null and unfavorable results to the file-drawer [24, 25].

The *winner's curse* [3] is a specific kind of publication bias referring to the phenomenon that low-power studies only reach statistically significant results on large effects and, thereby, tend to overestimate the observed effect sizes. They, hence, perpetuate inflated effect estimates in the field.

We chose them as lens for this paper because they both operate on the interrelation between sample size (impacting standard error and power) and effects observed and emphasize different aspects of the overall phenomenon. The publication bias is typically visualized with funnel plots [20], which pit observed effect sizes against their standard errors. We shall follow Sterne and Egger's suggestion [28] on using log odds ratios as best suited x-axis. If no publication bias were present, funnel plots would be symmetrical. Hence, an asymmetry is an indication of bias. This asymmetry is tested with the non-parametric rank correlation coefficient Kendall's τ [2]. We note that funnel-plots as analysis tools can be impacted by the heterogeneity of the effect sizes investigated [29] and, hence, need to be taken with a grain of salt.

3 Related Works

3.1 Appraisal of the Field

Usable security, socio-technical aspects in security, human dimensions of cyber security and evidence-based methods of security are all young fields. The Systematic Literature Review (SLR) by Coopamootoo and Groß [6], hence, zeroed in on cyber security user studies published in the 10 years 2006–2016. The field has undergone some appraisal and self-reflection. The mentioned Coopamootoo-Groß SLR considered completeness indicators for statistical inference, syntactically codeable from a study's reporting [8]. These were subsequently described in a reporting toolset [9]. The authors found appreciable weaknesses in the field, even if there were cases of studies excelling in their rigor. Operating from the same SLR sample, Groß [14,15] investigated the fidelity of statistical reporting, on completeness of the reports as well as the correctness of the reported p-values, finding computation and decision errors in published works relatively stable over time with minor differences between venues.

3.2   Guidelines

Over the timeframe covered by the aforementioned SLR, a number of authors offered recommendations for dependable, rigorous experimentation pertaining to this study. Peisert and Bishop [23] considered the scientific design of security experiments. Maxion [21] discussed dependable experimentation, summarizing classical features of sound experiment design. Schechter [26] spoke from experience in the SOUPS program committee, offering recommendations for authors. His considerations on multiple-comparison corrections and adherence to statistical assumptions foreshadow recommendations we will make. Coopamootoo and Groß [7] summarized research methodology, largely focusing on quantitative and evidence-based methods, discussing null hypothesis significance testing, effect size estimation, and statistical power, among other things.

4   Aims

Effect Sizes. As a stepping stone, we intend to estimate *observed* effect sizes and their standard errors in a standardized format (log odds ratios).

RQ 1 (Effect Sizes and their Confidence). *What is the distribution of observed effect sizes and their 95% confidence intervals? How are the confidence intervals affected by multiple-comparison corrections?*

$H_{mcc,0}$: The marginal proportions of tests' statistical significance are equal irrespective of per-study family-wise multiple-comparison corrections.
$H_{mcc,1}$: Per-study family-wise multiple-comparison corrections impact the marginal proportions of tests' statistical significance.

Statistical Power. We inquire about the statistical power of studies independent from their possibly biased observed effect size estimates.

RQ 2 (Statistical Power). *What is the distribution of statistical power vis-à-vis parameterized effect size thresholds? As an upper bound achievable with given sample sizes as well as for the actual tests employed?*

Given the unreliability of post-hoc power analysis, we pit the sample sizes employed by the studies and individual tests against the small, medium, and large effect size thresholds according to Cohen [4]. The actual thresholds will differ depending on the type of the effect size.

Publication Bias. We intend to inspect the relation between effect sizes and standard errors with funnel plots [20], asking the question:

RQ 3 (Publication Bias). *To what extent does the field exhibit signs of publication bias measured in terms of relation between effect sizes and standard errors as well as asymmetry?*

We can test statistically for the presence of asymmetry [2] as indicator of publication bias, yielding the following hypotheses:

$H_{bias,0}$: There is no asymmetry measured as rank correlation between effect sizes and their standard errors.
$H_{bias,1}$: There an asymmetry measured as rank correlation between effect sizes and their standard errors.

The Winner's Curse. We are interested whether low-powered studies exhibit inflated effect sizes and ask:

RQ 4 (Winner's Curse). *What is the relation between simulated statistical power (only dependent on group sizes) and observed effect sizes?*

$H_{wc,0}$: Simulated power and observed effect size are independent.
$H_{wc,1}$: There is a negative correlation between simulated power and observed effect size.

5 Method

This study was registered on the Open Science Framework (OSF)[1], before its statistical inferences commenced. An extended version of this work is available on arXiv[2], including additional analyses and a brief specification of the underlying SLR [16]. Computations of statistics, graphs and tables are done in R with the packages statcheck, metafor, esc, compute.es, pwr. Their results are woven into this report with knitr. Statistics are computed as two-tailed with $\alpha = .05$ as reference significance level. Multiple-comparison corrections are computed with the Bonferroni method, adjusting the significance level used with the number of members of the test family.

5.1 Sample

The sample for this study is based on a 2016/17 Systematic Literature Review (SLR) conducted by Coopamootoo and Groß [6]. This underlying SLR, its search, inclusion and exclusion criteria are reported in short form by Groß [14] are included in this study's OSF Repository. We have chosen this SLR on the one hand, because its search strategy, inclusion and exclusion criteria are explicitly documented supporting its reproducibility and representativeness; the list

---

[1] https://osf.io/bcyte/.
[2] https://arxiv.org/abs/2010.02117.

of included papers is published. On the other hand, we have chosen it as sample, because there have been related analyses on qualitatively coded completeness indicators as well as statistical reporting fidelity [14] already. Therefore, we extend a common touchstone for the field. The overall SLR sample included $N = 146$ cyber security user studies. Therein, Groß [14] identified 112 studies with valid statistical reporting in the form of triplets of test statistic, degrees of freedom, and p-value. In this study, we extract effect sizes for t-, χ^2-, r-, one-way F-tests, and Z-tests, complementing automated with manual extraction.

5.2   Procedure

We outlined the overall procedure in Fig. 1 and will describe the analysis stages depicted in dashed rounded boxes in turn.

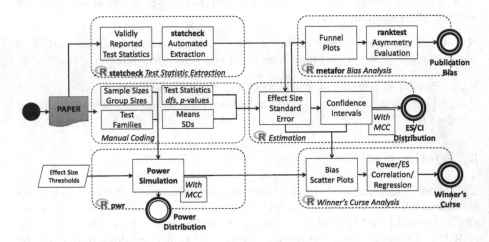

Fig. 1. Flow chart of the analysis procedure

Automated Test Statistic Extraction. We analyzed the SLR sample with R package statcheck proposed by Epskamp and Nuijten [12]. We obtained cases on test statistic type, degrees of freedom, value of the test statistic and p-value along with a correctness analysis. This extraction covered correctly reported test statistics (by APA guidelines) and t-, χ^2-, r-, F-tests, and Z-tests at that.

Manual Coding. For all papers in the SLR, we coded the overall sample size, use of Amazon Mechanical Turk as sampling platform, and the presence of multiple-comparison corrections. For each statistical test, we also coded group sizes, test statistics, degrees of freedom, p-values, means and standard deviations if applicable as well as test families. For the coding of test families, we distinguished different studies reported in papers, test types as well as dimensions investigated.

Test Exclusion. To put all effect sizes on even footing, we excluded tests violating assumption and ones not constituting one-way comparisons.

Power Simulation. We conducted a power simulation, that is, we specified effect size thresholds for various effect size types according to the classes proposed by Cohen [5]. Table 1 summarizes corresponding thresholds.

Table 1. Effect size thresholds for various statistics and effect size (ES) types [4]

ES type	Statistic	Threshold		
		Small	Medium	Large
Cohen's d	t	0.20	0.50	0.80
Pearson's r	r	0.10	0.30	0.50
Cohen's w	χ^2	0.10	0.30	0.50
Cohen's f	F	0.10	0.25	0.40

Given the sample sizes obtained in the coding, we then computed the *a priori* power against those thresholds with the R package pwr, which is independent from possible over-estimation of observed effect sizes. We further computed power analyses based on group sizes for reported tests, including a power adjusted for multiple comparisons in studies' test families with a Bonferroni correction. We reported those analyses per test statistic type.

Estimation. We computed a systematic estimation of observed effect sizes, their standard errors and confidence intervals. This estimation was either based on test statistics, their degrees of freedom and group sizes used for the test or on summary statistics such as reported means, standard deviations and group sizes. We conducted the estimation with the R packages esc and compute.es for cases in which only test statistics were available and with the package metafor if we worked with summary statistics (e.g., means and standard deviations). As part of this estimation stage, we also estimated 95% confidence intervals (with and without multiple-comparison corrections).

Publication Bias Analysis. We used the R package metafor to compute analyses on the publication bias. In particular, we produced funnel plots on effect sizes and their standard errors [20]. For this analysis, we converted all effect sizes and standard errors irrespective of their origin to log odds ratios as the predominant effect-size form for funnel plots [28]. Following the method of Begg and Mazumdar [2], we evaluated a rank correlation test to ascertain the presence of asymmetry.

Winner's Curse Analysis. To analyze for the winner's curse, we created scatterplots that pitted the simulated power of reported tests against the observed effect sizes extracted from the papers. We applied a Loess smoothing to illustrate the bias in the distribution. Finally, we computed a Kendall's τ rank correlation to show the relationship between absolute effect size and power. We employed a robust linear regression using an iterated re-weighted least squares (IWLS) fitting to estimate the expected effect size of the field at 100% power.

6   Results

6.1   Sample

The sample was refined in multiple stages, first establishing papers that are candidates for effect size extraction, their refinement shown in Table 2 in Appendix A. In total, we retained a sample of $N_{studies} = 54$ studies suitable for effect size extraction.

Secondly, we set out to extract test statistics and effect sizes with statcheck and manual coding. Table 3 in Appendix A gives an overview how these extracted tests were first composed and then pruned in an exclusions process focused on statistical validity. After exclusion of tests that would not yield valid effect sizes, we $N_{es} = 454$ of usable effect sizes and their standard errors.

We include the descriptives of the complete sample of extracted effect sizes grouped by their tests in Table 4 of Appendix A. The table standardizes all effect sizes as log odds ratios, irrespective of test statistic of origin.

6.2   Effect Size Estimates and Their Confidence

In Fig. 2, we analyze the effect size estimates of our sample with their confidence intervals in a caterpillar plot: estimated effect sizes are plotted with error bars representing their 95% confidence intervals and ordered by effect size. Two thirds of the observed effects did not pass the medium threshold: (i) 37% were trivial, (ii) 28% were small, (iii) 15% were medium, and (iv) 20% were large.

The figure underlays the uncorrected confidence intervals (gray) with the multiple-comparison-corrected confidence intervals in red. While 54% of 431 tests were statistically significant without MCC, only 38% were significant after appropriate MCC were applied.

The multiple-comparison correction significantly impacted the significance of the tests, FET $p < .001$, $OR = 0.53$, 95% CI $[0.4, 0.7]$ We, thereby, reject the null hypothesis $H_{mcc,0}$.

6.3   Upper Bounds of Statistical Power

We estimate the upper-bound statistical power studies can achieve had they used their entire sample for a single two-tailed independent-samples t-test versus a given standardized mean difference effect size. Thereby, Fig. 3 offers us a first characterization of the field in a beaded monotonously growing power plot.

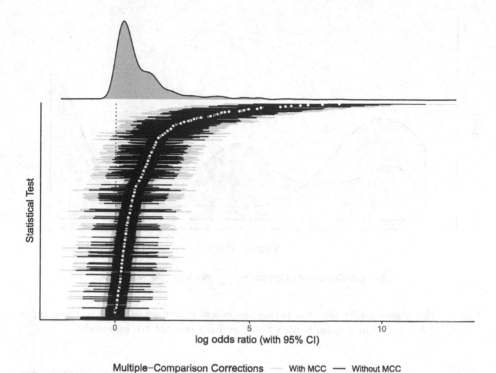

Fig. 2. Caterpillar forest plot of $n = 431$ log odds ratios and their 95% confidence intervals, ordered by log(OR).

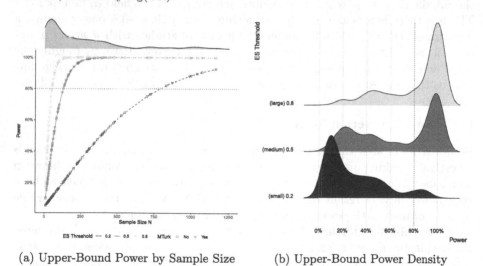

(a) Upper-Bound Power by Sample Size   (b) Upper-Bound Power Density

Fig. 3. Upper-bound of power against Standardized Mean Difference (SMD) effects and 112 observed study sample sizes N in SLR. (*Note:* Only studies with $N < 1250$ are shown for visual clarity, excluding 14 from the view)

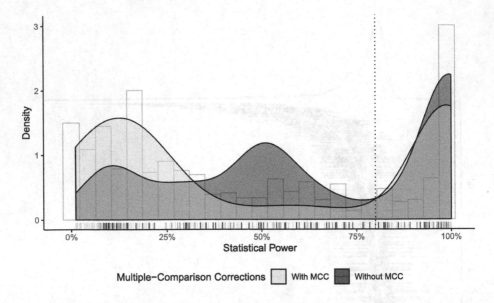

Fig. 4. Histogram-density plot comparing statistical power for all tests in the sample by MCC. *Note:* The histogram is with MCC and square-root transformed.

Let us unpack what we can learn from the graph. Regarding the sample size density on the top of Fig. 3a, we observe that the sample sizes are heavily biased towards small samples ($N < 100$). Considering the ridge power plot in Fig. 3b, the middle ridge of power versus medium effects shows the field to be bipartite: There is there is a peak of studies achieving greater than 80% power against a medium effect. Those studies match the profile of studies with *a priori* power analysis seeking to achieve the recommended 80% power. However, roughly the same density mass is in smaller studies failing this goal. The bottom ridge line tells us that almost no studies achieve recommended power against small effects.

6.4 Power of Actual Tests

Figure 4 illustrates the power distribution of all tests and all ES thresholds investigated taking into account their respective group sizes, comparing between scenarios with and without MCC. Notably, the studies tests designed to have 80% power largely retain their power under MCC. We observe a considerable number of tests with power of approx. 50% which falter under MCC.

Distinguishing further between different test types, we considered independent-samples t- and 2×2 χ^2-tests as the most prevalent test statistics. Their respective power simulations are included in the extended version of this paper [16].

In both cases, we observe the following phenomena: (i) The density mass is on smaller sample sizes. (ii) The ridge-density plots show characteristic "two-humped" shapes, in exhibiting a peak above 80% power, but also a density mass at considerably lower power. (iii) Both t-tests and χ^2-tests were largely ill-equipped to detect small effect sizes. Overall, we see a self-similarity of the MCC-corrected power of actual tests vis-à-vis of the upper-bound power considered in the preceding section.

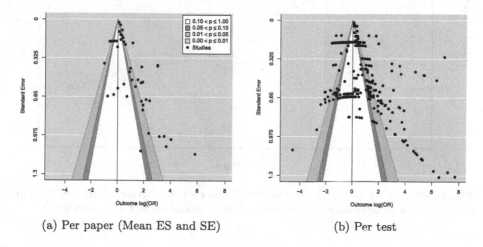

(a) Per paper (Mean ES and SE)   (b) Per test

Fig. 5. Funnel plots of $\log(OR)$ effect sizes and their standard errors

6.5 Publication Bias

The funnel plots in Fig. 5 shows the results for 47 papers and a total of 431 statistical tests. For the aggregated plot Fig. 5a, we computed the mean log odds ratio and mean standard error per paper. We observe in both plots that with greater standard errors (that is, smaller samples), the effect sizes become more extreme. Hence, we conjecture that smaller studies which did not find significant effects were not published.

By the Begg-Mazumdar rank-correlation test [2], there is a statistically significant asymmetry showing the publication bias in the per-paper aggregate, Kendall's $\tau(N = 47) = .349$, $p < .001$, Pearson's $r = .52$, 95% CI [.52, .52]. We reject null hypothesis $H_{\text{bias},0}$.

6.6 The Winner's Curse

In Fig. 6 depicts the winner's curse phenomenon by pitting the simulated power against a threshold medium effect against the observed effect sizes. We observe that at low power, extreme results were more prevalent. At high power, the results were largely clustered closely around the predicted mean log odds.

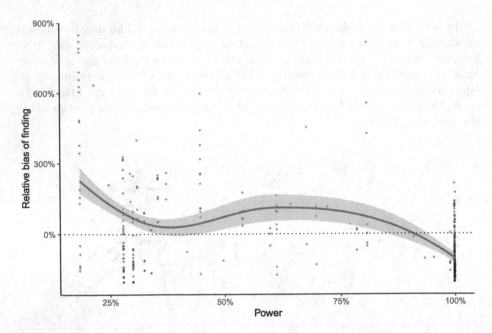

Fig. 6. ES Bias by Power illustrating the Winner's Curse. *Note:* Entries with more than 1000% bias were removed for visual clarity without impact on the result.

There was a statistically significant negative correlation between power and observed effect size, that is with increasing power the observed effect sizes decrease, Kendall's $\tau(N = 396) = -.338$, $p < .001$, corresponding to an ES of Pearson's $r = -.51$, 95% CI $[-.51, -.51]$ using Kendall's estimate. We reject the winner's curse null hypothesis $H_{wc,0}$.

We evaluated an iterated re-weighted least squares (IWLS) robust linear regression (RLM) on the $ES \sim power$ relation mitigating for outliers, statistically significant at $F(1, 394) = 114.135$, $p < .001$. We obtained an intercept of 1.6 95% CI $[1.44, 1.76]$, $F(1, 394) = 331.619$, $p < .001$. For every 10% of power, the measured effect size decreased by -0.11; 95% CI $[-0.13, -0.09]$, $F(1, 394) = 114.135$, $p < .001$. The simulated-power regression explained approximately $R^2 = .08$ of the variance; the standard error of the regression was $S = 0.19$.

We can extrapolate to the expected mean log odds ratio at 100% power $\log(OR) = 0.47$, 95% CI $[0.21, 0.72]$. This corresponds to an SMD estimate in Cohen's $d = 0.26$, 95% CI $[0.12, 0.4]$.

7   Discussion

The Power Distribution is Characteristically Two-Humped. We found empirical evidence that a substantive number of studies and half the tests extracted were adequate for 80% power at a medium target effect size. Hence, it is plausible to conjecture an unspoken assumption in the field that the population effect sizes in cyber security user studies are medium (e.g., Cohen's $d \geq .50$). The good news here is that studies that were appropriately powered, that is, aiming for 80% power, retained that power also under multiple-comparison corrections. Studies which were under-powered in the first place, got entangled by MCCs and ended up with negligible power retained (cf. Fig. 4, Sect. 6.4).

Having said that, the power distribution for the upper bound as well as for actual tests came in two "humps." While we consistently observed peaks at greater than 80% power for medium effect sizes, there was a density mass of under-powered tests, where the distribution was roughly split half-half. Typically, tests were altogether too under-powered to detect small effect sizes. Overall, we believe we have evidence to attest a power failure in the field.

Population Effect Sizes May Be Smaller Than We Think. The problem of power failure is aggravated by the mean effect sizes in the SLR having been close to small, shown in the caterpillar forest plot (Fig. 2) and the ES descriptives (Table 4). In fact, our winner's curse analysis estimated a mean Cohen's $d = 0.26$, 95% CI $[0.12, 0.4]$. Of course, it is best to obtain precise effect size estimates for the effect in question from prior research, ideally from systematic meta-analyses deriving the estimate of population effect size $\hat{\theta}$. Still, the low effect size indicated here should give us pause: aiming for a medium effect size as a rule of thumb might be too optimistic.

Cyber Security User Studies Suffer From a Host of Biases. We showed the presence of an appreciable publication bias (cf. Fig. 5, Sect. 6.5), that is, the phenomenon that the publication of studies was contingent on their positive outcomes, and found evidence of the winner's curse, that is, the phenomenon that under-powered studies yielded exaggerated effect estimates (cf. Fig. 6, Sect. 6.6).

Taken together with the likely close-to-small population effect sizes and the diagnosed power failure, we need to conclude that the field is prone to accept publications that are seemingly "positive" results, while perpetuating biased studies with over-estimated effect sizes. These issues could be resolved with a joint effort by field's stakeholders—authors, gatekeepers and funders: paying greater attention to statistical power, point and interval estimates of effects, and adherence to multiple-comparison corrections.

7.1 Limitations

Generalizability. We observe that we needed to exclude a considerable number of studies and statistical tests. This is consistent with the observations by Coopamootoo and Groß [6] on prevalent reporting completeness, finding that 71% of their SLR sample did not follow standard reporting guidelines and only 31% combinations of actual test statistic, p-value and corresponding descriptives. Similarly, Groß [14] found that 69 papers (60%) did not contain a single completely reported test statistic. Hence, we also observe that meta research is severely hamstringed by the reporting practices found in the field.

We note, further, that we needed to exclude 104 extracted statistical tests and effect sizes due to problems in how these tests were employed, leading to 17 less represented. Studies that inappropriately used independent-sample tests in a dependent-sample research designs or violated other assumptions by, e.g., using difference-between-means test statistics (expecting a t distribution) to test differences between proportions (z-distribution), needed to be excluded to prevent perpetuation of those issues. Finally, we needed to exclude 74 tests because papers reported tests with degrees of freedom $df > 1$ without the summary statistics to establish the effect sizes. Even though those studies contained complete reports the auxiliary data to estimate the effects were missing.

These exclusions on empirical grounds limit generalizability. The retained sample of 431 tests is focused on the studies that were most diligent in their reporting. This fact, however, makes our investigation more conservative rather than less so.

This Is Not a Meta-analysis. Proper meta-analysis combines effect sizes on *similar* constructs to summary effects. Given that studies operating on the same constructs are few and far between in cyber security user studies, we standardized all effects to log odds ratios to gain a rough overall estimate of the field.

8   Concluding Recommendations

We are the first to evaluate the statistical reliability of this field on empirical grounds. While there is a range of possible explanations of the phenomena we have found—including questionable research practices in, e.g., shirking multiple-comparison corrections in search of significant findings, missing awareness of statistical power and multiplicity, or limited resources to pursue adequately powered studies—we believe the evidence of power failure, possibly close-to-small population effect sizes, and biased findings can lead to empirically underpinned recommendations. We believe that these issues, however, are systemic in nature and that the actions of different stakeholders are, thereby, inter-dependent. Hence, in the following we aim at offering recommendations to different stakeholder, making the assumption that they aim at advancing the knowledge of the field to the best of their ability and resources.

Researchers. The most important recommendation here is: *plan ahead with the end in mind.* That starts with inquiring typical effect sizes for the phenomena investigated. If the reported confidence intervals thereon are wide, it is prudent to choose a conservative estimate. It is tempting to just assume a medium effect size (e.g., Cohen's $d = 0.5$) as aim, but there is no guarantee the population effect sizes are that large. Our study suggests they are not.

While it is a prudent recommendation to conduct an *a priori* power analysis, we go a step further and recommend to anticipate multiple comparisons one might make. Adjusting the target significance level with a Bonferroni correction for that multiplicity can prepare the ground for a study retaining sufficient power all the way. This kind of foresight is well supported by a practice of spelling out the research aims and intended statistical inferences *a priori* (e.g., in a pre-registration). Taken together these measures aim countering the risk of a power failure.

Speaking from our experience of painstakingly extracting effects from a body of literature, we are compelled to emphasize: One of the main points of strong research is that it is *reusable* by other scientists. This goal is best served by reporting effect sizes and their confidence intervals as well as full triplets of test statistic, degrees of freedom and exact *p*-values, while also offering all summary statistics to enable others to re-compute the estimates. It is worth recalling that *all* tests undertaken should be reported and that rigorous, well-reported studies have intrinsic value, null result or not. This line of recommendations aims at enabling the gatekeepers of the field to do their work efficiently.

Gatekeepers. It bears repeating that the main goal of science is to *advance the knowledge of a field*. With reviewers, program chairs and editors being gatekeepers and the arbiters of this goal, it is worthwhile to consider that the goal is not served well in pursuing shiny significant results or valuing novelty above all else. Such a value system is prone to fail to ward against publication and related biases. A well-powered null result or replication attempt can go a long way in initiating the falsification of a theory in need of debunking. Because empirical epistemology is rooted in falsification and replication, we need the multiple inquiries on the same phenomena. We should strive to include adequately-powered studies of sufficient rigor irrespective of the "positiveness" of the results presented, exercising the cognitive restraint to counter publication bias.

Reviewers can support this by insisting on systematic reporting and on getting to see *a priori* specifications of aims, research designs, tests conducted, as well as sample size determinations, hence creating an incentive to protect against power failure. This recommendation dovetails with the fact that statistical inference is contingent on fulfilling the assumptions of the tests used, where the onus of proof is with the researchers to ascertain that all assumptions were satisfied. Those recommendations are in place to enable the gatekeepers to effectively ascertain the statistical validity and reliability of studies at hand.

Funders. With significant investments being made in putting cyber security user studies on an evidence-based footing, we recall: "*Money talks*." On the one hand, we see the responsibility with the funders to support studies with sufficient budgets to obtain adequately powered samples—not to speak of adequate sampling procedures and representativeness. On the other hand, the funders are in a strong position to mandate *a priori* power analyses, pre-registrations, strong reporting standards geared towards subsequent research synthesis, published datasets, and open-access reports. They could, furthermore, incentivize and support the creation registered-study databases to counter the file-drawer problem.

Acknowledgment. We would like to thank the anonymous reviewers of STAST 2020 for their comments. Early aspects of this study were in parts funded by the UK Research Institute in the Science of Cyber Security (RISCS) under a National Cyber Security Centre (NCSC) grant on "Pathways to Enhancing Evidence-Based Research Methods for Cyber Security." Thomas Groß was funded by the ERC Starting Grant CASCAde (GA n°716980).

A   Sample Characteristics

We offer a detailed sample refinement on papers in Fig. 2 and extracted statistical tests and corresponding effect sizes in Fig. 3.

Table 2. Sample refinement on papers

Phase	Excluded	Retained
Source SLR [6]		
Search results (Google Scholar)	–	1157
Inclusion/Exclusion	1011	146
Refinement in this study		
Empirical studies	2	144
With sample sizes	21	123
With extractable tests	69	54

Table 3. Sample refinement on extracted effect sizes

Phase	Excluded	Retained
Total effects extracted	0	650
statcheck automated extraction		252
Test statistic manual coding		89
Means & SD manual coding		309
Refinement in this study		
Independent-samples test on dependent sample	46	604
Treated proportion as t-distribution	8	596
Reported dependent-samples test w/o correlation	62	534
Reported χ^2 without *df*	5	529
χ^2 with *df* > 1 without contingency	72	457
Multi-way F-test	22	435
Yielded infinite ES or variance	3	432
Duplicate of other coded test	1	431

Table 4. Descriptives of the observed absolute effect sizes as log odds ratios.

Statistic	n	Min	Q:25	Mdn	Q:75	Max	IQR	M	SD
Chi2	102	0.07	1.05	1.38	1.74	3.73	0.69	1.40	0.90
F	42	0.04	0.31	0.73	1.57	7.71	1.26	1.43	1.81
r	6	−1.03	1.02	1.33	1.86	2.15	0.84	1.40	0.60
t	317	−4.58	0.21	0.43	0.99	8.35	0.78	0.85	1.18
Z	33	0.07	0.31	0.66	1.59	7.17	1.29	1.37	1.57

References

1. American Psychological Association (ed.): Publication Manual of the American Psychological Association (6th revised ed.). American Psychological Association (2009)
2. Begg, C.B., Mazumdar, M.: Operating characteristics of a rank correlation test for publication bias. Biometrics **50**, 1088–1101 (1994)
3. Button, K.S., et al.: Power failure: why small sample size undermines the reliability of neuroscience. Nat. Rev. Neurosci. **14**(5), 365–376 (2013)
4. Cohen, J.: A power primer. Psychol. Bull. **112**(1), 155 (1992)
5. Cohen, J.: Statistical power analysis. Curr. Dir. Psychol. Sci. **1**(3), 98–101 (1992)
6. Coopamootoo, K., Groß, T.: Systematic evaluation for evidence-based methods in cyber security. Technical Report TR-1528, Newcastle University (2017)
7. Coopamootoo, K.P.L., Groß, T.: Evidence-based methods for privacy and identity management. In: Lehmann, A., Whitehouse, D., Fischer-Hübner, S., Fritsch, L., Raab, C. (eds.) Privacy and Identity 2016. IAICT, vol. 498, pp. 105–121. Springer, Cham (2016). https://doi.org/10.1007/978-3-319-55783-0_9
8. Coopamootoo, K.P., Groß, T.: A codebook for experimental research: the nifty nine indicators v1.0. Technical report TR-1514, Newcastle University (November 2017)
9. Coopamootoo, K.P.L., Groß, T.: Cyber security and privacy experiments: a design and reporting toolkit. In: Hansen, M., Kosta, E., Nai-Fovino, I., Fischer-Hübner, S. (eds.) Privacy and Identity 2017. IAICT, vol. 526, pp. 243–262. Springer, Cham (2018). https://doi.org/10.1007/978-3-319-92925-5_17
10. Cumming, G.: Understanding the New Statistics: Effect Sizes, Confidence Intervals, and Meta-Analysis. Routledge (2013)
11. Dickersin, K.: The existence of publication bias and risk factors for its occurrence. Jama **263**(10), 1385–1389 (1990)
12. Epskamp, S., Nuijten, M.: statcheck: Extract statistics from articles and recompute p-values (R package version 1.0.0.). https://cran.r-project.org/web/packages/statcheck/index.html (2014)
13. Gardner, M.J., Altman, D.G.: Confidence intervals rather than p values: estimation rather than hypothesis testing. Br. Med. J. (Clin. Res. Ed.) **292**(6522), 746–750 (1986)
14. Groß, T.: Fidelity of statistical reporting in 10 years of cyber security user studies. In: Groß, T., Tryfonas, T. (eds.) STAST 2019. LNCS, vol. 11739, pp. 3–26. Springer, Cham (2021). https://doi.org/10.1007/978-3-030-55958-8_1
15. Groß, T.: Fidelity of statistical reporting in 10 years of cyber security user studies [extended version]. Newcastle University (2020). arXiv Report arXiv:2004.06672

16. Groß, T.: Statistical reliability of 10 years of cybersecurity user studies [extended version]. Newcastle University (2020). arXiv Report arXiv:2010.02117

17. Hoekstra, R., Morey, R.D., Rouder, J.N., Wagenmakers, E.J.: Robust misinterpretation of confidence intervals. Psychon. Bull. Rev. **21**(5), 1157–1164 (2014)

18. Howell, D.C.: Fundamental Statistics for the Behavioral Sciences (8th international ed). Cengage Learning (2014)

19. Ioannidis, J.P.: Why most published research findings are false. PLoS Med. **2**(8), e124 (2005)

20. Light, R.J., Pillemer, D.B.: Summing Up; The Science of Reviewing Research. Harvard University Press, Cambridge (1984)

21. Maxion, R.: Making experiments dependable. In: Jones, C.B., Lloyd, J.L. (eds.) Dependable and Historic Computing. LNCS, vol. 6875, pp. 344–357. Springer, Heidelberg (2011). https://doi.org/10.1007/978-3-642-24541-1_26

22. Morey, R.D., Hoekstra, R., Rouder, J.N., Lee, M.D., Wagenmakers, E.J.: The fallacy of placing confidence in confidence intervals. Psychon. Bull. Rev. **23**(1), 103–123 (2016)

23. Peisert, S., Bishop, M.: How to design computer security experiments. In: Futcher, L., Dodge, R. (eds.) WISE 2007. IAICT, vol. 237, pp. 141–148. Springer, New York (2007). https://doi.org/10.1007/978-0-387-73269-5_19

24. Rosenthal, R.: The file drawer problem and tolerance for null results. Psychol. Bull. **86**(3), 638 (1979)

25. Scargle, J.D.: Publication bias (the "file-drawer problem") in scientific inference. arXiv preprint physics/9909033 (1999)

26. Schechter, S.: Common pitfalls in writing about security and privacy human subjects experiments, and how to avoid them (2013). https://www.microsoft.com/en-us/research/wp-content/uploads/2016/02/commonpitfalls.pdf

27. Sterling, T.D., Rosenbaum, W.L., Weinkam, J.J.: Publication decisions revisited: the effect of the outcome of statistical tests on the decision to publish and vice versa. Am. Stat. **49**(1), 108–112 (1995)

28. Sterne, J.A., Egger, M.: Funnel plots for detecting bias in meta-analysis: guidelines on choice of axis. J. Clin. Epidemiol. **54**(10), 1046–1055 (2001)

29. Terrin, N., Schmid, C.H., Lau, J., Olkin, I.: Adjusting for publication bias in the presence of heterogeneity. Stat. Med. **22**(13), 2113–2126 (2003)

Privacy, Security and Trust in the Internet of Neurons

Diego Sempreboni and Luca Viganò(⊠)

Department of Informatics, King's College London, London, UK
{diego.sempreboni,luca.vigano}@kcl.ac.uk

Abstract. Arpanet, Internet, Internet of Services, Internet of Things, Internet of Skills. What next? We conjecture that in a few years from now, we will have the Internet of Neurons, in which humans will be able to connect bi-directionally to the net using only their brain. The Internet of Neurons will provide new, tremendous opportunities thanks to constant access to unlimited information, but it will also bring along enormous challenges, especially concerning security, privacy and trust. In this paper we discuss the main technological (and neurological) breakthroughs required to enable the Internet of Neurons, the new opportunities it provides and the security challenges it raises. We also elaborate on the novel system models, threat models and security properties that are required to reason about privacy, security and trust in the Internet of Neurons.

Keywords: New internet paradigm · Brainwaves · Human computer · Security · Privacy · Trust

1 Introduction: From the Human Computer to... the Human Computer

We all carry around a computer: our *brain*. The term "computer" has been in use from the 17th century, way before electronic computers became available. It was introduced simply to mean "one who computes", namely a person whose job is to perform complex mathematical calculations. In that sense, people often speak of "human computer" to make this distinction clear[1]. Throughout the centuries, human computers, working alone or in teams, have begotten groundbreaking scientific discoveries, ranging from trigonometry to astronomy, to the dawn of nuclear energy and nuclear weapons (e.g., the complex computations crucially related to nuclear fission in the Manhattan Project) and to the space race [36].

When electronic computers became available in the second half of the 20th century, human computers became useless, and "human computer" is nowadays mainly used to refer to individuals with prodigious powers of mental arithmetic

---

[1] In [39], Turing wrote: "The human computer is supposed to be following fixed rules; he has no authority to deviate from them in any detail".

© Springer Nature Switzerland AG 2021
T. Groß and L. Viganò (Eds.): STAST 2020, LNCS 12812, pp. 191–205, 2021.
https://doi.org/10.1007/978-3-030-79318-0_11

who display their abilities in theaters or TV shows. Electronic computers also brought along a revolution that has transformed the economic, social, educational, and political landscape in a profound and indelible manner: the *net*.

The technical foundations of the Internet were laid by the *ARPANET* in the 1960s. The creation of new overseas nodes of the network and the definition of the standard TCP/IP officially launched the *Internet* as a set of interconnected networks through these packet switching protocols. Advances in hardware and software at the end of the 20th century enabled mobile connectivity to billions of laptops and (smart)phones. This *Mobile Internet* gave rise to the *Internet of Services (IoS)*, with the flourishing of e-commerce, health-care portals, booking services, streaming websites and social networks. This redefined entire segments of the economy in the first decade of the 21st century, and was soon followed by the *Internet of Things (IoT)*, a network of physical devices, vehicles, home appliances and other items embedded with electronics, software, sensors, actuators, and connectivity which enables these objects to connect and exchange data.

The next evolution of the Internet will be the *Tactile Internet*, which has been defined by the International Telecommunication Union (ITU) as a network that is based on 5G and combines ultra-low latency with extremely high availability, reliability and security [20][2]. The Tactile Internet will encompass human-to-machine and machine-to-machine interaction, enabling tactile and haptic sensations and the control of the IoT in real time. It will unleash the full potential of the fourth industrial revolution (a.k.a. Industry 4.0), and revolutionize the way we learn and work through the *Internet of Skills* (a.k.a. Human 4.0, [13]), which will enable the real-time delivery of skills in digital form remotely and globally.

What next? We conjecture the return of the human computer, but in a different guise. We predict the coming of the next, and maybe ultimate, phase of the Internet evolution: the *Internet of Neurons (IoN)* will rest upon a novel paradigm in which humans are able to connect bi-directionally to the net using (only) their brain. The IoN will provide new, tremendous opportunities thanks to constant access to unlimited information. It will empower all those outside of the technical industry, actually it will empower all human beings, to access and use technological products and services as everybody will be able to connect, even without possessing a laptop, a tablet or a smartphone. The IoN will thus fulfill the democratization of knowledge and technology, but it will also bring along enormous challenges, especially concerning privacy, security and trust.

In the following, we speculate on the forthcoming deployment of the IoN and discuss the technological (and neurological) breakthroughs required to enable it, as well as the new opportunities it provides and the challenges it raises. We also elaborate on the novel system models, threat models and security properties that are required to reason about privacy, security and trust in the IoN.

---

[2] Note, however, that more work is needed to tackle 5G's security challenges [1, 7].

2   The IoN: From brainwaves to packets, and Vice versa

In 2014, Stephen Hawking said "*We are all now connected by the Internet, like neurons in a giant brain*" [40]. Although Hawking is famous for his predictions (as well as for his scientific results, of course), in this case he was not prophesying the advent of what we call the IoN. However, it is interesting to note that he used the same keywords (we found this quote when we googled "Internet of Neurons" to see if somebody had already had the idea) and that, in a brain, like in the Internet, it is actually all a matter of connectivity.

How would connectivity work in the IoN? At the root of our thoughts, emotions and behaviors is the communication between neurons within our brains. *Brainwaves* are produced by synchronized electrical pulses from masses of neurons communicating with each other. Hence, to realize the *brain-net*, which is one of the frontiers of *brain-computer interaction* and thus of human-computer interaction, we need to interface brainwaves with the packets that are received and sent by computers or other external devices[3]. Some approaches have already been proposed, and prototypical devices built, for the realization of *brain-computer interfaces (BCIs)* [15]. The methodology behind brain-computer interaction, through a BCI, can be summarized as the following sequence of steps:

(1) Collect brainwaves by recording activity directly from the brain (invasively or non-invasively) in real-time.
(2) Convert the complex waveforms of brainwaves into data.
(3) Encode the parsed information and issue action instructions.
(4) Feed back the externally perceived information in real-time in the form of signals that the brain can read (possibly through a stimulating device).

Note that the system must rely on intentional control, i.e., users must choose to perform a mental task whenever they want to accomplish a goal with the BCI.

Nowadays, it is already possible to detect and process brainwaves (e.g., using EEG sensors placed on the scalp) and a number of solutions have been proposed to provide a form of uni-directional communication and thus address at least Steps (1) and (2) of this methodology. Let us consider three interesting examples. The neurotechnology company "Neuralink" was founded in 2016 by Elon Musk and others with the aim of developing an ultra-high-bandwidth implantable BCI to connect humans and computers [30]. While Neuralink is still work in progress, the "Brainternet" project [29] has developed an apparently more rudimentary but effective technology that streams brainwaves onto the Internet (by converting brainwaves into signals and streaming them to an online server using a Rasperry Pi computer). The startup "Neurable" created the VR game "Awakening" in which the gamer's brain essentially acts as mouse thanks to a brain-scanning headband paired with software that interprets the neural signals, thus allowing for hands-free control [37]. Other application areas that BCIs are currently

---

[3] Note that we are here assuming that the "normal" network will still be operating through packets, although by then advances in quantum computing might have provided for new modes of data transmission. But this is a topic for another paper.

being developed for are, for instance, education (e.g., for monitoring of students' attention in real time) and medical care (e.g., for monitoring and treatment of Parkinson's and other serious brain diseases, with the eventual goal of human enhancement as aspired by Neuralink and other projects).

These technologies are promising, but are still quite far from addressing Steps (3) and (4). The IoN will require more than a uni-directional information flow; it will require a bi-directional information flow, in which (i) brainwaves are translated into data and (ii) data is translated into signals that the brain can parse.

Some exploratory research has been carried out attempting to bridge neuroscience with computer science and telecommunications, but brain-computer bi-directional information flow is still largely unchartered territory. Nonetheless, we conjecture that in a few years from now[4], advances in neurology and in brain-computer interaction, combined with technological innovations, will have led to the creation of a device able to connect the human brain to the Internet bi-directionally, and without resorting to any invasive surgical operations [14]. This device won't be bulky; it will be portable, light and chargeable inductively so that we will be able to connect to the Internet anywhere anytime. It could take the form of a lightweight headphone like in Fig. 1, or more likely simply be a button-like pod that we will attach to our temples. Or it could even be a tiny implant, although non-invasive procedures are typically to be preferred.

The device will communicate bidirectionally with the brain via brainwaves (as illustrated by the brainwave symbol on the forehead of the human in Fig. 1) and with the Internet via wireless communication (as illustrated by the standard symbol) to and from appropriate routers. The device ought thus be capable of reading the brainwaves in real-time, more or less like EEG readers are capable of doing now, but it ought also be capable of interpreting the brainwaves and transform them into their digital version, sending the coded version to the Internet. The device ought also be capable of receiving incoming data, convert it into brainwaves (Step (3)) and send them to the brain (Step (4)).

Being able to convert data into brainwaves and vice versa is necessary in this phase. Progress in Machine Learning, AI and Big Data have made it possible to interpret brainwaves [43] mapping them with words or pictures creating a valid and applicable brainwaves-to-digital and digital-to-brainwaves codification. Feeding back the converted data into the brain requires techniques capable of stimulating the brain with signals. *Electroconvulsive therapy, rapid transcranial magnetic stimulation* and *magnetic seizure therapy* are techniques able to deliver stimulation pulses through the tissue directly to the brain, even wirelessly [17].

---

[4] It is not really important whether it will be in 5, 10 or 30 years, but rather that it will happen for sure, in one form or the other. And this time we should do it right, considering security from the start, unlike what happened when Internet was first designed as pointed out Danny Hills in [11]: *"Because the Internet was designed for a community that trusted each other, it didn't have a lot of protections in it. We didn't worry about spying on each other, for example. We didn't worry about somebody sending out spam, or bad emails, or viruses, because such a person would have been banned from the community"*.

Fig. 1. Configuration 1 – Bi-directional brain-Internet connection by means of a wearable device

Fig. 2. Configuration 2 – Bi-directional brain-Internet direct connection

We also conjecture that advances in software and hardware will remove the need for any wearable device to connect: as depicted in Fig. 2, humans will be able to connect to the Internet directly with their brainwaves, possibly through routers that "read" brainwaves remotely (say from a distance of a few meters like wireless routers do now with wireless signals), and transform the brainwaves into data and vice versa (i.e., brains will download/upload information from/to the network)[5]. Research is ongoing on developing sensors to monitor the electroencephalogram without electrical or physical contact with the body (e.g., [33]), but there is a long way to go until these sensors are able to do more than just monitor and actually allow for the full realization of the four steps that we described above. However, several foundation stones for the IoN have been laid so it is necessary that we start thinking about the privacy, security and trust challenges that will plague the IoN. Some of these will mirror the challenges affecting the Internet as we know it today, but others will be novel and even more intriguing.

3   Privacy, Security and Trust

The potential offered by the technological revolution underlying the Internet of Neurons will be as varied as the problems related to privacy, security and trust that it will cause. To reason about these problems, we will need to provide suitable definitions, where a security definition is typically provided by combining a system model with a threat model and with one or more security properties that the system should guarantee even in the presence of an attacker. In the following, we discuss the main features of such models and properties for the IoN. In our analysis, we thus take into account the two configurations suggested in the previous section, where the connection is made with or without a device, pointing out analogies with, and differences from, current research and technologies.

3.1   System Model

To provide a model of the system means to give a clear, and preferably formal, definition that provides enough detail to be able to understand and specify how

---

[5] This may sound like the killing argument of "tin-foil-hat conspiracy theorists", who wear hats made of aluminum foil in the belief that will shield the brain from threats like electromagnetic fields, mind control, mind reading.

the system behaves, encompassing both when it behaves correctly and securely, and when it behaves in unexpected and insecure ways.

In the literature, security models have been formulated in a number of different ways. For instance, encryption and decryption operators are typically described by means of mathematical formulas along with some algebraic structure to capture the operators' properties; security protocols are typically described by means of state transition systems that specify how the knowledge of the protocol agents evolves over time; firewalls are typically described by means of sets of rules regulating how packets are filtered; software systems are typically described directly by their source code (or by the specification that can be learned or inferred by interacting with the code) or by dataflow and/or control flow specifications. These are just some examples, but all of them have in common the need to represent the infrastructure and how information flows among the system's agents (a.k.a. principals or entities).

For example, for Configuration 1 (Fig. 1), we can identify four agents, (i) the human being, (ii) the device, (iii) the router(s), (iv) the Internet, connected by three communication channels, (i) a short-range channel between human being and device, (ii) a medium-range channel between device and router, (iii) a long-range (possibly wired) channel between router and Internet. Different protocols will be used to transmit information over these channels. The channel between the device and the router and the channel between the router and the Internet might actually employ protocols similar to the wireless protocols that we are already using today—in fact, if we are interested in a formal analysis of the system, we could even abstract away the channel between the router and the Internet and simply consider a medium–to–long-range channel between device and Internet. The channel between the human being and the device will, however, require new protocols able to translate between brainwaves and data packets, as the technologies that we discussed in the previous section are attempting to do.

For Configuration 2 (Fig. 2), we can identify three agents, (i) the human being, (ii) the router(s), (iii) the Internet, connected by two communication channels, (i) a medium-range channel between human being and router, (ii) a long-range (and possibly wired) channel between router and Internet. As before, different protocols will be used to transmit information over these channels. It will likely be possible to generalize to this configuration the protocols developed for the short-range brain-device communication in Configuration 1.

In both cases, the model of the configuration will need to be extended with models of the agents (including their actions and their states), of the security protocols used (including routing protocols), of the messages being sent, of the cryptography used and so on. Many of the modeling languages and techniques that are in use today will be applicable with reasonable extensions, except of course for the translation brainwave-data, which will require considerable work. A starting point could be the formalization of this translation as a new cryptographic operator that encodes brainwaves into data along with the inverse operator that decodes data into brainwaves; identifying and formalizing the properties of these operators won't be easy though.

3.2   Threat Model

A number of questions need to be answered in order to provide a threat model:

- *Who is the attacker?* An outsider or an insider? Is he an agent (a human or a machine) trying to attack the communication between the human and the Internet? Is he perhaps the router, or even the human itself? What if the human behaves honestly but makes mistakes, or thinks "wrong thoughts" (whatever they may be) that make the system vulnerable? How would social engineering look like in this case?
- *Where is the attacker?* For instance, can the attacker attack all communication channels in the two configurations as in Fig. 3 and Fig. 4? Or can we assume that the system contains a trusted network area? For example, Fig. 5 assumes that the short-range channel between brain and device cannot be attacked, perhaps supposing that the device itself is able to provide a kind of shield creating some "noise" that isolates the human brain and prevents remote reading (and writing) of brainwaves, like noise-cancellation headphones do with the urban noise. Another approach could be to establish some kind of "encryption" between brain and device, mapping device signals to a specific person's individual brainwaves. Alternatively, a more radical way would be to "implant" the device preventing possible substitutions with tampered devices. Other approaches could be possible. This situation is similar to the assumptions that are currently often made when reasoning about the security of complex security protocols, such as those built by composing sub-protocols [2], or of cyber-physical systems [26], where the attacker can only tamper with some, but not all, channels and devices.

What is the power of the attacker? What are his computational resources? Does he possess a certain amount of computation time to devote to his attack? Does he possess, or control, devices that allow him to access the different channels and the messages sent on them? Or perhaps should we assume that the attacker can inject some malicious code in the device or the router? In that way, he could harm the system or even spoof a router to gain access to the human brain, and perhaps also physically harm the human, by tampering with the device that has direct access to the brain. The attacker could also spoof another human to gain access to a router. We will return to this when we discuss security properties in the next subsection. In fact, we must also answer the question: *What is the attacker trying to achieve?* What can he do on the different channels? Read, replace, modify, intercept messages and perhaps even brainwaves? To that end, we need to consider the security properties that the system is trying to achieve.

3.3   Security Properties

Let us now discuss the main security properties that we could ask the IoN to guarantee. Note that although we focus on the traditional security properties, it is obvious that the categorical imperative of the IoN is actually the *safety*

Fig. 3. Possible attacker locations in Configuration 1

Fig. 4. Possible attacker locations in Configuration 2

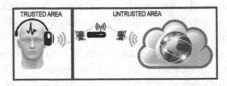

Fig. 5. Trusted area in Configuration 1

of the human being, i.e., no harm should occur to the (brain of the) human being. The Internet is already putting human safety at risk in several ways (e.g., [24]), but in the IoN failure to guarantee one or more security properties (e.g., consequences of the Internet "tampering" directly with the human brain) might expose, directly or indirectly, humans to novel and much more dangerous risks.

Privacy, Confidentiality and Authentication. *Information privacy* (a.k.a. *data privacy*) is the relationship between the collection and dissemination of data, technology, the public expectation of privacy, and the legal and political issues surrounding them. *Internet privacy* is a subset of information privacy that concerns the storing, repurposing, provision to third parties, and displaying of information pertaining to oneself by means of the Internet. In the IoN, our "persona" is using one of the most private information we have: our thoughts.

Thoughts and emotions are intrinsically and intricately related. In psychology, emotions are described as unconscious feelings that are the result of mostly unconscious thoughts [31]. A number of works have been published on how to extract human emotions from brainwaves using EEG [19,41]. What would happen if the attacker were able to extract our emotions from the brainwaves that we are sending in the IoN? How can we protect them from being stolen?

In Configuration 1 (as shown in Fig. 3), the attacker could intercept the brainwaves received by the device before they are coded and transmitted to the router and then the network. Already in 2011 a study demonstrated technologies able to reconstruct images from brainwaves [10], so that, also thanks to some spoofing techniques, the attacker could intercept our communication, reverse it into brainwaves and thus obtain the raw data of our thoughts, even in their binary version. This hypothesis becomes even stronger if we consider a device-less configuration (as shown in Fig. 4) where there is no encoding of brainwaves and they are broadcast over the air to the Internet. This is reminiscent of the attacks that can be carried out by eavesdropping from a distance on the sound emanated by different keyboard keys [45] or by eavesdropping from a distance on the data that is displayed on a computer screen [6]. In these two kinds of attacks, the attacker learns how to recognize and reconstruct the sound or image generated. We expect that advances in machine learning, coupled with those in neuroscience and brainwave-data translation, will make brainwave eavesdropping and reconstruction possible with affordable attacking devices.

Another major issue concerns *location privacy*. Several indoor and outdoor location techniques can be used to trace our position [8,44], which can have positive or negative consequences. For instance, in 2011, the Chinese government announced that it would track people's movements through their cell phones for better traffic control [25], while a study of the Haitian population after the 2010 earthquake showed that similar tracking is extremely useful in informing where people are and where relief aid should go [9]. The IoN won't be exempt from mass surveillance issues, allowing attackers, including governments or Internet providers, to violate the users' location privacy.

We could assume that every brainwave-data device will have a unique identifier like most of the devices have, such as a uuid [27] or a global identifier that is created when the device accesses some services [18]. Tracking these identifiers will be possible, e.g., along the lines of [22]. Removing the device (and its identifier) as is done in Configuration 2, will help mitigate these problems, but still it won't guarantee location privacy. It is namely possible to create brainwave patterns to identify users, and thus use *brainprinting* as a biometric *authentication* factor [4,23,34][6]. In both of the configurations that we considered, with or without a device, the attacker could then track a specific user relying just on her brainprint. To that end, the attacker would, of course, need to know the user's brainprint, but, mimicking how authentication is done today, we could imagine a sort of brainprint certificate issued by a certification authority of a public-brainprint infrastructure[7], or we could simply consider the Internet or the Internet provider as the attacker able to track the movement of its users.

In this case, in order to attempt to achieve location privacy, users should try to change their brainprint. One way to alter one's thought pattern would be to learn to think differently than usual, e.g., thinking "happy thoughts" that obfuscate the normal pattern. This sounds a bit "mystical", but maybe one could indeed learn to confuse one's own brainwaves while still functioning normally as a human being. Alcohol and drugs might help here (although it might then be

---

[6] Other studies [28,38] have investigated *pass-thought authentication*, which allows users to submit both a knowledge factor (i.e., a secret thought) and an inherence factor (i.e., the unique way that thought is expressed) in a single step, by performing a single mental task.

[7] The process behind the brainwave authentication methods that have been proposed requires the registration of a brainwave pattern: a sequence of images or a sequence of words are shown to a user and her brainwaves are stored as her brainprint. This process has to be done in the same way for each user in order to obtain an impartial brainprint. Through this brainprint, an authentication system is able to recognize a user and then, if desired, to authenticate her requests. Configuration 1 will also need to authenticate, and protect, the pairing of brain and device.

difficult to remember one's password [21]) or also physical exercise, workout, fatigue, hunger and stress, which all have been shown to alter one's EEG [12].

Another solution for privacy and location privacy, as well as for confidentiality, would be to encrypt. However, while we could use standard encryption algorithms (such as RSA, Triple DES or AES) to encrypt the wireless communication from device to router and from router to Internet, it is at best unclear how to encrypt the actual brainwaves, which are transmitted from brain to device in Configuration 1 or broadcast over the air in Configuration 2. But maybe one day somebody will devise an algorithm that allows humans to carry out mental encryption similar to the way one can learn how to carry out mental calculations.

The device of Configuration 1 could raise other privacy questions. For instance, it could determine health-related issues while it is reading the user's brainwaves and provide, or sell, such information to health-insurance companies or the government. Could it also determine the user's emotions and thoughts? Will the user trust the device? How could we protect information that we know (e.g., passwords or other confidential data) from being read and distributed by the device? One could, similar to "happy thoughts" above, try to suppress one's thoughts about such confidential information when wearing the device, but this will be difficult if not impossible[8]. Or one could learn to store some thoughts in *private mental drawers*, like some mentalists are (supposedly) able to do. In any case, to ensure that users will trust the device, it will be necessary to carry out a strict procedure of testing and certification of the device before it is deployed. Similar comments apply also for Configuration 2, but referring to the router rather than to the wearable device.

Integrity. What does integrity mean in the IoN? How can we protect thoughts and brainwaves? The attacker will attempt to tamper with all communication channels, the digital and the mental ones. In the case of digital channels (device-to-router or router-to-network), we will likely be able to use integrity-preserving solutions similar to the ones that are available now (cryptographic checksums, hash functions, message authentication codes, digital signatures, and so on)[9]. There is of course also the question of the integrity of the human mind itself, i.e., protecting the brain from "malicious brainwaves" generated from malicious data from the network. In this case, we will need techniques for mental firewalls, input sanitization, sandboxing or Chinese-walling, thereby ensuring the security of the information contained in the other parts of the brain.

---

[8] This is reminiscent of the *paradox of thought suppression* [42], which originates from a challenge that Fyodor Dostoevsky posed in his 1863 essay "Winter Notes on Summer Impressions": *Try to pose for yourself this task: not to think of a polar bear, and you will see that the cursed thing will come to mind every minute.*

[9] In the case of analog channels and signals (from the device to the brain or from the brain to the router), integrity of analog brainwaves could be evaluated in the same way in which we recognize a friend's voice: first by recognition of familiar analog speech sounds, then by recognition of familiar linguistic patterns, and eventually by recognition of familiar behavioral cues and, if needed, through private shared history.

Availability. Besides for malfunctioning of the device and the router, and of jamming of the wireless signals, availability in the IoN can be threatened by a *Distributed Denial of Service (DDoS)* attack when the brain is overwhelmed by the amount of incoming information, thus putting the human at risk. Filtering mechanisms will be necessary to control the flow of data. On the other hand, the IoN will enable opportunities that are unthinkable now. For instance, studies about sleep-learning [3,5] have shown that our mind is able to learn if it is stimulated during the night under certain conditions. The IoN would enable us to learn while we are sleeping thanks to the direct connection of our brain to the Internet. Actually, we could be learning in every waking moment, committing part of our brain to learning and leaving the remaining part untouched for everyday operations, i.e., for our brain's normal daily activity. We could even commit part of our brain as a CPU, e.g., for mining and other cryptographic calculations, as imagined in [35].

Anonymity. One way to achieve at least some degree of anonymity in today's Internet is to use an anonymizing service (such as Mixes, I2P or TOR) that addresses the issue of IP tracking by encrypting packets within multiple layers of encryption. Anonymity is achievable because, as the packet follows a predetermined route through the anonymizing network, each router sees the previous router as the origin and the next router as the destination, and no router knows both the true origin and the true destination of the packet.

In Configuration 1 of the IoN, some of the nodes of the network are actually other users with their devices, whereas other nodes are classic nodes like routers, computers and so on. In this case, the device could negotiate a preemptive path passing through a number of other devices creating a sort of onion routing. However, this kind of solution might not be applicable in Configuration 2 because it is unclear who would actually negotiate a route and apply multiple layers of encryption, unless we assume that brains are able to connect directly with each other, which is something that we will discuss in a bit more detail as we draw our conclusions.

4   Conclusions

The seeds of the IoN are already present in several of the technologies that are being used today or are under development. The opportunities will be prodigious, but repercussions for privacy, security and trust will be enormous and tremendously scary. We have tried to dissect some of those challenges that researchers will have to face once all of this is real (in one form or the other), but we have only skimmed the surface.

More work is needed to fully understand and reason about system and threat models and security properties, specifying the ones we discussed above in more detail but also considering other properties that could be relevant for the IoN. Moreover, we have made the quite strong assumption that brainwaves will need to be translated to data (and vice versa) as the Internet will still transmit packets. But in the future it could well be that the network will follow a radically different model, perhaps thanks to advances in quantum computing or in "brainwave computing" (a discipline that we invented just now), allowing the network to directly process brainwaves as shown in Fig. 6. But why stop here? If brainwave transmission protocols are possible, then it means that the network is able to read the brainwaves that a brain is emanating, but also that the brain is able to receive brainwaves in input. How long will it then take before we find a way for brains to connect not only to the network but also to each other? Some research in this direction is ongoing [16,32] and the ultimate IoN might then simply be based on direct brain-brain connections as the one in Fig. 7.

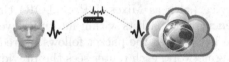 

Fig. 6. Bi-directional brain-Internet connection by means of brainwaves

Fig. 7. Bi-directional brain-brain direct connection

Finally, there is an elephant in the room that we have not addressed in this paper. In addition to technological and neurological questions, some of which we discussed above, there are a huge number of economical, political and ethical issues that we don't really feel competent to address, but that will have to be tackled before we open our mind to the Internet. Who will pay for the IoN? Will all citizens be taxed? Will governments or perhaps corporations provide it for free? Given that nothing is actually free, what will they want in return? In the wake of the recent scandals on data collection (such as the Facebook–Cambridge Analytica data scandal that involved the collection of personally identifiable information of up to 87 million Facebook users), we are skeptical that the IoN will be exempt from massive personal data collection and mining, possibly opening up the possibility for big-brother scenarios in which citizens are always surveilled and tracked in order to control and influence their thoughts, opinions, votes, in brief, their whole life.

References

1. Ahmad, I., Kumar, T., Liyanage, M., Okwuibe, J., Ylianttila, M., Gurtov, A.: Overview of 5G security challenges and solutions. IEEE Commun. Stan. Mag. **2**(1), 36–43 (2018)

2. Almousa, O., Mödersheim, S., Modesti, P., Viganò, L.: Typing and compositionality for security protocols: a generalization to the geometric fragment. In: Pernul, G., Ryan, P.Y.A., Weippl, E. (eds.) ESORICS 2015. LNCS, vol. 9327, pp. 209–229. Springer, Cham (2015). https://doi.org/10.1007/978-3-319-24177-7_11
3. Antony, J.W., Gobel, E.W., O'hare, J.K., Reber, P.J., Paller, K.A.: Cued memory reactivation during sleep influences skill learning. Nat. Neurosci. 15(8), 1114 (2012)
4. Armstrong, B.C., Ruiz-Blondet, M.V., Khalifian, N., Kurtz, K.J., Jin, Z., Laszlo, S.: Brainprint: assessing the uniqueness, collectability, and permanence of a novel method for ERP biometrics. Neurocomputing 166, 59–67 (2015)
5. Arzi, A., et al.: Humans can learn new information during sleep. Nat. Neurosci. 15(10), 1460–1465 (2012)
6. Backes, M., Dürmuth, M., Unruh, D.: Compromising reflections-or-how to read LCD monitors around the corner. In: IEEE Symposium on Security and Privacy (S&P), pp. 158–169. IEEE (2008)
7. Basin, D.A., Dreier, J., Hirschi, L., Radomirovic, S., Sasse, R., Stettler, V.: A formal analysis of 5G authentication. In: CCS, pp. 1383–1396. ACM (2018)
8. Benavente-Peces, C., et al.: Global system for localization and guidance of dependant people: indoor and outdoor technologies integration. In: Mokhtari, M., Khalil, I., Bauchet, J., Zhang, D., Nugent, C. (eds.) ICOST 2009. LNCS, vol. 5597, pp. 82–89. Springer, Heidelberg (2009). https://doi.org/10.1007/978-3-642-02868-7_11
9. Bengtsson, L., Lu, X., Thorson, A., Garfield, R., Von Schreeb, J.: Improved response to disasters and outbreaks by tracking population movements with mobile phone network data: a post-earthquake geospatial study in Haiti. PLoS Med. 8(8), e1001083 (2011)
10. Berkley News, Yasmin Anwar, Media Relations: Scientists use brain imaging to reveal the movies in our mind (2011). http://news.berkeley.edu/2011/09/22/brain-movies/
11. Herzog (directed by), W.: Lo and Behold, Reveries of the Connected World (2016). https://www.imdb.com/title/tt5275828/
12. Chuang, G., Chuang, J.: Passthoughts on the Go: Effect of exercise on EEG authentication. In: 38th Annual International Conference of the IEEE Engineering in Medicine and Biology Society (EMBC) (2016)
13. Dohler, M., et al.: Internet of Skills, where Robotics meets AI, 5G and the Tactile Internet. In: EuCNC, pp. 1–5. IEEE (2017)
14. Edelman, B.J., et al.: Noninvasive neuroimaging enhances continuous neural tracking for robotic device control. Sci. Rob. 4(31), (2019)
15. Graimann, B., Allison, B., Pfurtscheller, G.: Brain-computer interfaces: a gentle introduction. In: Graimann, B., Allison, B., Pfurtscheller, G. (eds.) Brain-Computer Interfaces: Revolutionizing Human-Computer Interaction. FRONT-COLL, pp. 1–27. Springer, Heidelberg (2010). https://doi.org/10.1007/978-3-642-02091-9_1
16. Grau, C., et al.: Conscious brain-to-brain communication in humans using non-invasive technologies. PLoS One 9(8), e105225 (2014)
17. Grossman, N., et al.: Noninvasive deep brain stimulation via temporally interfering electric fields. Cell 169(6), 1029–1041 (2017)
18. Jones, A.R., Quah, E.E.L., Nielsen, D.J., Eminovic, L.: Creating a globally unique identifier of a subscriber device (2012). US Patent Application 20100167734
19. Kao, F.C., Wang, S.P., Chang, Y.J.: Brainwaves analysis of positive and negative emotions. WSEAS Trans. Inf. Sci. Appl. 12, 1263–1266 (2015)
20. Kavanagh, S.: What is the Tactile Internet (2018). https://5g.co.uk/guides/what-is-the-tactile-internet

21. Kobie, N.: Brainwaves could act as your password – but not if you're drunk. New Scientist (2017)
22. Koneru, S., Tuchen, M.H.: Tracking a user across both secure and non-secure areas on the internet, wherein the users is initially tracked using a globally unique identifier (1999). US Patent 5,966,705
23. Kumari, P., Vaish, A.: Brainwave based authentication system research issues and challenges. Int. J. Comput. Appl. **4**(1), 2 (2014)
24. Kuss, D.J., Griffiths, M.D., Binder, J.F.: Internet addiction in students: prevalence and risk factors. Comput. Hum. Behav. **29**, 959–966 (2013)
25. Landwehr, C., Boneh, D., Mitchell, J.C., Bellovin, S.M., Landau, S., Lesk, M.E.: Privacy and cybersecurity: the next 100 years. Proc. IEEE **100**, 1659–1673 (2012)
26. Lanotte, R., Merro, M., Munteanu, A., Viganò, L.: A formal approach to physics-based attacks in cyber-physical systems. ACM Trans. Priv. Secur. **23**(1), 3:1–3:41 (2020)
27. Leach, P.J., Mealling, M., Salz, R.: A Universally Unique IDentifier (UUID) URN Namespace (2005)
28. Merrill, N., Curran, M.T., Chuang, J.: Is the Future of Authenticity All In Our Heads?: Moving Passthoughts From the Lab to the World. In: NSPW, pp. 70–79. ACM (2017)
29. Minors, D.: Can you read my mind? (2017). https://www.wits.ac.za/news/latest-news/research-news/2017/2017-09/can-you-read-my-mind
30. Musk, E.: An integrated brain-machine interface platform with thousands of channels. J. Med. Internet Res. **21**(10), e16194 (2019)
31. Pettinelli, M.: The psychology of emotions, feelings and thoughts. Connexions (2011)
32. Rao, R.P., et al.: A direct brain-to-brain interface in humans. PLoS One **9**, 1–12 (2014)
33. Rendon Morales, E., Prance, R., Prance, H., Aviles-Espinosa, R.: A novel non-invasive biosensor based on electric field detection for cardio-electrophysiology in zebrafish embryos. Procedia Technol. **27**, 242 (2017)
34. Ruiz-Blondet, M.V., Jin, Z., Laszlo, S.: Cerebre: a novel method for very high accuracy event-related potential biometric identification. IEEE Trans. Inf. Forensic Secur. **11**(7), 1618 (2016)
35. Sempreboni, D., Viganò, L.: May I mine your mind? In: 2nd Re-Coding Black Mirror workshop, Companion of The Web Conference (WWW), pp. 1573–1576. ACM (2018)
36. Shetterly, M.L.: Hidden Figures: The Story of the African-American Women Who Helped Win the Space Race. W. Morrow & Co., New York (2016)
37. Strickland, E.: Mind games. IEEE Spectrum **55**(1), e109678 (2018)
38. Thorpe, J., van Oorschot, P.C., Somayaji, A.: Pass-thoughts: authenticating with our minds. In: NSPW, pp. 45–56. ACM (2005)
39. Turing, A.M.: Computing machinery and intelligence. Mind **59**, 433–460 (1950)
40. USA Today: Q&A with Stephen Hawking (2014). https://www.usatoday.com/story/tech/2014/12/02/stephen-hawking-intel-technology/18027597/
41. Wan Ismail, W., Hanif, M., Mohamed, S., Hamzah, N., Rizman, Z.I.: Human emotion detection via brain waves study by using electroencephalogram (EEG). IJA-SEIT **6**(6), 376 (2016)
42. Wegner, D.M.: White Bears and Other Unwanted Thoughts: Suppression, Obsession, and the Psychology of Mental Control. The Guilford Press, New York (1994)

43. Wen, H., Shi, J., Zhang, Y., Lu, K.H., Cao, J., Liu, Z.: Neural encoding and decoding with deep learning for dynamic natural vision. Cerebral Cortex, pp. 1–25 (2017)
44. Werner, M.: Basic positioning techniques. In: Werner, M. (ed.) Indoor Location-Based Services. Springer, Cham (2014). https://doi.org/10.1007/978-3-319-10699-1_3
45. Zhuang, L., Zhou, F., Tygar, J.: Keyboard acoustic emanations revisited. ACM Trans. Inf. Syst. Secur. **13**(1), 1–26 (2009)

Author Index

Butler, Simon   135

Carlsson, Marcel   63
Chua, Yi Ting   23
Condori-Fernandez, Nelly   3

Daneva, Maya   3
Derakhshan, Ali   63

Furman, Susanne M.   107

Groß, Thomas   171

Haney, Julie M.   107
Harper, Scott   85
Harris, Ian G.   63

Indig, Balázs   121

Jamroga, Wojciech   45

Kurpiewski, Damian   45

Lendák, Imre   121

Mace, John C.   85
Malvone, Vadim   45
McBurney, Peter   154
Mehrnezhad, Maryam   85
Muñante, Denisse   3

Palkó, Gábor   121
Parkin, Simon   23
Platt, Moritz   154

Sempreboni, Diego   191
Suni-Lopez, Franci   3

Viganò, Luca   191

Printed in the United States
by Baker & Taylor Publisher Services